Walking by Faith

Women's Diaries and Letters of the South
Carol Bleser, Series Editor

A Woman Doctor's Civil War: Esther Hill Hawks' Diary
Edited by Gerald Schwartz

A Rebel Came Home: The Diary and Letters of Floride Clemson, 1863–1866
Edited by Ernest McPherson Lander, Jr., and Charles M. McGee, Jr.

The Shattered Dream: The Day Book of Margaret Sloan, 1900–1902
Edited by Harold Woodell

The Letters of a Victorian Madwoman
Edited by John S. Hughes

A Confederate Nurse: The Diary of Ada W. Bacot, 1860–1863
Edited by Jean V. Berlin

A Plantation Mistress on the Eve of the Civil War: The Diary of Keziah Goodwyn Hopkins Brevard, 1860–1861
Edited by John Hammond Moore

Lucy Breckinridge of Grove Hill: The Journal of a Virginia Girl, 1862–1864
Edited by Mary D. Robertson

George Washington's Beautiful Nelly
The Letters of Eleanor Parke Curtis Lewis to Elizabeth Bordley Gibson, 1794–1851
Edited by Patricia Brady

A Confederate Lady Comes of Age: The Journal of Pauline DeCaradeuc Heyward, 1863–1888
Edited by Mary D. Robertson

A Northern Woman in the Plantation South: Letters of Tryphena Blanche Holder Fox, 1856–1876
Edited by Wilma King

*Best Companions: Letters of Eliza Middleton Fisher and Her Mother, Mary Hering Middleton,
from Charleston, Philadelphia, and Newport, 1839–1846*
Edited by Eliza Cope Harrison

Stateside Soldier: Life in the Women's Army Corps, 1944–1945
Aileen Kilgore Henderson

From the Pen of a She-Rebel: The Civil War Diary of Emilie Riley McKinley
Edited by Gordon A. Cotton

Between North and South: The Letters of Emily Wharton Sinkler, 1842–1865
Edited by Anne Sinkler Whaley LeClercq

A Southern Woman of Letters: The Correspondence of Augusta Jane Evans Wilson
Edited by Rebecca Grant Sexton

Southern Women at Vassar: The Poppenheim Family Letters, 1882–1916
Edited by Joan Marie Johnson

Live Your Own Life: The Family Papers of Mary Bayard Clarke, 1854–1886
Edited by Terrell Armistead Crow and Mary Moulton Barden

The Roman Years of a South Carolina Artist: Caroline Carson's Letters Home, 1872–1892
Edited with an introduction by William H. Pease and Jane H. Pease

Walking by Faith: The Diary of Angelina Grimké, 1828–1835
Edited by Charles Wilbanks

Walking by Faith

The Diary of
Angelina Grimké
1828–1835

Edited by
Charles Wilbanks

University of South Carolina

© 2003 University of South Carolina

Published in Columbia, South Carolina, by the
University of South Carolina Press

Manufactured in the United States of America

07 06 05 04 03   5 4 3 2 1

Library of Congress Cataloging-in-Publication Data

Grimké, Angelina Emily, 1805–1879.
  Walking by faith : the diary of Angelina Grimké, 1828–1835 / edited by Charles Wilbanks.
  p. cm. — (Women's diaries and letters of the South)
  Includes bibliographical references and index.
  ISBN 1-57003-511-3 (alk. paper)
  1. Grimké, Angelina Emily, 1805–1879—Diaries. 2. Grimké, Angelina Emily, 1805–1879
—Psychology. 3. Grimké, Angelina Emily, 1805–1879—Religion. 4. Women abolitionists
—South Carolina—Diaries. 5. Abolitionists—South Carolina—Diaries. 6. Women—South
Carolina—Charleston—Diaries. 7. Charleston (S.C.)—Biography. I. Wilbanks, Charles.
II. Title. III. Series.

E449.G855A3 2003
973.7'114'092—dc21
[B]
                                                        2003047343

Contents

Illustrations

Series Editor's Preface

Walking by Faith: The Dairy of Angelina Grimké, 1828–1835 is the nineteenth volume in what had been The Women's Diaries and Letters of the Nineteenth-Century South Series. This series has been redefined and is now titled Women's Diaries and Letters of the South, enabling us to include some remarkably fine works from the twentieth century. Published by the University of South Carolina Press, this series includes a number of never-before-published diaries, some collections of unpublished correspondence, and a few reprints of published diaries—a potpourri of nineteenth-century and, now, twentieth-century southern women's writings.

The series enables women to speak for themselves, providing readers with a rarely opened window into southern society before, during, and after the American Civil War and on into the twentieth century. The significance of these letters and journals lies not only in the personal revelations and the writing talent of these women authors but also in the range and versatility of the documents' contents. Taken together these publications will tell us much about the heyday and the fall of the Cotton Kingdom, the mature years of the "peculiar institution," the war years, the adjustment of the South to a new social order following the defeat of the Confederacy, and the "New South" of the twentieth century. Through these writings, the reader will also be presented with firsthand accounts of everyday life and social events, courtships and marriages, family life and travels, religion and education, and the life-and death matters that made up the ordinary and extraordinary world of the American South.

Walking by Faith is the first publication of the diary kept by Angelina Grimké, which she started in 1828 when she was twenty-three and which she stopped keeping seven years later. One of the best-known antebellum abolitionist reformers, Grimké was born in 1805 in Charleston, South Carolina. Her work as an abolitionist is told in a myriad of history textbooks read by students from coast to coast. Yet, as these works point out, she seemed an unlikely supporter of the pre–Civil War antislavery movement in the North.

Angelina and her older sister, Sarah (also active in the antislavery movement), were the daughters of Oxford-educated Judge John F. Grimké of the South Carolina Supreme Court. When Judge Grimké died in 1819, he left his family well provided for—two homes in Charleston, two plantations, fifty slaves, and enough income for the family to live an extravagant lowcountry lifestyle.

Walking by Faith reveals the very spiritual and intellectual seven-year journey this privileged daughter of the planter class traveled to become a Quaker, an outspoken opponent of slavery, and a permanent resident of the North. Late in the summer of 1829, while still at her Charleston home, she wrote in her diary that she was not going North in expectation of being "exempt from trials, far from it, yet it looks like a promised land; a pleasant land, because it is a land of Freedom and it seems to me that I would rather bear much deeper spiritual exercise, than day after day and month after month to endure the countless evils which incessantly flow from Slavery." A few months later, she moved to Philadelphia to join her sister Sarah. She never returned to South Carolina. In Philadelphia she joined the Society of Friends, and she and Sarah engaged in charitable work. Not until 1835 did she begin her public career by writing in a letter to William Lloyd Garrison that abolitionism "is a cause worth dying for." Garrison published her letter in *The Liberator* and it was reprinted in other reform publications. Angelina Grimké had come to the end of her personal journey and stepped confidently onto the public stage of history, where her public person remains. She had no further use for her private diary.

Charles Wilbanks has skillfully edited and presented this very private diary, an important document, not previously published, that illuminates the decisions taken by one woman faced with the moral quandaries of the slaveholding era.

                                                                                      Carol Bleser

Introduction

On the evening of 16 May 1838 the Convention of Anti-Slavery Women met at Pennsylvania Hall in Philadelphia. The throng of people who gathered at the newly constructed hall numbered in the thousands. The crowd was so large that it spilled out the door and filled the grounds, which were still littered with the residue of fresh construction. It was a "promiscuous" audience, both men and women. The crowd included blacks and whites, and both abolitionists and reportedly some slaveholders visiting from the South.

There had been threats of violence against the women: placards warning of "forcible interference" had been seen throughout the city.[1] As the crowd became increasingly vocal, Maria Chapman rose to speak, but she could not be heard. Voices of opposition would not allow her to continue. However, a short time later a voice was heard, a voice that would bring the crowd to its feet. Angelina Grimké of Charleston, South Carolina, rose to address the hall even as some in the crowd inside and some outside became more aggressive. She spoke in a calm, firm, and measured voice: "As a southerner I feel that it is my duty to stand up here tonight and bear testimony against slavery. I have seen it—I have seen it. I know that it has horrors that can never be described."[2] Shortly after those words, stones were thrown and made it through some of the windows, causing even more of a disturbance in the hall. Grimké was unshaken. She asked, "What is a mob? What would the leveling of this hall be? Any evidence that we are wrong? or that slavery is a good and wholesome institution?"[3] After a loud crash heard by everyone inside the hall, Grimké continued, "I thank the Lord that there is yet life enough to feel the truth, even though it rages at it—that conscience is not so completely seared as to be unmoved by the truth of the living God."[4]

The powerful public persona that Grimké exhibited that evening was, in a sense, an example of great promise unfulfilled. Sadly, after the Pennsylvania Hall address Angelina Grimké ended her appearance on the public stage, much to the detriment of the slaves' cause. During her active struggle, however, she was more effective than most abolitionists, and her legacy was ensured.

Angelina Emily Grimké was an unlikely abolitionist. She was born in Charleston, South Carolina, in 1805 to John Faucheraud and Mary Smith Grimké. John Grimké would become a justice of the South Carolina Supreme Court. Angelina's brother Thomas would become a state legislator and educational reformer. Her uncle Benjamin Smith was governor of North Carolina. Her brother Frederick would write publicly in support of the institution of slavery, and she would become occasionally estranged from another brother, Henry, because of her anti-slavery militancy. Henry was a prominent lawyer who for a time ran his late father's affairs while maintaining a large plantation of his own which was located some distance from Charleston. Frederick also was an attorney who eventually became a judge in Ohio. All except her brother Thomas would remain slave-holders despite Angelina's efforts.

The influence of her sister Sarah is widely known. Sarah had almost constant contact with Angelina from the time of her birth throughout the latter's child-hood. The two sisters maintained a strong mutual devotion throughout their lives. Besides Sarah, Judge Grimké had the most influence on young Angelina. Accord-ing to Ellen Todras, Judge Grimké reflected qualities of intelligence, honesty, and a high work ethic to all who knew him.[5] In an early biography of the Grimké sis-ters, Catherine Birney wrote this about Angelina's father: "Judge Grimké inher-ited not only intellectual qualities of a high order, but abiding consciousness of his right to think for himself, a spirit of hostility to the Roman Catholic priesthood and church, and a faith in Calvinistic theology."[6] Certainly this independence of thought was passed down to Angelina. She reflected the strength of her father's religious beliefs. Birney reports another quality of Judge Grimké that is reflected in Angelina's diary: "From a diary kept by him, it appears that his favorite subject of thought for many years was moral discipline."[7]

In 1811 the Grimké family endured a traumatic ordeal that certainly tested their unity and that probably later, as she came to understand it more fully, helped to form Angelina's unyielding determination. In that year Judge Grimké was impeached. The charges against him were personal: some thought him to be "imperious" and "arrogantly secure in the rightness of his judgment."[8] He barely survived the votes for removal from the court. Allegations about his character had surfaced years earlier, and his response to them had led to a duel with Henry Laurens in 1775, from which both survived unhurt. Years later, when Angelina faced expulsion from the Presbyterian Church and when she faced the challenge at Pennsylvania Hall, it is likely that memories of her father's self-confidence and steadfastness served her well.

Judge Grimké accumulated much wealth, and when he died in 1819 he owned two homes in Charleston and two plantations (Belmont in Union District and Grange in Barnwell District). He owned fifty slaves to support the family's prosperous enterprises. Angelina's mother apparently had little influence on Angelina's maturity, at least in a positive way. As Angelina reports in many diary entries, she and her mother clashed often, and the two showed little outward affection toward each other. In fact, Birney reports: "As children multiplied, Mrs. Grimké appears to have lost all power of controlling either them [her children] or her servants. She was impatient with the former and resorted with the latter to punishments commonly inflicted by slaveowners. These severities alienated her children still more from her, and they showed her little respect or affection."[9]

Angelina came of age in Charleston as the city was undergoing major changes that threatened the economic well-being of the community as well as the comfortable social climate of the city. By the time Angelina began her diary, Charleston had declined. According to Robert Rosen, "Trade had decreased, population growth had leveled off, and Charleston's position in the union was less secure"; he concludes that "Charleston's golden era was coming to a close."[10] A century earlier Charleston had easily been the fifth or sixth largest city in the colonies. By the 1820s, however, it did not rank even among the fifteen largest.

By the early decades of the nineteenth century Charleston had begun a period of unease. There was a barely hidden anxiety based largely on racial tensions and threats of slave unrest. This anxiety was caused by news of slave rebellions elsewhere, such as in Jamaica and Santo Domingo. David Robertson explains: "To white residents, and some visitors, Charleston in the late eighteenth and early nineteenth centuries was a city of remarkable charm and beauty. But . . . the white charm was like a grin frozen in the face of an anticipated horror."[11] The fear of slave revolts was real, and in 1822 a nearly successful slave uprising led by freed slave Denmark Vesey rocked Charleston. The Vesey affair sent shock waves through the slaveholding community. Their security was threatened, and the resulting unease took its toll. Slaves were at least initially more closely watched, and any who were unattended in the city, with or without proper documents, were under suspicion.

Grimké matured in a society in which slavery was as fundamental as fine homes, sea air, and fashionable dress. Every aspect of daily life was in some way affected by the institution. As members of the plantation class, the Grimké family could not escape the spoils and costs of slavery even if they had wanted to. By the time Angelina was grown and had started her journal, the Grimkés lived on East Bay just outside Charleston's chief retail area. Slaves were bought and sold within an easy stroll from the Grimké house. Reminders of slavery awaited anyone who happened to glance out of the parlor window down East Bay.

The courage and determination that supported Grimké as she faced the mob at Pennsylvania Hall in 1838 was born a decade earlier during a difficult period of young adulthood. During most of those years she kept a journal, and that journal provides a glimpse into the development of her character and faith. Thanks to recent publications, the nature of her public persona has become clear. Her diary reveals her private persona.

The purpose of this text is to provide the evidence necessary to answer the important question: How does Grimké's private persona inform our understanding of her public rhetoric? It is likely not coincidental that her diary closes almost precisely at the moment that her public life began. Her diary, her period of self-expression, ended as her consuming need for public expression became too much to resist. Our understanding of this transition, which should be demonstrated in rhetorical terms, necessitates a consideration of the whole span of her journal. Only that way can we fully understand the motivation and the meaning of her public rhetoric. Recently, Stephen Howard Browne has rightly proposed that "Grimké's public self, her *ethos*—was symbolically fashioned and put to the purposes of moral reform"; he suggests that "so much that was significant about her rhetorical practice pressed on questions of self, being, and being-with-others" and that an important question occurs: "Who, then, was Angelina Grimké?"[12] That Browne has certainly aimed true in his development of the relationship between "human agency" and Angelina's rhetoric is undeniable. However, the question suggested by Browne can never be completely answered by analysis of her public acts only. Angelina Grimké was always struggling to define her private self, and not at any time more so than between 1828 and 1835.

The Search for a Resurrected Self

Kenneth Burke has written, "The attempt to discuss the symbolic acts of art or life involves us in a kind of pursuit that radiates in many ways at once."[13] This supports the notion that the feelings Grimké expressed privately, once expressed, were transformed from a wholly emotional apprehension to a more rational cognition that eventually necessitated action. Private expression, therefore, cannot be separated from our consideration of rhetoric. This analytic radiation mandates its inclusion.

Certainly diaries are rhetorical. Richard Gregg has written that "a person may choose to address himself, and that regardless of his reasons for such behavior, this primary transaction of self with self may properly be designated 'rhetorical.'" He terms this intrapersonal transaction an "ego-function" of rhetoric. To

Gregg, an important aspect of the ego function of rhetoric has to do with "constituting self-hood through expression."[14]

In Grimké's diary we see the evolution of Angelina's selfhood. Written prior to her appearance in the public forum, the diary is self-persuasive. Even though Gregg's analysis was not aimed at rhetoric that was only self-directed, he does suggest that if one's self were the primary audience, others would identify with it as they identified with the same or similar ego-concerns.[15] Gregg refers to self-persuasion that is produced in the public forum, and Angelina Grimké's diary was not. Despite the likelihood that Gregg did not intend to apply his approach to private writing, Grimké's journal seems to reflect a process similar to the one he describes. Moreover, there is evidence that Angelina recognized the likelihood that others would read her diary, so it does have a public character.

In fact, I propose that Grimké's diary can be understood, not as a chronicle of her aspirations and trials (because that may be intended only for others to read), but as a sort of psychological and spiritual self-portrait. As Gregg points out, "What is at stake is not the nature of the rhetorical claims or the sense and probity of the appeals and arguments," but simply that the "rhetoric must be verbalized."[16] As the diary unfolds, Grimké's self-portrait comes into sharper focus and becomes less introspective and more publicly self-affirming, similar to Gregg's analysis of protest rhetoric. When Angelina began her journal she lamented her limited abilities to change herself. Within a short time, however, she recognized the imperative to change others. Because of the richness of this rhetorical act, we can identify an emerging private persona.

Angelina Grimké's diary reveals the self-confirming aspects of the ego-function of rhetoric. Moreover, viewing the diary as a rhetorical act, rather than merely a chronicle, allows a fuller understanding of the motivation for the personal renewal she seeks. Gregg refers to this sought-after renewal as a "struggle for a resurrected self."[17] In the Grimké diary the notion of redemptive sacrifice is a recurring theme. Unless the diary is read within the context of her struggle for a resurrected self, the instances of redemptive sacrifice she often records would be seen as a series of interesting but disconnected events reflecting a troubled, almost tormented individual. The truth is, the acts of sacrifice reflected in Grimké's diary are not disconnected, and they mirror not merely torment but guilt and recognition for the need for atonement.

Until 10 January 1828 Angelina Grimké was not devoted to keeping a journal. Only sporadically did she make diary entries earlier, and only fragments of those survive. But on that date an emotional and troubled young woman began a diary that she would keep regularly for the next seven years. In January 1828 Angelina was struggling with a host of conflicts. She was desperately searching for the springs of a spiritual renewal. She was in turmoil with her mother, whom she believed to be cold and uncaring; she was quarreling with her brothers; and she was impatient with her family's extravagant lifestyle and often wondered what of value there was for her to do in Charleston.

She also condemned herself. From the first entry of the diary Angelina articulated her own shortcomings, real and perceived, and began to search for ways of atoning for her transgressions. Indeed, the first entry reflected her felt need for sacrifice when she wrote, "Today I have torn up my novels." She explained that she "had long been troubled about them" but did not have the courage to destroy them until that morning "when in much mercy strength was granted." For some months Grimké had felt guilty for her perceived adherence to the "customs" of the world. In an unpublished and undated autobiographical sketch that she probably wrote in the summer of 1828, Grimké gives us some insight as to the motivation for the destruction of her novels. She explains: "During the winter I had felt the necessity of giving up the world and was glad that my situation (being in deep mourning for my brother) precluded even the propriety of my mingling in gay society, but still did not think I could possibly have strength to give it up entirely under all circumstances, nonetheless my earnest prayers ascended day and night that I might be a true Christian no matter what I may be called to suffer." In the sketch she explains that the death of her brother convinced her that her rather casual attitude toward worship had caused the tragedy. She believed that she should suffer, at one point writing, "I deserve it for I always said that nothing but affliction would ever bring me to God." So when she destroyed her novels she was at once proclaiming her guilt, the guilt of frivolity, and engaging in an act of self-sacrifice.

In the 10 January entry she reports that she had gotten rid of some of her clothes as well: "A great deal of my finery too, I have put beyond the reach of anyone. My hat also I have untrimmed and I have put nothing but a band of ribbons round it & taken the lace out of the inside." Grimké actually stuffed an ottoman with the finery and sewed it up so as to be "out of reach." It is interesting that she found the courage to destroy the books completely but could not destroy the clothing. In several instances in her diary she writes of the difficulty of dressing plainly. Despite those difficulties she was steadfast in her determination to follow what she believed to be her duty. She stated simply, "I do want if I am a Christian to look like one." She explained, "I think every professor ought so to dress that wherever they are soon all around may feel that they are condemning the world & all its trifling vanities." She was determined to dress plainly regardless of, or perhaps because of, what others might imply about it. Her motive seems clear: "I believe this alteration in my dress will tend to make me more watchful for the more we are unlike the world the more it will sensitise us & the more it will hate us; every direct deviation from its customs places us one step higher on a conscience that will expose us to its shafts of ridicule & display more fully our real defects. I think I am willing to bear or forebear for all the ill natured remarks I hear often remind me of what I once was, this is profitable because it is humbling." She had expressed an acknowledgment of her sin (a lack of seriousness toward God) and had destroyed things she had loved so that she could "demonstrate" her newfound seriousness, so the first entry in her diary is an example of redemptive sacrifice. She claimed that the comments she received from others "remind me of what I once was." Already she was beginning to acknowledge a resurrected self.

There is little doubt that Grimké was sincere in acknowledging her sin, but it was not long before she indicated that the sacrifices she was making were extremely taxing for her. She at least once expresses resentment for having to make them. She complains: "It seems as tho' the more I give up the more I am called to relinquish, & every surrender only prepares the way for another and a greater sacrifice. The yoke of Jesus Christ is not easy to me now. It is harder for me to kick against the pricks than to yield & therefore I give up what is demanded, but O how little satisfaction flows into the mind from such a surrender of the will." Grimké had not yet completed the redemptive process; she still had not fully accepted the liberating redemptive nature of the sacrifices she was making.

Just a month later, however, on 10 February, she seems to have strengthened her willingness to bear the necessities of the sacrifice. She explains: "My attention has lately been called to the duty of Christians dressing quite plain. When I was first brought to the feet of Jesus I learned the lesson in part, but I soon forgot much of it & now I find my views stricter and clearer than they ever were. The first thing I gave up was a Cashmere mantle which cost $20. I had not felt easy with it for some months and being encouraged by a friend determined never to wear it again tho' I had no money at the time to get it replaced by anything else, however I gave it up in faith and the Lord provided for me." Obviously she eventually felt better about her regimen of sacrifice, but Grimké went through a brief period of doubt about the course of suffering she had chosen.

In this early part of the diary the only mention of slavery is brief but reveal-ing. The subject that would engender so much passion from her and so much elo-quence just a few years later was not a subject that she discussed with much conviction at the time. Grimké had long been uncomfortable with slavery. She had not embraced the elite society of antebellum Charleston as other young women of her age and station had eagerly done. Early in 1828 she had developed a sense that slavery was unnatural and inconsistent with Christian teaching. In a passage dated 11 January 1828 Grimké describes an incident that reveals her growing antislavery feelings:

> I have great cause of gratitude for spiritual blessings tonight. I have
> conversed with my servant & find that her mind is perfectly calm, her
> soul seems stayed on God's & yet she is distrustful of herself the circum-
> stances through which she came to belong to me are singular and are as
> follows. I had determined never to own one but finding that my mother
> could not manage her I undertook to do so. If I could have her without
> any interference on her part, this I could not do unless she was mine
> and purely from motives of duty I consented. Soon after this one of my
> mother's servants quarreled with her & beat her & I determined that she
> should not be subject to such abuse thinking it really sinful to subject
> her to such treatment. I therefore determined to go out & get her a
> place in some religious family; my steps were ordered by the Lord. I
> succeeded in my design & placed her with a friend.

What makes this passage most interesting is that Grimké describes her behavior toward the servant in a way that she would not have entertained later. After she became a public figure she would never have consented to own a slave, even if it meant protecting them from abuse. She would argue that there was no justifica-tion either for owning slaves or for tolerating those who did. In the manuscript of the diary the above entry had been X'd over. No one knows who made the mark or when the edit was attempted.

The Fellowship of Suffering

Angelina Grimké felt powerless in the face of the momentous changes that were taking place in her life. She was convinced that she had not been worthy of God's benevolence. She accepted blame for the several misfortunes that had lately come her way. For a time she focused her response on the atonement for those shortcomings by dressing plainly, as she thought all Christians ought to dress. She was willing to endure the reactions of others in order to win redemption.

Grimké was not simplistic in her faith. The foundation of her religious conversions was solid. She had been intrigued by the preaching of William McDowell, the pastor of Third Presbyterian Church in Charleston. Just a year before her diary began, Grimké had shocked her mother and friends when she ceased attending St. Philip's Episcopal Church and joined the Presbyterian congregation. However, her attraction to the Presbyterian Church began to weaken quickly, and by March 1828 Grimké openly questioned some of that church's doctrine. For a time she became interested in a doctrinal position to which a Methodist friend had introduced her. The Doctrine of Perfection was originally put forward by Rev. John Fletcher, a Methodist.[18] Essentially the doctrine states that people were once perfect or otherwise we would never have manifested God's glory. According to the doctrine, if we were once perfect, it is possible to attain perfection again, and if it is possible to attain perfection, we must strive to do so. Grimké became convinced that the Doctrine of Perfection was enlightenment. This was the blueprint for her to create her new self—a perfect self. She wrote of the doctrine and explained her reasons for embracing it in the following passage dated only March 1828: "I do feel astonished that so many Christians reject the doctrine of Perfection. I am more & more convinced of it from reading the Bible. One exclaimed the other day David says, 'I have seen an end to all perfection.' And so have I, of the perfection of human nature without the cleansing influences of the Holy Spirit." Grimké's self-image was influenced by her understanding of Fletcher's doctrine. In her autobiographical sketch she describes its importance in detail. She reports that "it was from looking at myself in the perfect mirror that I began to see the glaring inconsistencies of my character and that this doctrine of indwelling sins was not scriptural." After studying Fletcher's writings, Grimké's "opinions were shaken to pieces," and she eventually fully embraced his teaching.

This was also about the time she became more fully dissatisfied with the Presbyterian Church. The fellowship that had once excited her greatly now did not. By April she entertained the notion of leaving the church, but contemplating such a course was painful for her. She had been drawn to William McDowell and the Presbyterian Church as a surrogate family. Grimké had believed that McDowell's words spoke to her and validated her aspirations. She eloquently articulated the pain of the separation on 20 April 1828:

> My mind is composed & I cannot but feel astonished at the total change which has passed over me during the last 6 months. Then I delighted in going to meeting 4 & 5 times every week, but now my Master says "be still" & I would rather be at home, for I find that every stream from

which I used to drink the refreshing waters of salvation is dry & that I
have been led to the fountain itself. Once, Oh how precious were the
means of grace to my soul with how much power did sermons come
home to my heart, but now I sometimes wish I could close my ears to
the preacher's voice and retire into the closet of my heart & hold converse with Him who speaks as never man spake. And is it possible I
would ask myself tonight, is it possible that today is the last time I
expect to visit the Presbyterian Church, the last time I expect to teach
my interesting class in Sabbath School and is it right that I should separate myself from a people whom I have loved so tenderly & who have
been the helpers of my joy, is it right to give up instructing those dear
children whom I have so often carried in the arms of faith & love to a
throne of grace.

It was a painful realization for Grimké that she no longer "belonged" in the Presbyterian Church. She no longer belonged there because she had spiritually out-
grown it and was no longer the person she once was. She had certainly redefined
herself in a short period of time. She had recognized her faults (at least as she
saw them) and would take action to set them straight. In the same diary entry
Grimké clarifies her motivation for leaving: "It has been clearly shown to me that
the 3rd P. C. was the cradle into which my soul was put by my Heavenly Father,
then I was fed by the 'sincere milk of the word,' but now its pastor can do no
more for me he knows nothing about the exercises of my mind & he can teach
me no more, I need a higher teacher." Grimké recognized that she, not McDowell or the Presbyterian Church, had changed. Leaving the church and McDowell
was more significant than destroying her novels, more permanent than hiding her
finery, and more courageous than being seen in plain dress. She decided that she
could not fully reach perfection under the guidance of William McDowell. Once
again she decided to sever her affiliation with a church she once loved.

The act of publicly removing herself from the fellowship of the church was
evidence that Grimké had taken an important and necessary step toward her
entrance onto the public stage. She had first *expressed* contrition, and that necessitated physical action rather than a solely spiritual change. The construction of
her diary provided the necessary bridge from private to public, from the intuitive to the rational, and from the contemplative to the active.

Resurrection and Conversions

By the end of May 1828 Angelina had started down a path of self-affirmation that
would eventually have her courageously facing the mob at Pennsylvania Hall. In

July 1828 Grimké left Charleston to spend the summer in Philadelphia with her sister Sarah. While there she made only four entries in her diary. One of those entries was recorded the day after she arrived, and the last was written only a few days before she returned to Charleston.

Her visit to Philadelphia was a salve to Grimké's torment—it at least provided temporary relief. She was with people who did not believe her attitudes and behavior were unusual, which must have been invigorating for her. She dreaded her return to South Carolina; in her final entry while in Philadelphia she wrote, "I think much suffering awaits me." She was right. However, momentous changes also awaited her.

Angelina Grimké's diary reveals that she struggled mightily with three life-changing decisions. Three conversions took place over a period of just a few years. Between 1826 and 1829 she converted from Episcopalian to Presbyterian to Quaker. Over a period of just a year she was transformed from being merely uncomfortable with slavery (but still willing to own slaves) to being an outspoken opponent. Finally, in the course of less than six months she had permanently broken the bonds that held her to a large and powerful family, gaining independence at the age of just twenty-four.

Conversion to the Society of Friends

By December after her return, Grimké had clearly been strengthened in her adherence to the notion of Christian simplicity. Her affinity to the Quakers in speech and dress had become more pronounced, and by March her commitment to Quaker expectations was strengthened. Even though for some time she had dressed plainly, she realized that her wardrobe would still not be acceptable among the Friends. On 13 March 1829 she reported: "Today for the first time I ruined my clothes, & I felt as though it was an acceptable sacrifice, this seemed to be part of the preparation for my removal to the North." Moreover, for the first time in the journal she articulated the likelihood that she would leave Charleston permanently. For the first time she recognized that being a Quaker and living in Charleston would not be possible.

Interestingly, despite Grimké's decision to leave the Presbyterian Church, the church would not allow her to quit. Instead the Session filed charges *against her* for not worshiping on a regular basis and thereby neglecting the solemn vows she had made when joining. In May 1829, after a hearing of the Session, Angelina was asked to leave Third Presbyterian Church. Even though she had already removed herself from fellowship, the action was devastating. Her response to the Session's action was decisive.

In a rather emotional entry dated 27 April 1829 she recognized the absolute necessity of joining formally the Society of Friends. Thinking back on her initial attraction to the Presbyterian Church, she wrote: "I desire not to glory . . . but to be low in the dust remembering I was & still am nothing but a woman— this was the infancy of a new born soul, a time of much joy, but great ignorance, of fervent feeling, but little experience—it was spring to the tender tree which had just been planted in the Lord's vineyard, the great Husbandsman watched and watered it daily but it should wither and die—soon under his fostering care it put forth leaves & was decked with blossoms but they soon withered and fell to the ground so that very little fruit in a very imperfect state was gathered, the root was not deep enough to bear the body of the tree." If she were to survive spiritually, and to be more solidly rooted, the root must take hold through adherence to Quaker doctrine.

Conversion to Abolition

Her first clear condemnation of slavery was recorded in her diary on 6 February 1829. This marked a departure from previous references to slavery as only troublesome and uncomfortable. Grimké was worried about one of her brother's slaves. It is clear that she and her brother Henry at this point had vastly different opinions about slavery and about how slaves should be treated. She wrote: "I have been suffering for the last two days on account of H[enry]'s boy having run away because he threatened to whip him. O who can paint the horrors of slavery & yet so hard is the natural heart that I am continually told that their situation is very good much better than that of their owners, how strange that anyone should believe such an absurdity or try to make others credit it." After considering the situation with John, Henry's runaway slave, Grimké decided to confront her brother. It was not a pleasant encounter and on its face did not appear to have been successful. Upon John's return, however, Henry did not whip him but sent him on to his quarters. Angelina appears to have been relieved and somewhat self-satisfied with the outcome. On 7 February she wrote: "Surely my heart ought to be lifted to my blessed Master in emotions of gratitude and praise. Henry's boy came home last night a short time after I had spoken to him & instead of punishing him as I was certain he ment [*sic*] to do merely told him to go and do his business."

As in her diary entries pertaining to her religious conversion, Grimké ultimately concluded that because of her revulsion in the face of slavery she could not remain in South Carolina. On 23 April 1829 she lamented: "None but those who know from experience what it is to live in a land of Bondage can from any idea of the weight of exercise which is endured by those whose eyes open to the enormities of slavery & where hearts are tendered so as to feel for these miserable creatures. . . . Sometimes I felt as though I was needing to fly from Carolina, but the consequences be what they might, at this it seemed as though the very exercise I was suffering under was preparing me for future usefulness to them [slaves]." She had recognized the difficulty of remaining in South Carolina as long as it was a land of bondage. She had to leave if she were to live as a Quaker. She had to leave if she were to continue to work on behalf of the slaves.

Conversion to Independence

Angelina's strongest anchor to South Carolina was her family, particularly her mother. She had not gotten along well with her mother, but obviously they had strong feelings for each other. Her mother was controlling, and Angelina often bristled at her harshness. But the occasional tenderness that Angelina and her mother exchanged made a separation painful to contemplate. Consider the entry of 19 April 1829: "This morning mother woke me with a kiss. I do desire to be grateful for every little mark of her affection. I do not know whether my feelings are right but it appears to me that these things do not proceed from _love_ in her heart but from a conviction of duty since I told her how very hard her coldness & indifference had been for me to bear."

Katherine DuPre Lumpkin, Grimké's biographer, believes that when Angelina finally left Charleston in September it was her intention to return someday.[19] However, it seems more likely that, given her expressed beliefs and intensity of feeling about her spiritual conversion and her antislavery sentiments, she knew as she sailed for Philadelphia that she would not see Charleston again. In fact in the first entry in her diary after she arrived in Philadelphia, she wrote that she expected her mother to move to Philadelphia. Angelina recounted her conversations with her mother and her sister Eliza before leaving Charleston. She wrote of an emotional farewell to her mother:

> The evening before I sailed as we were sitting together Mother said
> something of her trials and she would be enabled to bear them seeming
> to think she would never be released from them but by death. With
> tears of emotion and pity I told her I did not believe that these family
> trials were to last always, but if she was faithful these burdens would be
> removed and I believed that a happy old age was before her, a period in
> which she would enjoy far more real solid happiness than she had ever

done before—thou seemed to think I continued that necessity is laid upon thee to live just where as thou hast been accustomed to and that will have to drag out an instance of continual trial, but it is not so—she made no reply and silence followed. E[liza] and myself were soon after left alone and I opened to her my belief that Mother would in time feel it right to leave Carolina and that it had appeared to me that my going away would be the means of breaking some of the cords which bound her there and that this change would contribute greatly to her happiness.

Clearly, Grimké believed that leaving would bring not only a release from her own personal trials but a release for her mother from trial as well.

From Redeemed to Redeemer

It was a critical aspect of Grimké's personal identity that she was able to demonstrate her own redemption through public acts of sacrifice. As it developed, Angelina wanted to be *redeeming* as well. Not only was she committed to her own redemption, but she wanted to be the instrument for the redemption of others.

She came to believe that she was given a "high and holy" calling. She wrote of this as early as February 1828. She maintained at that time that she was willing to endure the ridicule of others if that were part of the calling God had given to her. On several occasions afterward Angelina spoke of this calling. She was not content merely to improve her own standing with God; she must also "save" others. She put this feeling into action for the first time in April 1829: "Of late I feel the necessity of dear Mother's seeing the bitter fruit of her system of education. I want her instead of priding herself on the morality of her sons to see and acknowledge that tho' far from gross crimes they are <u>not</u> moral men that is they do <u>not</u> fill their respective stations in the domestic circle." In this one brief passage Angelina characterizes her brothers in rather condemning language and suggests that her mother's moral confusion was at fault. Later in the same entry she even more directly questions her mother's moral standing. To Angelina, personal shortcomings were to be expected, but neither to acknowledge them nor to atone for them was unacceptable. Grimké wrote: "I want her to see & feel that it is in a great measure <u>her</u> fault that we have always lived in strife and contention—caring too much to place ourselves to care for each other. Let everyone do as they please has been her motto & we have been too willing to adapt & act upon it too." Angelina was convinced that she was destined to win some divine battle. To her, nothing was more admirable than helping God save the souls of others.

After she had returned from Philadelphia, left the Presbyterian Church, and alienated many of her friends, she found herself without much to do. By March 1829 she had relinquished much of what had occupied her life just a few months prior. She complained that for someone with such a divine calling, the inactivity was unbearable. On 11 April 1829 she questioned why God allowed her to be inactive. She wrote, "It is hard for <u>me</u> to be & to do nothing, my ambitious temper craves high duties & high attainments & I have at times tho't that this <u>ambition</u> was a motive to me to do my duty & submit my will."

This belief that the souls of others were entrusted to Grimké became a defining philosophy that is increasingly apparent as the diary unfolds. It becomes more and more a defining element of her private persona. Her use of the diary began as she struggled with inconsolable and irreconcilable emotions. It ended as Angelina became a public figure. When that happened there was no longer the need for that kind of expression. Her eventual public rhetoric, seen up to now largely as purely political and within a frame of public policy, can be seen in light of her diary as perhaps political but framed in more spiritual and social terms. As she gradually became a public figure and her diary concluded, she turned her instrument of redemption from the circle of friends and family that surrounded her in her parlor and aimed it at a larger audience watching her upon the public stage.

Description and Editorial Method

Angelina Grimké's diary exists almost in its entirety. The first entry is dated 10 January 1828 and the last October 1835. The diary is continuous except for an almost one-year hiatus between fall 1830 and summer 1831. Only fragments of the manuscript survive from the years 1834 and 1835. During the first five years of the diary entries' span, Grimké wrote three other "life accounts." The first was a sketch of her life (particularly her religious life) probably written sometime during summer 1828. She also kept a journal during a brief trip she took to New England in July 1831. Finally, she compiled a rather emotional account of the death of Edward Bettle, her lover, written between December 1832 and May 1833. Of these additional accounts, this volume includes only the journal entries from her trip to New England. Neither the biographical sketch nor the account of her bereavement was written as a diary. Moreover, she did not consider those accounts to be part of her diary. These manuscript materials are part of the Weld-Grimké Papers at the William C. Clements Library, University of Michigan.

The diary is written in several bound "notebooks" and, considering its age, is in remarkably good condition. The quality of the paper varies, and some of the entries are more difficult to read than others due to the bleeding of the ink through to the back sides, which Grimké invariably used as well. The transcription of the diary was completed largely from microfilm copies that allowed for enlargement when needed.

I attempted the most literal textual treatment possible. Some editorial intervention was necessary because of certain textual peculiarities. For example, there are inconsistencies in punctuation, particularly missing periods and odd slashes that are sometimes used in the place of periods. To improve the readability of the text, those irregularities have been regularized by the substitution of periods when needed. Larry Ceplair, who edited *The Public Years of Sarah and Angelina Grimké: Selected Writings, 1835–1839,* made the same choice.

Another characteristic of Grimké's writing that presented a challenge was the unique system of spelling developed by her brother Thomas. This truncated spelling began to appear in Angelina's diary in 1834. I felt that it was important to leave the spelling as it was. To impose modern standard spelling only slightly improves readability and sacrifices an important visual element of the diary.

Some annotations were necessary. Biblical references fill the pages of the diary. I have identified scripture passages to which she refers. It should be pointed out, however, that almost all of her scripture references were apparently from memory. Hence, there are many incomplete or misquoted passages. I have cited only those passages that could be identified with relative confidence; otherwise I did not cite them at all. Many of the quoted references have missing quotation marks. I have inserted them in those instances indicated within brackets. A segment of the diary that required some annotation chronicled her trip to New England from 4 July until 28 July 1831. She visited locations that would eventually become more meaningful to her, and she would meet people who would eventually play important roles in both her private and public lives. On this trip, for example, she would meet for the first time Catharine Beecher, with whom she would later become engaged in a public dispute. When they could be deciphered, I have included words and phrases that Grimké struck through.

The entries from 1834 and 1835 are incomplete and not continuous. Fairly frequent annotations connect these otherwise disconnected entries. Other annotations were necessary where Grimké refers to individuals with only initials. All editorial interventions on my part were guided by the principle that readability and appreciation of the text should be afforded without sacrificing the diary's historical and personal character.

Walking by Faith

1

Purification and Perfection

January 10, 1828–May 7, 1828

A Quaker minister, Anna Braithwaite, and her husband visited Charleston in the closing days of 1827. They stayed with the Grimkés. At first Angelina did not want them there, but soon she went to hear her guest preach, and as Angelina put it, Braithwaite "opened the state of my mind as fully as if she had my heart in her hand." Apparently, Anna quickly became an important influence on the development of young Angelina's religious beliefs. Angelina was struck with Braithwaite's piety and simplicity and was impressed when she was told that Braithwaite had a sister who, like Angelina, had been brought up an Episcopalian and became a Presbyterian and then a Quaker. It was perhaps the first time that Angelina had been told that the religious conversions she had experienced were not peculiar. Braithwaite touched Angelina's heart and sharpened her resolve. With her memory of Anna Braithwaite still fresh, Grimké penned the first entry in her diary.

The heading inscribed at the top of the first diary entry, "Take heed lest there be more of Self than of Christ in the diary," reflects precisely the fundamental character of the entries that follow and the message that Braithwaite left with Grimké. The inscription is an accurate mirror of Angelina's soul. The first sentence of the 10 January entry, "Today I have torn up my novels," speaks eloquently of Angelina's desire to relegate worldly activities and attractions to a position subordinate to her spiritual well-being. As she began her diary she seemed determined to demonstrate her Christian character and not simply to profess it. It is obvious that she was sincere but more than a little confused and uncertain. She believed that she was destined for some noteworthy Christian purpose—what it was she admitted she did not know. She nevertheless was convinced that the "duties & trials" she faced were only preparatory to the real "work" before her.

∽

Take heed lest there be more of Self than of Christ in the diary
1828

January 10   Today I have torn up my novels. My mind had long been troubled about them. I did not dare either to sell them or to lend them out, & yet I had not resolution to destroy them until this morning when in much mercy strength was granted. A great deal of my finery too, I have put beyond the reach of anyone. My hat also I untrimmed & have just nothing but a band of ribbon round it & taken the lace out of the inside. I do want if I am a Christian to look like one. I think every professor ought to dress that whenever they are soon all around may feel that they are condemning the world & all it's [*sic*] trifling vanities. I believe this alteration in my dress will tend to make me more watchful, for the more we are unlike the world the more it will sensitise us & the more it will hate us; every direct deviation from it's customs places us one step higher on an eminence which will expose us to it's shafts of ridicule & display more fully are real defects. I think I am willing to bear & forbear for the ill natured remarks I hear often remind me of what I once was, this is profitable because it is humbling.[1]

This text rests so much on my mind "I have many things to say unto you, but you cannot bear them now."[2] It does appear to me & has appeared to me since I had a hope that there was a work before me to which all my other duties & trials were only preparatory. I have no idea what it is & I may be mistaken but it does seem that if I am obedient to the still small voice of Jesus in my heart that he will lead into more difficult paths and cause me to glorify Him in more honorable & trying work than any which I have yet been engaged.

January 11   I have great cause of gratitude for spiritual blessings tonight. I have conversed with my servant & find that her mind is perfectly calm, her soul seems stayed on God's & yet she is distrustful of herself—the circumstances thro' which she came to belong to me are singular & are as follows. I had determined never to own one but finding that my Mother could not manage her I undertook to do so if I could have her without any interference on her part, this I could not do unless she was mine & purely from motives of duty I consented. Soon after this one of my Mother's servants quarelled with her & beat her & I determined that she should not be subject to such abuse, thinking it really sinful to subject her to such treatment. I therefore determined to go out & get her a place in some religious family; my steps were ordered by the Lord. I succeeded in my design & placed her with a friend. She was invited to a Methodist wedding about 3 weeks after where she became impressed & was invited by them to go to one of their watch night settings up, she went & was still more deeply convicted —she came to see me soon after & candidly told me all that passed and impressed her fear that I would not allow her to join the Sect. I told her that I felt so grateful to find her mind so solemn that I would not be a stumbling block in her way—indeed I do love the Methodists very dearly & can rejoice at the increase of their Church for it is the Church of my Redeemer. She now attends one of the Classes & appears to feel as anxious as I do that she should not deceive herself & should not join herself to that People until she feels her soul united by a living faith to Christ our living Head.[3]

January 12   Today I have been called to give up some trifles and wonder that I have not been able to do so cheerfully. I do not glory in the Cross as I once did, O no! It is my grief & shame that I find it so hard to yield willingly. I am tempted to have hard tho'ts of my Master & to think he requires a great deal of me. It seems as tho' the more I give up the more I am called to relinquish, & every surrender only prepares the way for another & a greater sacrifice. The yoke of Jesus Christ is not easy to me now. "It is harder for me to kick against the pricks"[4] than to yield & therefore I give up what is demanded; but O how little satisfaction flows into the mind from such a surrender of the will. Fear predominates here, but to yield being constrained by the love of Christ, this is sweet indeed. At dinner a few words that were said wounded me deeply—the tears started to my eyes, I left the table & retired when alone I could not help reflecting if such so trifle gave me pain, how often & how tho'tlessly I had pierced my Savior's side. Ah! how much it becomes us to pray for our enemies as Jesus did for his "Father forgive them for they know not what they do."[5] He would know not how many thorns they often plant in our hearts—our hearts of flesh are often wounded by what could not pierce their hearts of Stone.

January 14   Tonight I went to Teacher's Monthly Meeting. M. Kirk addressed us to the following effect. If any one had travelled thro' France before Napoleon Bonaparte began his expeditions of Ambition & had remarked that in every part of the Kingdom forces were gathering—ammunition was collecting and leaders were marshalled at the head of select lands; however sectored and inefficient these efforts might appear when viewed separately, yet he would doubtless have perceived in looking upon them as a whole that they were the united & consistent & powerful preparations of some giant work. Thus in passing thro' these United States I have perceived that there is no grand movement among Christians. More time I am called to attend the anniversary of a Bible or a Tract or a Missionary Society—at another I visit a Sabbath School. Today I hear of a Female Prayer Meeting—tomorrow the brethren of the Church are gathered of one accord into one place. Here I meet a poor widow who is desirous of casting into the Lord's Treasury her mite, there I hear the learned & polished Statesman conversing with the deepest interest in the Grand Scheme of Evangelising the World & yet in these diversified operations I find that our Spirit actuates all—& what does all this mean. Is it not plain that Zion's King is about to take possession of our World. He is now marshalling his forces & making preparation for a great and glorious conflict. He is calling forth the active energies of all the Soldiers of the Cross & the poor widow with her mite will be found to be no inefficient laborer in the Vineyard of her Lord. A battle must be fought & a bloody battle it will be. Gog and Magog must meet the Lamb. The Beast will also make great opposition—doubtless the fires of martyrdom will be lighted again & desperate indeed will be the struggle. Sabbath School Teachers remember you are training up the very individuals who are to go forth & stand the first onset of this great conflict perhaps you have never reflected what an important work you have engaged in. Your situation is awfully responsible. Sabbath School will produce a powerful influence on the system of education. Hitherto the intellectual faculties have been cultivated to the greatest extent, whilst the moral faculties have been almost entirely neglected—the powers of the mind have been trained, the affections of the heart noncultivated. Men are sometimes proficient in the Sciences who are totally ignorant of Religion & the true character of the Great Author. Such men are Monsters in the Moral World—they may be compared to a man who has one arm which has grown to its full size & possessed it's full strength whilst the other from some natural defect is withered & deformed & useless.

The following entry is dated "4th Mo. 1829." It appears that the entry was entered sometime between 14 and 17 January 1828, although the entry is clearly marked as dated. The errant date was perhaps written on the manuscript later. It is possible that Grimké left pages in the journal blank and returned fourteen months later to use them. The entered date is puzzling.

Is it not true that where there is no confidence there is no real love. Where there is rudeness there is no tender feelings of affection. That blessed light which is given us to walk by is so bright that we may see how to pick up a pin by it—it can direct even to a hairs breadth. We ought to be very careful lest we lose by unwatchfulness what we have gained by faithful suffering. I think much satisfaction is to be deprived from seeing others do their duty tho' we may not be at all interested in it. The truly humble believer can bear to have his faults exposed to him even by a slave & will freely acknowledge them & be thankful, because his first desire is to be pure, & from constant watchfulness & prayer he recognizes every reproof as designed to accomplish the death of self, it is the chastening rod of his Father laid upon him because he loves him & desires to carry forward the great work of salvation from sin in his polluted heart. How hard it is to bear interruption when the soul has been permitted to enter the place where prayer is wont to be made. Sometimes when an uncouth servant has thus disturbed me I have tho't it was like to the savage bear treading under his feet the delicate flowers of spring, without knowing or caring what he was doing.

January 17   Last night my dear sister [Sarah] spoke to me very faithfully as to my feelings & conduct toward my Mother.[6] My proud heart rose at every word she said. I excused myself and cast all the blame on her, but I felt all the time that these were Satan's temptations & it did appear to me that now was the time to shake the very foundation of his throne in my heart as to allow him to harden me in my sins more than ever. The tears forced themselves from my eyes, at one moment I tried to forget what had been said, at another I was made deeply sensible that I was resisting the spirit & of the danger of doing so, with this con- flict of feeling I fell asleep—my dreams were troubled & I woke with my heart as heavy as a stone & as hard. After breakfast I retired alone and began to reflect when I soon became completely overpowered with my guilt and found that something must be done. Conscience told me that at her feet was my proper place & confession and repentance my duty, but my pride resisted it, and I deter- mined to write to her, but I felt that I was wrong in the resolution for that I ought to have an interview with her. I determined I would tho' I knew it would cost me much. I heard her footsteps in the passage, opened the door & requested her to come in, before she could be seated I burst into a flood of tears, she eagerly asked what was the matter, I threw myself into her arms & exclaimed O my mother I have sinned so much against you. Can you forgive me? Can you love me? Her trembling arm supported my head—she said all I could desire & entreated me to be calm, for she would remember my sins no more, forever. I told her God had broken my heart in pieces. She pressed me to her bosom & rejoiced that He had done so before she was no more as she knew my repentance would have been far more bitter if she had not been here to pronounce her for- giveness. Let the remembrance of this day (continued she) tend to make us love each other more & to humble us I added. Much more passed, we embraced each other again and again & then parted. O God what hast thou done, Thou hast broken my heart, then hast smitten the rock with the rod of thine anger & the waters of repentance flowed out. Thou hast bowed my stubborn will—thou hast caused me to drink of a bitter cup. I have drunk it to the very dregs. O Lord I abhor myself in dust and ashes. O that Thou wouldest forgive me.

January 23   This evening begged Henry[7] to go to Lecture with me, he refused. I passed one hour in great agony of mind in pleading for his soul, I felt that he was more and more hardened, but seemed to pray with less faith than ever. O how hard to see any thing of mercy in our Father's refusing to grant an answer to such prayer. If I have ever put up the prayer of faith it has been for his soul but this evening I had many hard tho'ts of my blessed Jesus. I tho't it hard that tho' the power was his that he would not exert it to subdue the heart of one who was so dear to me & for whom I had frequently & fervently pled. O it is hard to say at such times "Thy will be done."[8]

February 1   After much rainy weather our sky has become perfectly clear & in gasing at it lately I have had peculiarly delightful feelings, it looks like heaven so pure, so calm, so lovely, & I have often exclaimed if this world in which we live is so beautiful what must heaven be, if our Sun can by his dazzling rays gladden all around us—what will be the effect of the Sun of Righteous which is to enlighten the New Jerusalem. If the influence of visible objects can so cheer the heart here, what will be the effect of the splendors of Mount Zion bursting upon the disembodied spirit.

February 2   My mind has been brought to feel of late the necessity of Union among Christians—not members of the same Church or denomination only, but of every Church or Denomination. Christians are like the rivers which flow thro' & fertalizes our land, taking their rise in different parts but all losing their waters in the same great Ocean & mingling them together there. The hearts of all Christians ascend like the drops of Ocean to the clouds—they are attracted by the same influence—their prayer ascend to heaven & like the drops of water descend again into their own bosoms & in blessings on the world. When the waters of tribulation roll around our trembling bank, how sweet to know that it is anchored on the Rock of ages, & that He who commands the winds & waves is our Pilot. The sword of justice which was stretched out to destroy us has been sheathed in a Savior's side. The tears of the penitent are sweeter than all the joys of the thoughtless soul, for it is sweet to weep at the feet of Jesus. The Commandments are the Christian's binding strings, whilst he swears them there is no fear of his falling tho' he may walk over slippery places where Satan has spread many snares for his feet, for it is God whose hand is leading him & whose right hand is holding him. As soon as our first Parents eat of the forbidden fruit, Justice locked the gates of Mercy but Jesus has opened them with the key of the Cross. The River of Salvation now flows freely thro' our guilty World & all who will stoop to drink of its life giving waters may live forever.

God's children sometimes wander from him, but as soon as they lay themselves at the Savior's feet—he will take them up and lay them on his bosom. The Bible is a precious book when we can read it by the light of that pure flame of devotion which the Spirit of God kindles in the heart. The Bible is the Sinner's death warrant signed & sealed with the blood of the Savior. It is the Christian's Title deed to that building of God, that house not made with hands eternal in the heavens. It is the last will & testament of the Christian's Father whereby an inheritance incorruptible, undefiled, & that fadeth not away is secured to him for all eternity. Jesus Christ (the light of the World) has been lifted up on the Cross as a Beacon to warn Sinners of the Shoals & Quicksands which lie beneath the Sea of life & to point them to Heaven the only Heaven of Eternal rest.

February 7   How delightful it is to trace the analogy which exists between the natural & spiritual World. With how much rapture does the eye sometimes linger on the bright clouds which float over the western Horizon when lighted up by the last rays of the departing Sun, we watch them until by degrees they lose all their beauty & the west is curtained in blackness & why this change?— it is because the Luminary of day has sunk so low that Ichabod is written on all that but a little while since was bright & lovely. And cannot the believer sometimes look back upon trials which came over his soul like dark clouds & yet was he not even then enabled to rejoice in God his Savior because the beams of the Sun of Righteousness shone bright in the Temple of his heart—but as soon as the Master withdraws the light of his countenance then his soul sits in darkness & faints beneath the Cross.

February 10   My attention has lately been called to the duty of Christians' dressing quite plain. When I was first brought to the feet of Jesus I learned this lesson in part—but I soon forgot much of it & now I find my views stricter & clearer than they ever were. The first thing I gave up was a Cashmere mantle & being encouraged by a friend determined never to wear it again tho' I had no money at the time to get it replaced by anything else—however I gave it up in faith & the Lord provided for me.[9] This part of Scripture came very forcibly to my mind & very sweetly too "And Dagon was fallen upon his face to the ground before the ark of the Lord."[10] It was then clearly revealed to me that if the true ark Christ Jesus was really introduced into the Temple of the Heart that every idol would fall before it.

February 13   This morning I enjoyed an unction in prayer. I thought of the 133d Psalm—what a beautiful figure—it is like the oil poured upon the head of Assan & descending even to the skirts of his robe—it is like oil—this will penetrate the rocky heart of man & calm the raging waves of sin and temptations. "It is like the dew of Hermon, and as the dew descending upon the mountains of Zion, for there the Lord commanded a blessing, even life for evermore."[11] When the dews of divine grace descends upon the mountains of sin in the heart—they are melted down, the fruitifying streams of repentance flow from them & tho' plants of faith & humility & love begin to spring up in that heart which was once a barren rock—& here the Lord commands a blessing even life forever more. Happy is the soul which is thus blessed now, for these delightful feelings are but a few drops of that over flowing cup of joy of which he will drink forever in his Father's Kingdom. O God thou art the well spring of all happiness, and yet how prone my heart is to wonder from thee—my soul still cleaves to the dust, my affections are still "earthly & sensual." Thou knowest it is the desire of my soul to be cleansed from all filthiness of the flesh & spirit & to be sanctified & made a vessel sent for the master's use but O my soul art thou willing to have "the affections & heart crucified"[12]—art thou willing to be baptised with the baptism he was baptised with & to drink of the cup which He drank of. Remember the path of purification is the path of deep humiliation & tribulation—art thou willing to be "made perfect thro' suffering."

February 23   My friends tell me that I render myself ridiculous and expose the Crown of Jesus to reproach on account of my plain dressing, they tell me that it is wrong to make myself so conspicuous, but the more I ponder on this subject the more I feel that I am called with a high and holy calling & that I ought to be peculiar & zealous of good works. I see nothing of that kind of policy in the Bible which is so prevalent among Christians, that of trying to win over the world by a conformity to it's fashions to such a degree as to rid ourselves of the Cross. When "Zion shall look forth clear as the Sun, fair as the Moon and terrible as an army with banners"[13]—then her children will not temporise but come out entirely from the world & be known everywhere & at all times by their appearance & dress & conversation & conduct to be decidedly on the Lord's side. I rejoice to look forward to the time when Christians will follow the apostolical injunction to "keep their garments unspotted from the world"[14] & is not every conformity to it a spot on the believer's character. I think it is & I bless the Lord that he has been pleased to lead my mind to the contemplation of the subject. I pray that He may strengthen me to keep the resolution of my dressing always in the following style. A hat over the face without any bows of ribbon or lace— no frills or train—may every part of my dress & material not the finest.

February 24 I have lately been deprived of some of the privileges to which I used to be accustomed—tonight (Sabbath) I tho't it duty to remain at home & teach two of the Servants—I feel assured this will work for my good & I sometimes feel ashamed that I am so unwilling to yield up my privileges when duty demands it—surely the Lord would not deprive me of them if they were necessary to my growth in grace. Lately this text of Scripture has rested much on my mind "Be still and know that I am God"[15]—since I entered the christian course I have been very active but now it appears to me that my warmest & most energetic feelings are subdued & that I do feel more like clay in the hands of the father than I ever did. I am more and more convinced that there are various dispensations thro' which the believer must pass & the more he advances the more he feels the worthlessness of work as a foundation of the necessity of throwing himself into the Redeemer's arms as a little child.

March I do feel astonished that so many Christians reject the doctrine of Perfection. I am more & more convinced of it from reading the Bible. One exclaimed the other day David says "I have seen an end to all perfection"[16]—& so have I of the perfection of human nature without the cleansing influences of the Holy Spirit. I have seen some very striking instances of the utter inconsistency & watchfulness of the most learned and refined people of the world. The most complete system of morality is tarnished gold, yes, worse it is sounding brass & a tinckling symbal.

March 24 It is a long time since I have written in my diary but to night I feel called upon to record the goodness of the Gods. This morning M. C. came to see me—I had visited her during a severe fit of illness on the Benevolent Society —she came to tell me that my conversations at that time & a Tract (Importance of distinguishing between False and True Conversions) I gave her, had convinced her that tho' a professor of Religion for some years that she knew nothing of the vital godliness—by this she was led to the Baptist Church & now given evidence of a change of heart & has united herself to it. I desire to feel grateful if I have been made in the least degree instrumental of good to any. Last night I began to feel very anxious about my Class in the Sabbath School. I felt that I had not prayed enough for them & had not been faithful to them. I carried my case to my heavenly Father & sought direction from him what to do for them. I felt directed to call them together & speak solemnly & affectionately to them about the salvation of their souls & to write them to come to me every Wednesday Afternoon in order that I might converse with them & pray for them. This morning one of them came to me deeply anxious. I gave her two Tracts—went to prayer & begged her to come on Wednesday—she was at times quite overcome. I urged her to immediate repentance & we parted. O God I beseech thee not to suffer her to go back to the beggerly elements of the world, but glorify Thyself in her conversion from sin to holiness.

March 27   Yesterday I met my Class for the first time & confessed my unfaithfulness & proposed that they should come to me every week—it was a profitable little meeting I hope to all. One of them has entertained a hope for about a year—she asked me with great simplicity whether I tho't it wrong to plant geraniums. I told her I had no time for such things—she then said that she had [once] taken great pleasure in cultivating them, but lately she had felt so much condemnation that she had given it up entirely. Another professed to have some little hope in the Savior, remarked that her views as to dress had changed very much—she had taken off her rings & flowers & hoped not to wear them again—her hat also distressed her, it was almost new & she could not afford to get another. I told her if she would send it to me that I would try to change it. A good work is I think evidently begun, may "it be carried on unto the day of Jesus Christ."[17] Two others came who felt a little but are still asleep.

March 29   My mind has been much exercised lately on the question—Are seasons of darkness always occasioned by sin. About six months ago I was thrown into this state, at first I was totally bewildered, & knew not what to make of it, I had heard that sin was invariably the cause of such effects & Satan who is still "the accuser of the brethren"[18] tormented me day and night after suffering for some weeks & finding that no one knew any thing about my feelings with whom I conversed & literally feeling that there was no eye to pity. My Heavenly Father was pleased no infinite condescension to appear & plainly showed me that this state was sent in answer to my own most earnest prayer. In state of rejoicing I was frequently told that I had not that virtue which was the brightest ornament in the Christian crown—or humility & I did incessantly beseech the Lord to make me humble as a little child. I felt deeply that I did need it, & made known my wants to Jesus & professed myself willing to pass thro' my trials He might be pleased to visit me, but how little did I think He would take from me the light of his countenance. I knew from sweet experience that no outward trials could disturb the peace & tranquility of that soul which was warmed by the rays of the Sun of

Righteousness, & imparted whilst passing thro' the furnace of purification to be able still "to rejoice with joy unspeakable & full of glory"[19] but He who is full of wisdom knew that as long as I was on the Mountain I would look with contempt on those who were walking in the valley of humiliation, they appeared little in ~~the~~ my eyes & it was necessary for me to go down into it in order to learn that she who knows not what it is "to wrestle not against flesh and blood, but against principalities against power," against the rulers of darkness of the world, against spiritual wickedness in high places, knows but little of christian experience & is a babe in Christ.[20] As soon as I was taught by the Spirit that this darkness was not occasioned by sins, but that God was turning his holy hand upon me & purging the pure gold of grace from the dress of corruption, then these texts came to me "Be still & know that I am God"[21]—What I do thou knowest not now, but thou shall know hereafter. "I have many things to say unto you, but ye cannot bear them now."[22]—It was not until this that I ever knew what was meant by the soul passing thro' the wilderness—I had before tho't it applied to fading pleasure of the world, the unsatisfying nature of every thing earthly, but now I know it is to be "led by the Spirit into the wilderness to be tempted of the Devil"[23]—Whilst rejoicing in "a hope full of immortality" I often asked myself where is the Cross Christians have to bear, for every thing I do however self denying is no cross, for it is "my meat & drink to do the will of my Heavenly Father." To me at that time the ways of wisdom were ways of pleasantness & "all her paths were pure"—but now I know what it is for my soul to faint beneath the Cross just as my Master did, and the more I examine my own feelings & the Holy Scriptures, the more I am convinced that every Christian must (spiritually) pass through the same dispensations he passed thro'. One day from outward trials & inward temptations I was thrown into an awful state of mind when I heard the Savior say to me "Beloved, think it not strange concerning the fiery trial that is to try you, as tho' some strange thing happened unto you:[24] But rather rejoice inasmuch as ye are made partakers of Christ's sufferings, that when his glory shall be revealed ye may be glad with exceeding joy."[25] My soul consciously inquired why so much suffering, it shuddered & fainted at the tho't, but I was answered "Fear not for I am with thee."[26] When thou passest thro' the waters I will be with thee, & thro' the rivers they will not overflow thee; when thou walkest thro' the fire thou shalt not be burned; neither shall the flames kindle upon thee. Now I understand what Moses meant when he said that "Abraham talked to God face to face as a man talketh with his friend" for I felt fully assured that the Master was close by me, tho' my eyes were held on that I could not see him with eyes of flesh, but the eye of faith was open. At this time I enjoyed no other evidence of discipleship but His teaching.

March 31   This morning I read the 22d Psalm. It is only lately that I have been able to enjoy this part of the Bible—it always appeared to me that David was passing thro' dispensations far too spiritual for me to understand & this was literally the case. It is generally believed by Commentators that the feelings expressed in the Psalm are nothing more than an exact prophecy of the sufferings of Jesus, but I do not think so. I am fully persuaded from a careful and prayerful perusal of Scripture that every real believer must pass thro' the same sufferings that he did-thro' at one time we may stand on Mt. Tabor & behold his glory and rejoice in the bright light of his countenance, yet we too must not only follow him to the Garden and the Cross, but we must be crucified with him. Paul says "I am crucified with Christ"[27] & so must we be. Now it seems to me that it was thro' this agonizing dispensation that David was passing at the time he exclaimed "My God my God, why hast thou forsaken me"[28] it was when he felt that his soul was encompassed by his spiritual enemies that he said "For dogs have compassed me"[29] &c.—& tho' there some expressions in this Psalm which can apply to none but the Savior, yet these are very few & most of it must be the painful experience of all who "come to in the unity of the faith, & of the knowledge of the Son of God, unto a perfect man, unto the measure of the fullness of the stature of Christ."[30] These tho'ts led me to reflect upon the import of this passage—"But God forbids that I shd—glory save in the Cross of our Lord Jesus Christ, by whom the world is crucified to me & I unto the world."[31] Now it occurred to me that a crucified man was raised above the world, he has it under his feet, a crucified man can no longer take any pleasure in the things of the world, for he is a dead man, if the wealth & honors of the world were poured at his feet, still he would be perfectly insensible to all their attractions. Now here is the state of the sanctified believer, he is raised above this poor worthless world of dust, he has it beneath his feet & its pleasures, honors, & riches have lost their fascinations to him, for he is dead. "And the world is crucified to him"—a dead man however beloved cannot impart happiness to his friends now, every stream of joy which once flowed thro' him entirely stopped & that body around which we once threw our arms in the fondest embraces, becomes an object from which we turn with disgust, thus it is with the world to the dedicated believer—the rivers of happiness from which the children of this world drink with avidity flow thro' the dark valley of sin & of vice but cannot ascend the elevation of that Rock upon which the feet of the traveller are placed, the pleasures of the world are dead to him & that world around which the affections of his whole heart once clung is now an object [of] pity & disgust.

April 10   This morning I read the 31st Psalm—many parts of it have come with power to my soul—he says I was "a fear to mine acquaintances: that they did see me without fled from me."[32] Alas! How little are christians a fear to their acquaintances now, David was so decidedly holy, that those who knew him were afraid to be in his company lest he should reprove there careless & prayerless lives, his purity of character was a bright & shining light which dazzled & confounded sinners & they fled from his presence. "I am forgotten as a dead man out of mind."[33] This holy man was never seen in the haunts of vanity or vice for he says "I have not sat with vain persons, neither will I go with dissemblers"[34] therefore ~~the~~ he was to those world beings "as a dead man, out of mind" because out of sight—it is impossible that he could have been so entirely forgotten by the world, if he had mingled as much with its notaries as some who ~~who~~ take the name, without carrying the Cross of Jesus. "I am like a broken vessel"[35] O! how often have I heard the despisers of Religion say of young converts that they were entirely missed, they were good for nothing since they had become pious—and is it not strikingly true that real believers are as useless to the world as broken vessels & like them they will be thrown away by their acquaintances and entirely neglected.

April 13   I found upon going to the Sabbath School that one of my Scholars had been taken from me. It is only three weeks since she came into my class & it appears that the serious impressions she had received about a year before under a Baptist Minister were received with more power than ever—she soon began to exhibit the fruits of the Spirit in her life & her Mother became so apprehensive that she would unite herself with the Presbyterian Church that in ~~th~~ a few weeks she persuaded her to go to the Baptist School tho' there was no class in it fit for her to enter. This was at first a great trial to me. I tho't it was very hard that just as I was reaping the fruits of my labor that they should thus be snatched out of my hand. I saw some time ago that the trial was approaching & I have been praying for resignation but I must acknowledge as yet that it has only served to show how much self there is in the best duties I perform. Ah! If it was the glory of my Master & not my own that I was seeking surely it would be immaterial to me in what Church the seed I have sown sprung up & bore fruit. I thank the Lord for this little incident it has been the means of exposing before my own view something more of the corruption of heart.

April 16   My mind has at times been much exercised as to the inconsistencies of christians. In my own church (the best I believe in town) professors are not to be distinguished from the world scarcely (in dress particularly). Friends are certainly the most spiritual and the most consistent christians. Lord I feel like clay in thy hands lead me just where & how thou pleasest.

April 18   Yesterday I was thrown into great exercise of mind. The Lord more clearly than ever unfolded his design of appointing me another field of labor & I clearly saw that I was about to pass thro' deep waters at the same time I felt released from the Cross of conducting family duty. I feel that very soon all my burdens will drop from my hands & all the cords by which I have been bound to many christian friends will be broken to pieces soon I shall be a stranger in the midst of those with whom I once took sweet counsel. I should have to tread the wine press alone—to be (like Jesus) forsaken of all & condemned actually crucified. I must be introduced into the fellowship of suffering. Thy will be done, my will is swallowed up in thine O God. I am willing to abide all the turnings of thy Holy hand if thou wilt only put my enemies beneath the Redeemer's feet & make me conqueror & more than conqueror thro' Him that loved me & gave himself for me. This morning I felt no condemnation when I went in to family worship & yet did not lead as usual in the duties. I felt that my Master had stripped me of the priests garments & put them upon my Mother—may he be pleased to anoint her for the sacred duties.

April 20   My mind is composed and I cannot but feel astonished at the total change which has passed over me during the last 6 months. Then I delighted in going to meeting 4 & 5 times every week, but now my Master says "be still"[36] & I would rather be at home, for I find that every stream from which I used to drink the refreshing waters of Salvation is dry & that I have been led to the fountain itself. Once Oh how precious were the means of grace to my soul with how much power did sermons come home to my heart, but now I sometimes wish I could close my ears to the preacher's voice & retire into the closet of my heart & "hold converse with Him who speaks as never man spake." And is it possible I would ask myself tonight, is it possible that today is the last time I expect to visit the Presbyterian Church—the last time I expect to teach my interesting Class in Sabbath School—and is it right that I should separate myself from a people whom I have loved so tenderly & who have been the helpers of my joy, is it right to give up instructing those dear children whom I have so often carried in the arms of faith & love to a throne of grace. Reason would sternly answer no, but the Spirit whispers "come out from among them."[37] O! God thou only knowest the conflict of soul I did suffer when from time to time thou didst unfold to my feeble mind thy mysterious purposes concerning me—thou only knowest how every feeling of nature was opposed to such an entire separation from what I clung to with eagerness & tenacity—when first I am Ichabod written on the walls of that Church which was the Cradle of my soul. It would be like a dagger to my heart & desolation and darkness covered my future prospects but Oh! The goodness, the tenderness of my heavenly Father—by degree the fiber of affection were loosened & I found the ends bursting asunder till now my soul is free from all incumbrance & I am sure that if I do refuse the call of my master to the Society of Friends that I shall be a dead member in the Presbyterian Chh. I have read none of their books for fear of being convinced of their Principles, but the Savior has taught me himself that "He who is head over all things to his Church"[38] has called me to follow him into the little silent meeting which is in this City. Oh! How strange this will appear to all my friends, I am ready to ask will I not be a stumbling block to many, but Jesus says what is that to thee, follow then me. It has been clearly shown to me that the 3d P.C. was the cradle into which my soul was put by my Heavenly Father, then I was fed by the "sincere milk of the word,"[39] but now its Pastor can do no more for me he knows nothing about the exercises of my mind & he can teach me no more, I need a higher teacher & these words of John have been sweet to my soul—"Ye need not that any man teach you but the same anointing teacheth you all things, & is truth & no lie,"[40]—Oh! It is well for me that I have a guide superior to the Bible itself for how should I ever know from reading it that I ought to take such a step as I now feel by divine power & divine teaching constrained to take, regardless of all consequences & leaving them entirely in the hands of him who "hath done all things well."[41]

April 25 I saw Wm. McDowell[42] day before yesterday & conversed with him on the subject of leaving his Church—we wept together for this is a painful separation to both—he is totally ignorant of the state of my mind & told me that he pitied me sincerely for that I was certainly under the delusions of the arch adversary, before going away he earnestly entreated me not to act precipitately, but to pray over this subject—when he was gone I began to think what an awful thing it would be if I really was deceived as to the source of my feelings—doubts & fear arose & casting myself at the feet of Jesus I besought him to teach me what was the real state of my heart. I begged him not to suffer me to be deluded & these words came again & again to my heart. Have you not been taught already, what else do you want the path of duty has been made plain & strength has been given what more can I do for you. Yesterday two of my female friends called about my leaving the Sabbath School, they tried to persuade me that I was under wrong influence & expressed some fear as to what would be the result of my wild notions—deceived I certainly was & they pitied me sincerely & (this they said I do believe with the tears of affection in their eyes) & they would pray that the Lord would bring me back to the paths of duty I had forsaken & plant me again in the midst of their Church—they would not give one up they said for they still loved me. No one can imagine how strange I felt under the expressions of such feelings—grateful I hope for their love but we were mutually pitying each other—mutually desiring that the eyes of the other might be opened. As to the exercises of my mind, it was useless to talk to them about them for they did not understand me & when I mentioned two or three particular instances of the teachings of the Spirit they would say that they were evidently temptations of Satan & that he was permitted to tempt me in this way in order to try my faith. This passage of Scripture seemed to suit my case for I said no more "as a lamb before her shearers is dumb, so opened he not his mouth"[43] & thinking of the light in which the teachings of the Holy Spirit were regarded I remembered the accusation of the Jews against our divine Master "he casteth out devils thro' Beelsebub the prince of the Devils["][44]—so now the influence of his spirit on my heart was attributed to the Prince of darkness. I felt firm whilst conversing with them but when they had gone I began to question again as to whether I was deceived or not & this threw into a state of deep exercise of mind but it did not last long, for I was relieved by the recollection of the impossibility of my enjoying any peace if I was doing anything wrong "Beloved, if our hearts condemn us not, then have we confidence towards God." This conversation took place in the afternoon & I had not got over the feelings it produced when at night one of my Sabbath School Scholars called to see me—she was converted in the School and when I told her the afternoon before of my change of sentiment and my determination to give up my class, she expressed much sorrow & when I mentioned the desolate feelings—I expected soon to ~~feel~~ have, her little heart overflowed with tenderness & she said never mind Miss Grimké tho' all your friends may forsake yet "the Lord will take you up"[45]—this seemed to be a drop of comfort sent by my Heavenly Father & it was peculiarly sweet coming from a child whom I believed He had condescended to make me the instrument of bringing to Jesus—but this interview was still more interesting. She said she was sure that she had passed thro' the same feelings with myself & that she had never had so great a weight upon her heart at that time—her sympathy was like balm to my wounded spirit & after mingling our tears together over each others trials we parted feeling much refreshed by these new proofs of affection.

Although the date of the next entry is not noted, it was probably the 28th, which would have been the Monday following the 25th.

April (Monday)   My mind has been in such a state of suffering since Friday that I could not write. On that day I received a letter from W. McDowell which awakened every tender emotion & pushed my heart to the very bottom he does not take a right view of the subject & indeed I cannot make him understand me "in my humiliation my judgment is taken away"[46] & I find that I must be content to be condemned & to be regarded as completely under the dominion of Satan. O that I might be purified whilst passing thro' the furnace. O that pride may be smitten in the dust & "every idol utterly abolished." I sat down to write an answer when Sister E[liza][47] came to ask me some trifling question—in the anguish of my spirit I begged her to leave me alone for I could not attend to anything & immediately burst into tears—she went out & closed the door, but soon returned & with deep feeling depicted in her countenance she threw her arms around me, we wept aloud—she then said she had not come to advise me for no human being could do this, but she tho't I must feel alone in my Father's house & she had come to weep with me. I showed her the letter I had received and after being encircled in each others arms & pouring out each others hearts for near two hours we parted, the better, I trust for these deep exercises of mind—never wide that day—forgotten by me. I returned to my desk & as strength and words were given continued to write until 5 O'Clock when the door was opened & the Superintendent of the S.S. entered—he met me with a smile but my poor broken heart felt no inclination for any such light feelings and as I offered him my hand, deep anguish filled my soul & I took my seat beside him convulsed with weeping—he appeared sorry for my distress & took this ground as an evidence of my doing what was wrong as the Christian was permitted to enjoy a peace whilst in the path of duty which nothing could destroy. I told him I did possess entire peace, why then he enquired this suffering? I tried to explain my feelings but it was useless—he could not understand me & I sat like a criminal condemned before her judge—he treated me tenderly however & I was not sorry we had the interview—as soon as he left me I finished my letter. I was very anxious to have a copy of it but my head and eyes were in such a condition that I could not write anymore & feeling anxious that Wm. McD. should no longer be kept in suspense I sealed it & sent it without even sharing it with any one & went to bed at 6 O'Clock being quite exhausted & really not from the deep exercise I had recently passed thro' whilst lying awake & thinking of what had passed this text was given to me "The like figure whereunto even baptism doth also now save us, (not the putting away of the filth of the flesh, but the answer of a good conscience towards God)"[48] the latter part felt like oil poured into my heart & I enjoyed much peace. Saturday afternoon I could not feel easy without a farewell address to the Teachers of the Sabbath School & sent it to the place of their meeting but do not know whether it was read. Sunday I went to Friends' Meeting all day—this text was continually on my mind "I will wait upon the Lord"[49] it was a season of barrenness to my soul, I felt that I was in my right place but no particular manifestation was given and in looking forward to the Summer I think that spiritual life will be born & that the Lord means to "let patience have her perfect work in my heart.["][50] I shall be stripped of every thing & made to feel that I "am poor and needy, blind & naked."[51] O that I might be still under this tedious & refining operation. O that I may yield myself as clay to all the turning of his holy hand & at last may my soul be "His workmanship"[52] & have the image of my meek & lovely Jesus. O that whilst in this furnace every shred of my own righteousness may be burned up & I may be "brought unto the King in raiment of needlework—having my clothing of wrought gold & being all glorious within."[53] Yesterday in meeting this text was also given "I have accepted thee in this thing also."[54]

May 1   This has been a day of inward trial—doubts and fears have arisen as to whether I have been directed by Jesus or prompted by the adversary to separate myself from the 3d Pres: Ch: This is Thursday night and Oh! When I look back to this time a year ago I cannot refrain from tears for then I would not have remained at home on any account & it is now my voluntary choice, or rather so completely is Ichabod written on all the services in that Church now that when I did go a fortnight since I always came out with a heavier heart than when I went in. Many trials are before me & I know not to what state of nakedness & famine my soul will be reduced to before I shall be favored to hear preaching—may my life be preserved thro' this dark dispensation & may the root of humility strike deep into my heart. "O Lord make plane my path before me, because of my enemies." I feel tried as to speaking the plain language. I think sometimes that if I were to do it my mind would be easier & yet I do not know that the command has gone forth yet, O that I might be enabled to do every thing at the right time & in the right way.

The date of the following entry would be 4 May.

May (Sabbath)   My spirit seems light this morning & the song of praise is put into my mouth, love springs up with my heart & flows out to all around. In thinking yesterday of the star which guided the wise men to the feet of Jesus I was led to reflect on the manner in which the Lord leads his people in the path of duty—it is only in the narrow way that Heaven be found & tho' no star appears in the natural horizon to direct their footsteps, yet the eye of faith can see the bright light of the Spirit still shining & shedding its beams of glory around his pathway—& still leading them to "the place where Jesus is within." In the beginning of my christian course—The star of the Spirit led me to the 3d Presbyterian Ch: & now since Ichabod has been written on it's walls—it has removed & rests on Friends meetings, it occurred to me, why then do you not receive more from Jesus there? I immediately recollected that when the wise men found the babe of Bethlehem they did not receive any thing from Him, but "when they were come into the house they fell down & worshipped him & when they had opened their treasure they presented unto him gifts"[55] & it does appear to me that I must go there (for the present, expecting to receive nothing, but to worship him & open my heart to him & present the sacrifices of "a broken spirit & a contrite heart"[56] which He will not despise; my duty ~~for the~~ now is to wait there (as the Apostles did at Jerusalem) for the promise of the Father.

I was struck this morning with this fact related in the 4 chap: Mark & "when they were alone he expounded all things unto his disciples.["][57] O how little do we learn in a crowd—how necessary is retirement to the cultivation of vital religion—it is in the stillness of the Christ that the Master breaks the seven seals of the Book & still speaks as never man spake. What privileges to be taught by Him in whom all the fulness of the Godhead dwells, will sway the balance. Apostles say to them who are thus instructed "you have no need that any man teach you."[58]

It is said that "Christ thro' the Eternal Spirit offered himself unto God"[59]— if I may so speak it was because the great sacrifice was offered thro' the Spirit that it was acceptable, & so it is with our poor offerings of prayer and praise they must be offered thro' the Eternal Spirit. If prayer is not the inwrought prayer of the Spirit, however eloquent it may be, still it is a "vain oblation."

It was remarked by a good old Quaker that he believed that the true Israel of God were still divided into Tribes. It is only embracing this opinion that I can account for the diversity of feeling & opinion which we find among Christians at the present day—do we not all know from experience that there are some whom we cannot but believe are sincere followers of the Lamb & yet with whom we have no fellowship, no clear communion of sentiment, their tho'ts are not as our tho'ts, nor their ways our ways. Here too I think we may discover why there are unhappy marriages even among true believers. The Israelites were positively commanded not to intermarry with each others tribes, & I believe if christians were at the present day to attend more to the internal manifestations of the Spirit that tho' there is outwardly no distinction of Tribe, no evidence why they might

Philadelphia

July 29   Seven weeks have elapsed since I wrote in my diary.[1] Very unexpectedly after having been brought into a state of calm submission to whatever
the Lord was pleased to lay upon me in Charleston the door was opened for me
to spend the Summer in Philadelphia. I think I was willing to go or stay just as
was right, feeling that in C[harleston] tho' I had much to bear yet strength was
granted equal to my day & that I enjoyed a peace which I never could feel in
P[hiladelphia] however free from outward trials I might be, if that was not my
proper place I prayed to be directed & an evidence was given that a time of rest
was before me & that if I sailed for the north, the master would be in the Ship
with his disciple & would abide with & direct me. My health required a change
of air for owing to the deep exercise of my mind & the active life I had led for
the last 2 years, my frame had been much weakened. My friends were all glad to
hear I was about to leave them being convinced that I had nothing at present to
do in Charleston & that my soul & body both needed rest. On my passage I felt
a delightful peace & when tossed on the waves in my birth felt like a little baby
rocked to Sleep by the kind hand of a parent. On leaving C[harleston] I could not
see a day before me & knew not whether a home was ready for me or not but
He who has said "My people shall have a place of refuge" has been pleased to open
many doors to me & I enjoy a home wherever I go. ["]Truly goodness and mercy
have followed me all the day long"[2] & the constant language of my heart is "What
shall I render unto the Lord for all his benefits"[3]—my only fear is that I may
abuse his mercies & the necessity of using my friends exactly in the capacity &
according to the design of the great & good giver has dwelt with much force on my
mind lately. "Preserve me O God, for in thee do I put my trust"[4] is the constant
prayer of a heart which looks with wonder love & praise at that cure which is daily
and hourly extended over a poor, sinful worm. The language of the Apostle has
been again & again ~~been~~ bro't sweetly to my mind. He "giveth you all things richly
to enjoy"[5] & the words of Jesus to my soul seems to be "take your rest."[6]

August 3   How beautiful and full is this expression of the prophet Isaiah
"I will extend peace to her as a river."[7] Is there a more lovely object in nature
than the lucid stream whose bosom glistens with the rays of the Sun & reflects
the asure of an unclouded sky. Whilst nothing passes over it how calm are it's
waters—& thus is it with the believer in Jesus, he enjoys a peace which the
world can neither give nor take away. Of Moses it was said that his face shone
after he held converse with God upon the mountain & so ought every christian

countenance to bewray him that he has been with Jesus, just as we may be assured that the Son is shining from seeing his rays reflected in the water & it will be so if we are faithful & abide in him. The different events of life too are like the ~~the~~ various objects which float on the stream for a moment they cast their shadows upon its' ~~& disturb~~ surface & ruffle the sameness of its waters but soon pass away & leave not a trace behind. But how changed is the scene when clouds & darkness cover the sky itself & the Sun no longer shines upon the river & the winds of heaven are let loose upon it then instead of its bosom glistening in the Sun beams, it is dark and gloomy instead of that peacefulness with whh it flowed in its channel, it's waves are tossed to & fro & all is confusion—& O how like this ~~is to~~ those hours of darkness which sometimes move over the soul, when the Sun of Righteousness hides his glorious face & our hearts are no longer cheered by the light of his countenance.

August 7   Since my arrival I have enjoyed an almost unbroken rest to my soul, truly in looking back I can say with the Psalmist "thou hast delivered my soul from death, my feet from falling & my eyes from tears."[8] But this is a season of strong temptation & often do I remember the exhortation of Jesus to his disciples —"pray that your flight be not on the Sabbath day"[9] this is a Sabbath to my soul and did I not believe that my frail back was anchored on the Rock of Ages I know I must inevitably sink to rise no more in this Sea of temptation. Many Friends have kindly invited me to take tea at their houses, I have done so 3 or 4 times but invariably such a depression seizes me that I cannot converse & sometimes the tears will fill my eyes; soon as I enter I feel impatient to be gone & this anxiety continues & increases the whole time, I cannot account for the feeling unless it is given to prevent my making many acquaintances, last night I staid at home & spent a delightful evening in reading to Dear Sister [Sarah] & the two girls, I went to bed with these words resting sweetly on my mind "peace be upon you."

October 31   In a few days I expect to leave this delightful land which has been an Elim unto my soul & body. I desire to be grateful for all I have enjoyed & still more grateful for the willingness I do sweetly experience to give up all my friends here & to go to Carolina not knowing what awaits me there. I have been plainly directed to "Return to the land of my fathers & to my kindred['] & the promise has been added "I will be with thee."[10] I think much suffering awaits me, but O Lord be thou my strength & shield my high tower & my refuge—this language appears to be addressed to me. "Verily verily I say unto you, ye shall weep & lament, & ye shall be sorrowful, but your sorrow shall be turned into joy."[11]

Charleston

30 November   I arrived a few days since from Philadelphia after a 2 weeks passage in which we encountered 3 Storms. In the first I was much alarmed, I believe I was left to feel my own weakness for wise purposes—during the second I was greatly depressed fearing that the tempest which howled around me then was typical of what I am to encounter in Charleston—still I was quite calm in both I did not desire that any thing might be altered, only that patience might be granted & I was enabled to say "The Lord is good & his mercy endureth forever."[12] In the third I still felt some anxiety but my situation appeared to be like one who holding something valuable in a trunk had in time of danger taken the treasure out & secured it & feeling the treasure was perfectly safe cared but very little about the trunk. My soul was the treasure, this I had long before committed to the care of my precious Savior. I could say with confidence "I know in whom I have believed, that He is able to keep that which I have committed unto Him["]—my body was only the empty trunk—& if we were wrecked—this only would be lost. But it has pleased my Father to spare my unprofitable life for which I desire to render thanks—and find myself again in the bosom of my family— the prayer of my heart is that our coming together may be ["]for the better not for the worse."[13] I see nothing for me to do here but it is comforting to reflect that—"they also serve who stand and wait." I began to feel the weight of this remark "Religion consists in what we are, not in what we do." O that I may only keep in my right place & be willing to be thought nothing but a poor deluded fool. Peter says "ye living stones are built up a spiritual house"[14]—now in every building there are different parts & I believe that this to share the different places of believers in the Church—each believer is a living stone in this spiritual house & no two stones can stand in exactly the same place yet they are all in their proper places, and I think there is a dispensation in which he is brought to feel that he is sure of the steps of the temple, made to be trampled upon. Some excitement still exists as to my having left the Presbyterian Society. May the Lord hide me in the secret of his pavilion from "the strife of tongues."[15] I desire to be a child in malice. This morning in reading was struck with the passage "The Lord shall fight for you & ye shall hold your peace."[16] I think it was given to me, may I not only be consoled but best profited by it.

December 12   Have but a few minutes to write but feel as if I must record the living kindness of the Lord. My unburdened heart exclaims in the language of the Psalmist "I will bless the Lord at all times, his praise shall continually be in my mouth.["][17] My soul shall make her boast in the Lord. Surely in my empty &

useless state I can boast in nothing but Him—for in myself I find nothing to feed spiritual pride upon. O I am nothing & willing to be nothing yea I rejoice in my nothingness.

December 14   I feel a renewed desire to be perfectly still before the Lord. I am more and more convinced that this state must be attained before I can be prepared to hear or to do his will—sometimes I am afraid that even my breathing may disturb the motions of his Spirit on my heart. How much the heart is like a vessel on the troubled Ocean—our earthly feelings & desires toss it to & fro just as the vessel is tossed on the waves, never still for a single moment but always in motion—but there is an influence which comes down upon the heart & stills its raging restless passions, it is like oil poured upon the billows which calms them into peace. O it is in this state that we are able to attest the truth of our divine Master's declaration "the words that I speak unto you they are spirit & they are life"[18]—it is in vain that we go about to hear human being proclaim the truths of the gospel unless our spiritual ears are also open to hear His words who still speaks in our hearts as "never man spake."[19]

December 16   Feel uncomfortable tonight & know not why except it be because I twice in the course of the evening called the 5th day & 6th day by the name the world has given them. I wish to excuse myself but think I did it not to avoid the Cross, but because I knew I should not be understood but O I know now from the reproofs of the blessed Spirit that I did what was wrong & that I must not bend to worldly customs in any thing—this deviation I suspect sprung from the want of the entire willingness to be tho't a fool—those who do not feel the necessity of making every thing after the pattern shown us in the Mountain of Holiness regard these things as too little to be of consequence but he who has not learned the importance of trifles has not yet learned one of the most important lessons in the natural & spiritual world. I well remember that I was greatly helped forward in the divine life last winter by tearing up my Novels & taking the bows off my shoes and cutting the border off my shawl, many laughed at what they tho't useless & foolish particularity, but I began to feel that neither the good nor bad opinion of any one altered my standing in the sight of God at all & that I was to act with single eye to Him & strictly to obey every requisition of his Spirit tho' I might by so doing forfeit the good opinion of those I loved & valued most. I once enjoyed a character for piety & zeal but now because I am a Quaker my friends think it impossible I can be in the right road, they think I have embraced dangerous errors & that I am saying peace, when the Lord says there is no peace. I have left the field of activity & therefore they think I cannot love my precious, precious Jesus but if I do not deceive myself I love him more than ever tho' I know there is not as great a contrast in my feelings towards him & towards human beings because I love all thro' him & for him whereas I once passed thro' dispensation in which I would not & did not love any but those who loved him & from believing in the Doctrine of Predestination Satan persuaded me that I was not required to love those whom I did not believe or had no evidence from their holy lives to believe He had loved & died for—at this time I felt, fully felt that enmity which it was foretold should exist between the seed of the woman and the seed of the Serpent. O there was a root of bitterness in my heart then—against a particular individual more especially which it cost me agony indescribable to pull up & cast out, this person was an inconsistent professor of Religion & it seems to me when I look back upon my feelings that I shrink from them with horror here was a dispensation like that of the Jewish in which it was said an eye for an eye & a tooth for a tooth, but I think I do now feel something of the dawning of a better & a brighter one, even the dispensation of the glorious Gospel of peace & love in which we are privileged to love our enemies & I can now take that person to my bosom & feel the sweet flowings of tenderness & affection towards them. Lord this is thy work in my heart & it is a great good word, "bless the Lord O my soul & all that is within me bless his holy name"[20]—truly I can say with David "Great & marvellous are Thy works & that my soul knoweth right well."[21]

December 18   I believe there is a dispensation of rest thro' which the believer passes which may be compared to the flowing of a river thro' a forest for tho' it bears no vessels on it's bosom yet it fertilizes the banks & causes them to bring forth abundantly—so the christian sometimes is required to bear no burdens at all, while at the same time, by his fife he "holds forth the word of life" & ["]shines like a light in the world"[22] directing those around him to the harbor of eternal rest.

December 19   A few short days have elapsed since my heart sung the anthem of praise for joy and gladness of heart, but O how different my feelings tonight, Lord help me to say "thy will be done, help me to be willing to drink one drop of that cup of suffering than drunk off to the dregs for human guilt & human woe.["] Since my arrival in C[harleston] I have enjoyed a continuation of that rest from exercise of mind which began last Spring until tonight but my soul is sorrowful & my heart bleeds. I am ready to exclaim, when shall I be released from the land of Slavery, but if my suffering for them can at all ameliorate their condition surely I ought to be quite willing & I can now bless the name of the

Lord that my "labour has not been in vain"[23] tho' much remains to be done yet. I sincerely desire to do all & say all "in meekness of wisdom."[24] Sanctify these things unto our Heavenly Father & enable me to say ["]Prepare me in any way thou pleasest for the work thou hast set before me—purify me like silver & make me just what thou wouldst have me to be & save me for thy mercy's sake." "How precious the promise I will not leave you comfortless I will send you another comforter."[25] I set to my seal that the Lord is true for tho' far from those who can sympathize fully in the feelings under which I now labor yet there is a Friend who sticketh closer than a brother—he is the Friend of Sinners therefore he is my Friend. I hold communion with him & the words of wisdom & consolation drops from his lips like honey from the honey comb. Tonight I look at the quiet comfortable little parlour in P[hiladelphia] where C[atherine Morris][26] & precious Sister [Sarah] & myself used to sit together on the Sofa & wait upon the Lord, yes I remember well how peaceful all within and without used sometimes to be & how tenderly we used to press each others hands & I lean upon C's bosom & find it a sweet home in a strange land. Lord, it was Thou who gave these blessings & I did & still do bless thee for them and in Thou who hast taken them away & I still can say blessed be thy Holy name—even so Father for so it seemed good in Thy sight.

December 20   This morning in reading part of the Epistle of John was struck with these words "Perfect love casteth out fear"[27]—do not think I ever understood them before but it appeared to me that the meaning was this. He who loves God perfectly feels no fear under any dispensation thro' which he may be passing, whether of joy or sorrow—fullness or emptiness—temptation or barrenness, feel no fear but that all things are ordered or permitted for his spiritual good, just as much as if there was not a being in the Universe but himself. In time of prosperity & temptation he holds the precious promises to his bosom. Because thou hast kept the word of my patience "I also will keep thee in the hour of temptation"[28] & "God is faithful and will not suffer you to be tempted above what you are able to bear, but will, with the temptation also make a way to escape."[29] In seasons of trial & sorrow he is at times permitted "to glory in tribulation knowing that tribulation maketh patience & patience, experience & experience hope that hope which maketh not ashamed."[30] In barrenness, he remembers the words of his master "blessed are the poor in spirit."[31] In emptiness he hears him saying unto him "Blessed are they who hunger and thirst after righteousness for they shall be filled."[32] He who is made perfect in love is not always suspecting the Lord's faithfulness, if He should be pleased to withdraw the light of his countenance & leave him to the buffettings of Satan for he loves him for himself alone, not for the joys of consolations of his spirit, not because he is shielded from the fiery darts of the Enemy. Oh no—he who is perfect in love, will as willingly follow his Lord into the howling wilderness to be tempted of the Devil & to the Garden of Agony & the Cross of Crucifixion as up to the Mount of Transfiguration on into Jerusalem ["]in the midst of the multitude shouting Hosannahs to the Son of David." It seems to me a great attainment to love Jesus for himself. The sinner says he loves him, but why, because the thinks he died for him, or perhaps he loves him for the blessings with which he is surrounded. The professor says he loves him & will sit around what he calls the Communion Table, whilst he folds the world in his arms & nurses sin in his heart—he loves him because he thinks "he is altogether such an one as himself"[33]—he follows him because it is the fashion to belong to some Church. The young convert loves him for the joys which flow into his soul—but he only who is perfect in love, loves him because He is the brightness of the Father's Glory & altogether lovely in himself—& he only will follow him whithersoever He leads him—& do whatsoever He commands—he only is willing to be any thing or nothing—a fool in the eyes of the world—a step in his spiritual temple made to trodden upon—the filth & off scouring of the earth. He only has his heart fixed & confers not with flesh & blood, but looks at the Cross as his Polar Star & feels that the life of Jesus in his heart is the only light by which he is to walk—when thrown into circumstances of difficulty he goes not to human beings to teach him what to do—O no, he goes to Jesus in his heart and as Jehovah was wont to make his will known in days that are past in a voice issuing from above the mercy seat—so he will now teach all by the voice of his Spirit for James says ["]if any man lack wisdom let him ask of God"[34]—not of priests & elders & christians in high repute, & the command of the Omnipotent is "This is my beloved Son, hear him.["][35] It is the hypocrite who is always looking at the rewards of humans—for the true believer enjoys the evidence that "his reward is with him"[36]—the love which his Master bears towards him is reward enough—he loves him for himself not because he will take him to heaven.

December 2   I have thought that the course of the Christian was like that of the planets—always progressive tho' sometimes apparently retrograde—for instance ~~when~~ if he ceases to work outwardly he is thought to have grown lukewarm, when he is only ceasing from the activity of self & obeying the divine command "Be still & know that I am God."[37] Do not multitudes of Protestants believe practically in the power of human beings to absolve them from their sins as much as Catholicks, for instance a person feels uneasy about some thing they are doing—instead of going to God to ask counsel, ~~they~~ he goes to his Minister or some valued friend & they tell him such scruples are altogether useless & persuade him the thing is quite allowable—he goes home perfectly satisfied & if reproved by one who knows something of the depths of the heart he replies my minister or such a friend says it is not sinful and therefore I mean to do it & does resolve to kick against the pricks of conscience more violently than ever until it ceases to reprove & he is more hardened than before—now what is this but virtually saying, Men are better judges of what is sin than the Light within me & if they do not think such actions sinful, I need not either, for it will not be counted unto me as sin. O when will the people consider that the life of Christ in the soul is the Light of men, that Light which ["]shines in the darkness of the heart & which is given to every man to profit withall & lighteth every man that cometh into the world"[38]—it is this which is given ["]as a light to their feet & a lamp to their paths"[39] & when our eye is fixed on this light all others fade before our view, the light of reason fades, the light of Philosophy flickers & dies—for this is the Sun of Righteousness & when it arises on the soul—the heart like the temple of old is filled with the Glory of the Lord. And as in the natural world when the Sun appears in the greatness of his strength, the lesser lights of heaven are extinguished the moon and the stars disappear so is it in the spiritual world. O when we feel that this ["]Light is the eternal word, the son of God revealed in us" & that the command from heaven is "Hear him"[40] how little will we care for the instructions of men, then it is we become fools in the eyes of men, for they are always running after human beings to teach them the very lessons which if they would only "be still"[41] the Lord would write with his own hand upon their hearts, but how can He write when the heart is never fixed, for in this glorious dispensation he writes his laws not upon tables of stone but upon fleshly tables of the heart—but before this is done we must go up into the mountain of retirement & separate ourselves as Moses did from the World, even from the elders of Israel and carry our hearts in our hands as he did the tables of stone & wait upon the Lord.

December 25   O that I might live religion—how striking the exhortation of the Apostle—present your bodies a living sacrifice, Lord enable me so to live that every day I may sacrifice my own will to thine. I desire to talk but little about religion, for words are empty sounds, but may my life be a living epistle known & read of all men. I desire to be "blameless & harmless a child of God without rebuke"[42] ["]O for that gentleness which alone can make me great[.]"

It is said of Simon of Cyrene "him they compelled to bear his Cross"—the Cross of his Master was laid upon him, by whom? by Jesus himself?—no, it was those who had condemned & were about to nail him to it—it was by the disorderly multitude, those who were his enemies & yet he bore it, but it would appear reluctantly, for he was compelled to do it—here I think is a dispensation which is sometimes experienced. There are evils which the christian has to bear from those around him which if he were not compelled to submit to ~~them~~ he would throw off & rid himself of—there are trials which I think we can plainly feel are laid upon us by human beings—not by God & these are the hardest to bear because Satan takes occasion to excite all manner of evil feelings in us against them, pride, anger, hatred, contempt suspicion &c.—but we must remember that we are just in the situation of Simon here—& tho' the enemies of Jesus may lay this Cross upon us, yet it is his Cross & therefore we ought willingly to bear it, endeavoring to lose sight entirely of the hands which have laid it upon us—how frequently have I heard expressions like these, if it were sickness or any affliction that the Lord had laid upon me, then I could bear it—but this is an evil which comes from man & I cannot bear it from a human being—but O if we had right feeling would we not cheerfully bear these sufferings, remembering that this is still the Cross of Jesus tho' laid upon us by a human creature.

December 26   It is sometimes said that all that is in our hearts naturally must be worked out, but I do not think so, there are some affections & feeling which ought still to live tho' they must be made subservient to the glory of God then the Gibeonites were not slain by Israel but they were made "hewers of wood & drawers of water."[43] On account of the sin of one individual Israel could not stand before their enemies at Ai & until the "accursed thing"[44] was removed from among them & Achain stoned to death they could not take the city & until the city was taken they could not proceed in their conquest of the land—then it is with us, one single sin indulged in, one root of bitterness cherished in the heart will effectually stop the progress of grace in the soul & until that sin is abandoned, that root of bitterness torn up, we cannot proceed one inch towards perfection—and who has not felt this, who has not had to bring Achain out from the camp of their hearts & stone him to death. He said that the Babylonish guildrents & the gold & the silver were hid beneath the earth in his tent. And O! have we not reason to believe that many covetous desires after the perishing riches of the world are now covered up under the earthly part of our hearts. Lord search me, & try me, for I know not myself, but do thou make me willing to go down into the depths of my own heart & search it as with lighted candles, and when I do see, make me willing to see & to believe & to bring out all that is offensive to thee & surrender it freely & wholly. Was it not the love of dress & the love of money that ruined Achain and are not these more generally united than we commonly imagine. He who is pure will be able to speak of the work of grace in his own soul just as if he was another person, & will feel no more propriety in the good that he has done or professes than he does in his neighbour's, for he will know that it is altogether the work of the Holy Spirit & can say from the heart "by the grace of God I am what I am."[45] I have done many good things from a good motive in a wrong spirit & I believe there is such a thing as doing wrong things in a right spirit for there are many things we really believe to be right whilst we are only as the man did who saw "men as trees walking"[46] which when we see all things clearly appear to us in a very different light & are therefore no longer right for us to do, tho' it might have been sinful for us at one time to have left them undone, & right for others to do them still.

Note: About here there is a margin notation written vertically "First day."

December 28   It is necessary for us to be as willing to be ignorant of the secret things of God, as to learn the things which are revealed & do his holy will just so far as he is pleased to manifest it and no further. It is regarded as an evidence of our faith if we do what we are commanded by the Spirit tho' he may inwardly explain why such an act of obedience is required & open our spiritual eye to me—but it is a far greater evidence of our faith of nothing but our ear is opened to hear the command & the eye remains entirely closed as to the reason as result of what is required—then it is that we understand the meaning of this saying "who is blind as the Lords servant.["][47] Went for meeting this morning— my soul was barren but I feel willing it should be so if it will teach me what a poor & needy creature I am without the Masters presence & comforts. O to be humbled in the very dust. Lord all means and ways are in thy hands, do I pray thee whatever will accomplish this great work & earnestly do I plead that thy hand may not spare me thine eye pity me until all the good pleasure of thy will shall be accomplished in me & by me, tho' in the depths of tribulation. I may be tempted to ask for a respite from suffering, yet Lord hear not such a prayer but continue thy works unheeded by my cries & glorify thy own great & glorious Name in the entire emancipation of my wretched, polluted soul from the bondage of sin and the love of myself & created objects. Give me nothing but what will draw me nearer to thee & O I tremble as I pray this prayer that thou wouldst take from me whatever stops the current of love to Thee O my blessed

Savior from flowing freely & fully from my heart only do Thou give me grace & strength to bear the fires of purification. Lord here am I—do with me whatever thou wilt only give me clean hands & a pure heart & be thou Lord of my affections & the main spring of all my tho'ts, desires & actions. I desire to give thee myself—it is all I have to give & a miserable offering it is—but do thou condescend to accept it for it is a free will offering. When applauded or reproached we should remember that neither at all alters our standing in the sight of God—this will teach us to receive the first with humility & the last with patience, it is not either the praise or dispraise of men which injures us, but the manner in which we receive it.

December 31   How hard it is to spend a day out and come home with a conscience void of offence towards God & man. My heart is burdened tonight for I feel that I have said many things I ought not to have said. I have talked much of the principles of Friends to those who could not understand me—how hard it is to be satisfied with the praise of God only, how prone we are to seek that of man too—this is a fearful evidence that the heart is not pure nor the eye single. Lord I am so selfish & sinful a creature that it is a wonder thou hast not cast me off before this—how strange after all thou hast done for me & the love wherewith thou hast loved me that I should ever seek myself in anything but so it is, I have awful reason to believe I love myself more than thee. Blessed Savior I pray that thou wouldst not give me up but as thou hast in infinite mercy begun a good work in my heart O carry it on for thy Great Name sake, perfect that which concerneth me & make me altogether such as thou wouldst have me to be. O grant that my will may be swallowed up in thine. Thou knowest how hard it is for flesh to bear my situation here—once so much beloved & bearing so high a character for zeal & piety—now regarded as a poor deluded creature who has strayed far from the path of duty & whose heart has been so blinded & hardened that she is saying Peace, Peace, when there is no peace, but Lord it is designed to humble me & I entreat thee that I may be laid as low as the dust I walk upon. I ask not to be released but I ask that thy holy will may be fully done in me & by me. I feel very much the necessity of living on the present & neither hoping nor fearing for the future, but committing myself unreserved & cheerfully into the hands of my Father in heaven. Some things try me very much here, but I pray for resignation & desire to receive every passing event & everything from his hand as designed to convey instruction to my mind & to soften & purify my heart & may this ever be my prayer, Lord if I cannot enjoy Thee let me not enjoy anything. O never leave me nor forsake me.

January 2, 1829   The secluded and inactive life I feel it my duty to lead does very much confirm the opinion of my Presbyterian friends that I have backslidden in the divine life, but whilst I am permitted to enjoy the testimony of a good conscience toward God I know that I have no cause to complain tho' it seems at times hard for me to bear the great change in my situation with patience & thankfulness. Here the great criterion by which anyone is judged as to his piety is activity in religious Societies, First day Schools &c.—whilst but little account is taken of those christian graces which alone mark the follower of the Lamb. I know from experience that it is comparatively very easy to perform all those outward duties & very pleasant too, because the applause of the nominally religious world is gained by it and spiritual pride is thus fostered and self exalted— but O how hard it is to "keep the heart with all diligence"[48] to subdue the passions & as Paul did, die daily on the Cross of self-denial & be content to forfeit the praise of men by becoming a "fool for Christ's sake"[49]—how trying to human nature "to have our faith towards God to ourselves"[50] without caring whether professors call us Christians, or backsliders, or deluded creatures. As to the grace of humility it is by many regarded as meanness & Satan has persuaded professors that they may dress as much like the world as they please, for that those who do, not only pride themselves on their peculiarity & in reality sin a great deal more than they do in adopting the late fashions & wearing lace veils & gay ribbons & it is their notion ~~of~~ not to render themselves conspicuous, entirely forgetting that the Lord will have "a peculiar people"[51] & that so far from descending to the manners & customs of the world, it is their duty to hear a decided testimony against them & to lift the standard of purity & simplicity & as to speak & dress & behave like those who are crucified to the world & have it entirely beneath their feet.

Note: About here there is a margin notation written vertically "First day."

January 4   This day is kept by hundreds of Christians in commemoration of the death of their Master by taking what they call the Communion. Friends do not keep this day thus & the question arose "how ought we and all believers to show our thankfulness for this great gift of himself as a ransom for sin["]—it appears to me that if we daily died unto sin & lived unto righteousness, if we daily gave up the old man of sin to be crucified on the Cross of self denial—if we so lived as to hold constant communion with him, so walk'd in the path of humility & simple obedience as to manifest that we always remembered the divine injunction "if ye love me keep my commandments"[52] that such sacrifices w'd be more acceptable—but I desire to say little about Religion, but so to live as to evidence its power & spirituality & its loveliness.

January 5   Spent the afternoon and evening out & desire to record with thankfulness the calmness I feel on my return home—this is uncommon for me, for I almost always speak unadvisedly with my lips, & feel the burden of a condemned conscience & heavy heart after being in company.

January 12   I do not agree with those who think it a proof of a bad state of heart if we cannot pray outwardly, for it appears evident from our being told that the Spirit is like the wind which bloweth where it willeth that the one is no more at our command than the other. What should we think of the Mariner who persisted in setting sail in a calm or when the wind was contrary—does the circumstance of his setting sail secure him a favorable gale or rather does it not evince his folly in supposing because he was anxious to be gone that of course the winds would favor him & yet is he not like many professors who persist in praying outwardly when they feel nothing of the influences of the blessed Spirit which alone can teach us how to pray. The experienced Mariner diligently gets every thing ready drops down the river & waits until a fair wind springs up, and then spreading his sails is rapidly borne on his way & gains more in one hour than ~~the~~ he who set out in a calm does in 24 or a great deal longer—thus it is with the experienced christian, he will endeavor by a life of holiness always to be prepared to receive the influences of the Spirit & by dropping into silence & retirement of mind will wait in patient expectation of its being granted & when it is given by yielding to it will make for greater progress in the divine life, than he who will pray outwardly let his state of mind be what it may. The vessels which set sail with a contrary wind, so far from gaining anything by it is continually driven back & is constantly losing ground whereas if it had remained in Port it should have lost nothing at any rate; so it is with those who whilst they ought to "be still" before the Lord, are constantly doing & speaking—so far from gaining in the divine life they are constantly losing—like the Israelites they are moving, but not going forward. Christ says take "my yoke upon you for it is easy"[53]— it is easy if we are wearing it willingly—the ox which is willing to be yoked & patiently labors will find the yoke set easy on his neck, but if he is constantly striving to be rid of it & is fractious under it, it will gall him severely & unfit him for labor—thus it is with the believer, if he willingly wears the yoke of Christ & patiently labors for him—he will scarcely feel the restraints which others are striving to be freed from & from his consistency of character & his entirely resigning everything he believes contrary to his will, will be better prepared to labor effectually & diligently. Two Hiscksites[54] came to see me yesterday & openly avowed their sentiments. I actually trembled from head to foot & tho' sitting very near the fire felt as cold as ice. I will gratefully record the mercy of the Lord in preserving me from the least degree of harshness—my heart was lifted in prayer for preservation whilst I listened to their subtel reasoning for really I could have formed no idea of their cunning craftiness. I gave them one text which they did not know what to do with, it was this—"Hereby perceive we the love of God that He laid down his life for us"[55] one of them said he had never heard of the text before & did not know how he could so entirely have overlooked it—but that it ~~carried a contradiction within it~~ implied an absurdity for if I believed that He who created the world & formed myself had actually died upon the Cross then no God existed now. I told him that I certainly must believe that the body of Christ who the Apostle told me "was over all God blessed forever more"[56] had been offered as an atonement for sin on the Cross & that as to reasoning about a thing so far beyond my capacity I could not do it but that I desired in the humility of a little child to believe all the bible taught.

January 15   I have lately been led to look at the awful declensions in pure spiritual religion & to entrust it with the state of Christianity in the days of the Apostles & the time of Persecution—how calmly settled down upon their law are professors now—they talk a great deal about Religion & are very actively engaged in working for Societies, teaching in first day Schools & but where is the self denial of "living, & dressing like believers & how much do they work in the vineyards of their own hearts—plowing up the fallow ground & rooting out the words of pride, selfishness, anger & the love of ease—where is the christian now whose life is a living epistle known & read of all men" & who is by his daily conduct constantly condemning the world & never helping others to do what the Bible forbids. People say persecution has ceased because the world is too enlightened now, but I do not see any thing in the lives of professors to provoke it—the Church & the world are as closely united now as the Church and State were formally—& neither Satan or worldlings care how much professors talk or how much they run to meetings, so long as they do not live godly lives & do not run in the way of God's commandments. I believe that one of the most powerful machines the Adversary has in motion in the world is the system of activity—it tends to keep professors quite at their ease, because all these good works are so many steps by which they may climb to Heaven & it tends to keep them out of their own hearts—& so long as this is done, whether it be by means of good books—or good works, or good preaching it is the same thing to him—for if the heart is not pure, if the inside of the cup & platter be not clean—it matters not what the outside is for "Blessed are the pure in heart, for they (& they only) shall see God." Is not the christian Church as much bound down to forms and ceremonies now as the Jewish was, when Christ came into the world. The Jews tho't that from their having the Scriptures & conforming to outward ceremonies & making long prayers and a great fuss about Religion that they would certainly be saved whilst they lived in the daily neglect of the great command "to do justly, love mercy & walk humbly with their God."[57] They despised & rejected him who was sent to teach that God was a Spirit & must be worshipped in spirit & in truth—that he dwelt not in temples made with hands but in the hearts of the humble—& that nothing they were accustomed to depend upon could save them. Are not professors now depending upon what they call the ordinances & upon their exertions in Societies & going to Meetings, whilst at home—to their children & domestics they evince but very little of that humility condescension & forbearance which is essential to the character of the real disciple. ["]The Pharisee in the temple justified himself by saying he was not like other men, extortioners, unjust, adulterers. he fasted twice in the week I gave tithes of all he possesses."[58] And are there not very many now who are rocking their souls to sleep by vindicating themselves from the charge of gross crimes & saying that they have been baptized with water, taken the sacrament, regularly attended meetings & subscribed to religious & charitable institutions. O when will the Lord raise up faithful witnesses who will not be afraid to tear the veil from the hypocrites face, & uncloak the formal professors showing them what they are in themselves & uttering the awful declaration that except their righteousness exceed the righteousness of the Scribes & Pharisees—except their religion be the circumci[si]on of their heart & their baptism that of the Holy Ghost & of fire they cannot enter into the kingdom of heaven.

January 20   Yesterday I received a precious visit from M H. I had not seen her since my change of sentiment—dear girl she seems to feel not at all less interest in, or affection for me. The Lord is turning holy hand upon her and leading her from outward things to himself manifested within—may she be faithful unto the death itself & be willing to suffer for Christ's sake. Since conversing with her I have felt apprehensive that there was a work for me to do here and that I shall be released as soon as I expected. I am much tried at times as to the manner in which I am compelled to live here in so much luxury and ease & raised so far above the poor & spending so much of my board. I want to live in plainness & simplicity & economy for such ought every christian to do. I am at a loss what to do about this, for if I live with Mother which seems to be the proper place for me I must live in this way in a great degree, it is true I can always take the plainest foods & that I do generally believing whether at home or abroad I ought to eat nothing I think too sumptuous for a servant of Jesus Christ—for this reason when I took tea at a Minister's house some time since I did not touch the richest cakes nor the fruit & nuts handed after tea—& when paying a visit the other morning refused the cake & wine tho' I felt fatigued & would have liked something plain to eat. But it is not only the food I disapprove of at Mother's but the whole style of living is a direct departure from the simplicity that is in Christ. The Lord's poor tell me they do not like to come to such a large house to see me & if they come, instead of being able to read a lesson of frugality & deadness to the world in the chairs & tables—carpet &c. they must go lamenting over the inconsistency of a sister professor. But I desire to be resigned—one thing however is hard to bear. I am obliged to pay $5 a week for board tho' I disapprove of the extravagance & I am actually accessory to maintaining this style of living when as a christian I know it is wrong & am thereby prevented from giving to the poor as liberally as I should like. How hard are the sayings of Jesus Christ to those who are not willing to give all for all they still exclaim "who can hear them or bear them.["][59] The standard of Perfection is too high for professors now for they are seeking to find a way of serving two Masters.

January 29   For the last week I have been a good deal with a sick friend & feel that I ought to be grateful for every opportunity I have of showing my Presbyterian friends that I am as willing to serve them as ever. I have had but very little given me to do & sincerely desire to be willing to do that little for my Master's sake & to His glory—feel in a barren state—spiritual feeling is almost dead.

February 6   I have been suffering for the last two days on account of H[enry]'s boy having run away because he threatened to whip him.[60] O who could paint the horrors of slavery & yet so hard is the natural heart that I am continually told that their situation is very good much better than that of their owners, how strange that any one should believe such an absurdity or try to make others credit it. No wonder poor John ran away at the threat of a flogging when H has told me more than once than when he H last whipped him, he felt it physically for one week afterwards, so I don't know how the boy must have felt indeed that night was a night of agony to me for it was not only dreadful to hear him beating him but the oaths & curses he uttered went like daggers to my heart—& this was done too in the house of one who is regarded as a light in the

Church. O Jesus where is thy meek and merciful disposition to be found now—
are the works of discipleship changed or where are thy true disciples ~~to be found~~.
Last night I laid awake weeping over the condition of John, it seemed as tho' it
was all I could do, but I seemed to be directed to go to H & tenderly remonstrate
with him. I sought strength & was willing to do so if the impression continues.
Today was somewhat released from this exercise tho' still suffering & almost
thought it would not be required, but at dusk it returned & having occasion to
go into his room for something, broached the subject as guardedly & mildly as
possible, first passing my arm around him & leaning my head on his shoulder—
he very openly acknowledged that he meant to give him such a whipping as
would cure him of doing the same thing again & that he deserved to be whipped
till he could not stand, I remarked that would be treating him worse than he
would treat his horse—he now became excited & replied that he considered his
horse no comparison better than John & I would not treat it so—by this time my
heart was full & I felt so much overcome as to be compelled to seat myself or
rather to fall into a chair before him. (I do not think he knew this), the conversation proceeded I pled the cause of humanity—he grew very angry & said I had
no business to be meddling with him, that he never did so with me. I said if I had
ever done any thing to offend him I was very sorry for it but that I had very careful to do every thing I could to oblige him—he said that I had come from the
No[rth] expressly to make myself miserable & every body in the house & that I
had much better go & live at the North. I told him that I was not ignorant that
both C & himself would be very glad if I did & that as soon as I felt released from
Carolina I would go, but that I had believed it my duty to return this winter tho'
I knew I was coming back to suffer—this appeared strange. I continued weeping
—he again accused me of meddling with his private feelings which he said I had
no right to do & that I made him miserable. I told him I could not but lift up my
voice against the memories of his beating John—he said rather than suffer the
continual condemnation of his conduct by me he would leave Mother's house—
at one time I applauded the witness in his own bosom as to the truth of what I
said, to my surprise he readily acknowledged that he felt something within him
which fully met all I asserted & that I had harrowed his feelings & made him
miserable—much more passed I alluded to his neglect of me & testified that I
had experienced no feeling but that of love towards him & all the family & a
desire to do all I could to oblige them & left the room in tears—and retired to
bless my Savior for the strength he had granted & to implore his continued support & could from my heart say I am willing to suffer any thing for thee O Lord.

I think that we may observe a great difference in our feelings under the commands of the Master—sometimes the influence of the Spirit is so powerful that we dare not & cannot refuse compliance, but at others it seems to be left at our option whether we will obey or not—these last were the feelings I had this afternoon but last winter all I did appeared to me be from absolute compulsion. I was then passing thro' a dispensation of fear.

February 7 Surely my heart ought to be lifted to my blessed Master in emotions of gratitude & praise. Henry's boy came home last night a short time after I had spoken to him & instead of punishing him as I am certain he ment to do merely, told him to go & do his business.[61] I was amazed last night after my sufferings were over & I was made willing to leave all things in my Father's hands to see him in the house—this was renewed proof to me how necessary it is for me to watch for the right time to do things in, for if I had not spoken just when I did, I could not have done so before his return. I found tonight that Mother also had been recommending mildness to him & he certainly did come back (I think) in exactly the best time & has escaped entirely. Lord I ought to be far more willing than I am to suffer exercise of mind. O make me willing to drink the bitter draughts to the dregs & again I pray that thy work of grace in my wretched heart may be fully done let the suffering be what it may, only glorify thyself and save me for thy mercies sake—but how my heart clings to created good. A letter from dear Sister this morning revived so many delightful recollections & bro't my beloved friends at the North very forcibly to my mind very warmly to my heart. O I do feel nothing but divine grace could have made me willing to return to Carolinas, and nothing but that can possibly make me willing to remain. O how earnestly two nights ago did I pray for a release from this land of Slavery— & how my heart still pants after it & yet I think, I trust, it is in submission to my Father's holy will. I feel comfortable tonight my release from suffering about John was so great that other trials seem too light to name—my spirit was as usual disturbed by B F's rude and unfeeling manner & conversation & H[enry] has had two young men drinking wine for the last 3 hours, & is 10 O'clock now & I know not when they will go away—this is trying, but I am not as much exercised about it as I have been at other times, they called, were not invited, I very much desire patience & quietness. But must record the condemnation I felt today at dinner for not sitting in silence as long as I knew & felt I ought, for fear of rendering myself conspicuous, but as it happened this would not have been the case—but I am grateful for this reproof of the faithful Spirit—may I learn ["]obedience by the things that I suffer."

February 8   My heart sings aloud for joy. I feel the sweet testimony of a ["]good conscience toward God" the reward of obedience in speaking to H[enry]—dear boy he has good tender feelings naturally but education has nearly destroyed them & his own false judgement as to what is manly & what is necessary in the government of slaves. Lord open then his eyes & may thy greatness make him great. I have just returned from meeting—had a feeling comforting happy time—this text was applied "Let not your heart be troubled neither let it be afraid."[62] I remembered the command which was given me before I left Phila—"Return unto the land of thy fathers, & to thy kindred & I will be with thee" & these words seemed to be added ["]& will bless thee."[63] I establish the work of thy hands upon thee—fall a little as if I was to be released next spring & the faithfulness of some tried by my removal. Lord let thy will be done I can ask for no more. Some remarkable circumstances there bro't to mind which occurred last summer & I desire felt to write them down. A friend of D H arrived here last week he seemed to wish to introduce him to me this morning but I rather avoided it for I feel the necessity in being circumspect in all things.

February 9   I feel a continuation of peace & have been permitted this morning to ask for a release from the land of bondage, to pray that my work here might be cut short, & that all the suffering I have to endure before I leave Carolina may be laid upon me this winter, & strength to bear it.

February 12   Yesterday went to meeting anticipating a comfortable time, but felt pressed down by a weight of exercise I know not for what, but was willing to bear it, D H came to meeting which tried me for I was sure no good motive carried them there & I felt disappointed at seeing them on 4th day, for no one but the two old Friends & myself are in the habit of meeting in the week.

February 13   I am permitted to enjoy increasing evidence that Charleston is my right place & that if I had remained at the North I could neither have enjoyed my friends nor peace of mind.

February 16   I have been told that the dear little girls I used to teach in 1st day School are all but 2 gone away or have left it. Some did intimate that I would have to answer for this, but it has been shown me that as Moses was not chargeable with the sin of the Israelites falling down & worshipping a golden calf whilst he was in Mount Horeb receiving the commandments, so I cannot be responsible for the evil that may accrue to them whilst from conviction of duty I remain inactive & in one sense useless. Moses was doing the will of the Lord as much when he waited for the tables of stone as when he was leading & instructing the children of Israel & accommodating their litigious differences. My mind this

morning forebode many trials from Sister's E[liza]'s return from the Country &
S[elina][64] coming to live with us. Lord I pray that I might keep in my right place
& bear an unyielding testimony to the truth desiring thy favor in preference to
the approbation of human beings, but give me gentleness, weakness holiness.

February 19   Have much reason to be humbled at my covetousness—
today I received $100 Santee CCCL I am so fearful that I love money too much.
I earnestly desire to experience that state of mind which led the Apostle to say
that "having food & raiment he was therewith content."[65] I have more & yet there
is an unpardonable desire after more. I owe $100 which I gave to Societies last
year—& I feel uneasy about it & wish I could pay it at once, but this is not right
for I feel that I have no cause to doubt but that the Master will make a way for
me to pay it this year. My mind is uneasy about Cha[rles][66]—he will not do anything to support himself & I am sure he feels tried when he sees me receive
money—but I think I see very plainly that I ought not and must not contribute
to his support for in so doing I am encouraging pride & idleness—he is too
proud to accept any but a gentleman's place & this he cannot obtain so he is living on Mother. I wish to feel more than ever my need of divine direction about
this & every thing else.

February 27   Yesterday brother Henry brought his wife up to live with us,
I went down & was the first to meet her & did so affectionately. I then offered
him my hand & he kissed me twice—this felt very gratifying—it was quite unexpected & the tho't occurred to me that he was then conscious that if he said I
had come back to make every body miserable, or had any feeling of retaliation
towards him that I would not have greeted S[elina] as kindly as I did. Lord help
me to do & say just what I ought & to be willing to be nothing here. I believe the
time is coming when I shall be, as foreseen before I came from Philadelphia, like
a step of the temple, much to be trampled upon. Last morning as I reflected
upon the trials I would probably have to bear in the lightness & fashion of my Sisters it was forcibly impressed on my mind how good it was for me to remember
["]the rock from whence I was hewn & the hole of the pit from whence I was
digged"[67] this morning feel some gladness of heart & desire reservedly to render
thanks for the strength which was granted on the 6th of this month. O' if I had
not been faithful here what a constant burden I should have had to bear—& what
self condemnation too—but since I spoke to H[enry] that night my mind has
been entirely released from all anxiety on that subject.

March 4   If those who have done much are commanded to confess themselves to be unprofitable servants—what must I do who am doing nothing at
all. Sometimes this sentiment of Matthew administers comfort to me "They also

serve who only stand and wait"[68] and yet I think there is a willingness to do if the
Master would speak—if I deceive not myself this is the language of my heart,
"Speak Lord for thy servant heareth."[69] Last first day for the first time I felt some
little exercise in meeting on account of the sad state of Society here—there
seemed to be no spring of life in the midst of us—our little meeting a week
without water & ourselves trees without fruit.

March 13 Today for the first time I ruined my clothes, & felt as tho' it was
an acceptable sacrifice, this seemed to be part of the preparation for my removal
to the North. I felt fearful least this object were a stronger incentive to me than
the desire of glorifying my divine Master. Was exceedingly tried today by the
conversation of two professors (cousins) an emptiness & vapidness seemed to
pervade all they said about religion. I was silent most of the time I fear that what
I said sprung from a feeling of too great indignation & just before they went away
I joined in a joke much condemnation was felt, for the language to me constantly
is, ["]I have called thee with a high & holy calling" & it seems as tho' solemnity
ought always too much to pervade my mind to allow me to joke, but my natural
vivacity is hard to bridle and subdue. I feel as though a work is before me as to
render the best deviation in me a great sin, a great stumbling block, O that I
might make use of the grace that is given & watch & pray always. Was favored to
receive a long letter from Dear Sister [Sarah] today, it was a privilege indeed.
Paid a visit to M W this afternoon. I think she begins to feel the need of more
spirituality, she seems teachable but wants to learn on instruments. May she be
directed aright.

March 14 Our happiness does not depend on the number of blessings we
have bestowed upon us, but on the measure of the gratitude we feel hence we
see some with every thing this world can bestow, uneasy and wretched, whilst
on the contrary there are others poor & rich & destitute of necessaries, who can
rejoice even in these trying dispensations of Providence & bless his holy name for
the little they do receive. Sometimes we are suffered to meet with ingratitude
from those upon whom we have conferred favor in order to shew us how much
of self there is in our good actions—if our eye had been kept single to the glory
of the Master we would not have been chagrined & wounded at the ingratitude
of the individual because the great aim & end of the deed is always accomplished
of his glory, but not our own gratification is sincerely & singly sought—yea
even more, for by permitting us to meet with ingratitude He furnishes another
& still greater opportunity of glorifying Him by our meeting it with gentleness

& patience & this would be another advance to the death of self that idol which must & will (if we are faithful) fall before the true Ark.

March 16   On the 7th day Wm McDowell & Tho's Napier called on me as a Committee from the Session of the 3rd P.C. to inquire whether I did not think I had broken some of the vows I made when I entered that Church & to remind me I had promised to submit to its discipline. I was better satisfied with this visit from Wm McDowell than any since I left the Church. I told him I was well aware what was the purport of his calling on me before he mentioned the subject, that I did respect the discipline of every Society & felt its Officers had a right to exercise it & I respected those who had strength & faithfulness to do it—that I believed if we kept in our right places this would not be a cause of separation between us, for I felt that they had come in the spirit of love & tenderness & were only doing what it was their duty to do. I promised to read over "the Profession & Covenant" & to write to him on the subject, when they were going away I affectionately thanked them both for their visit & I think we parted with mutual feelings of love I attempted to write him this morning, but was not able to do so satisfactorily & therefore laid down my pen. O for strength, for that wisdom which cometh down from above, for preservation & divine direction in every line, above all for that "charity that never faileth."[70] Today I received a precious letter from R. S. I could but weep over it & bless my Master for this gift of a friend in one who seems so sweetly united to Him & his cause.

March 17   I have just written a note to Wm McD simply saying that I do not think I have broken any of my vows & requesting to know in what particulars I am regarded as having done so. I also submitted the querie to the Session, whether I do not, as having voluntarily withdrawn from Membership stand on very different ground from an individual who while continuing within that faith of the Church should incur its censures. O for preservation.

3

Trial and Triumph

March 19, 1829–April 27, 1829

Angelina was clearly heartened by her intervention on behalf of Henry's slave John. She saw it as a "reward of obedience." Her apparent success in saving the runaway from his torture bolstered her conviction that she was to achieve something of great importance. It gave her renewed patience to remain "still" and to wait on God's time to pursue her "high and holy" destiny fully.

She faced many trials in the spring of 1829. Perhaps the most difficult burden was her inactivity. In the diary she laments, "What must I do who am doing nothing at all." Just as success with her brother Henry had empowered her, a passage from the book of Matthew had comforted her: "They serve who only stand and wait." As she remained "still" and waited for divine guidance, she continued to have difficulties with her family. Besides the earlier clashes with her mother and brother Henry, she also attempted to confront her brother Charles over what she perceived to be his laziness. At one point she not only concluded that she "would have to speak to C about doing nothing & living on Mother as he did," but she immediately confronted him. She also agonized over her agreement to help an elderly couple with their affairs. She apparently did not approve of the couple's lifestyle and resisted contributing to it in any way. She still longed to go north but nevertheless believed it to be God's will for her to stay for a while longer in Charleston. She also faced the agonizing inevitability of leaving the Presbyterian Church permanently.

Despite these difficulties, Grimké's outlook brightened during March and April. Even though she was still inactive, still faced difficulties with family relationships, and began to face a fresh confrontation with her former pastor and church, she seems to have been remarkably cheerful and self-assured. Over the following weeks and months she would come to terms with the strained personal relationships she endured with her mother and brothers, and she would steadfastly and bravely deal with the Presbyterian Church's efforts to exclude her from membership. By the end of April her spirit had been renewed. More significantly, she quietly prepared to leave "the land of her fathers and kindred." As spring 1829 ended, Grimké had become stronger in her religious faith and seemed to be preparing for her eventual relocation to the North.

March 19   There is an island about 7 miles from our city which of a clear day seems to be within a stones throw so very near does it appear to be—if a person thus deceived should set sail for it expecting to be there in a few minutes, his patience would be much tried at finding that it was so much farther than he had expected. Is it not true that there are seasons of divine illumination in which coming events are so plainly seen, that like the little island they seem to be very near when in reality some years may intervene, & our patience is so much tried previous to their fulfillment as that of the person who sat out expecting to reach the island in a few moments, both are surprised at the space to be passed over & the variety of circumstances which occur & the objects which are brought to view. I have many times had occasion to admire the condescension of our divine Master in teaching his ignorant children by, passing events as a tender Mother does her children by pictures. One evening as we were sitting in the parlour together some one inquired the hour & some anxiety was expressed to hear the 9 O'Clock bell ring in order that it might be actually ascertained. In a short time it did begin, all of us voluntarily ceased from our different employments, every one was but to watch the seconds & a profound stillness reigned around—after this each was anxious to set their watch. I was much interested in those little circumstances on the subject of prayer. I thought how necessary it was for us to listen to the Holy Spirit, before we could know what was required of us to do—& how impossible it was to listen whilst we were ourselves speaking—just as we could not know the hour until the bell rung & could not have heard it if we had not ceased to speak & listened attentively for the windows were closed, therefore the sound was very indistinct it was like the "still small voice" our attention must be directed to that above, as we could not hear that one or the other & then as willing each was to set their watch & tho't what a pity it was we were not willing to do what the Spirit required of us.

March 24   I am sure I do not feel grateful enough for the blessing of preservation, the exemption from the oppressing feeling of condemnation—it is hard to the activity of self seeking nature to do nothing and still harder to be

willing to be nothing in the eyes of others—here is the spot I stand on now & I
have lately been shown how necessary this discipline is to me, "just & true are all
thy way, Lord God Almighty" seems to be the language of my heart to night;
Today I ruined my clothes again: & cannot but think this little act is a stepping
stone in the way of my reward—but I earnestly pray I may not go unless it
becomes a manifest duty to do so.

March 31   Yesterday I received a letter from dear Sister—there is now no
prospect of any return to the North & this morning I felt increasingly tried about
many things under my return desirable to me but I find on a careful examination
that all my motives are selfish, there is nothing disinterested in my feelings about
it—it is true none here can enter into the exercise of mind I at times experience
but I have been thinking how unreasonable I was to wish for any one but Him
who is a high priest ~~who is~~ ["]touched with a feeling of our infirmities." O I do
earnestly desire entire resignation to His holy will & the language of my heart is
that of Moses "if Thy presence go not with me take me not up hence."[1] Of late I
feel no satisfaction in reading the Bible, it is no better than a blank book to me &
a fear with the morning felt that the Master was given about to hide his face—
what shall I do in this desert land without my Star & Shield, my rock & healing
place. Lord preserve me in the hollow of thy hand, keep me under the shadow
of thy wings.

April 3   H[enry] & S[elina] have just gone into the country. I feel condemnation for not kissing him. I know I ought to have done so, & I believe it would
have been a good influence. I feel as tho' I am a thing of naught here & instead of
this leading me to the Fountain of all good, instead of casting myself into His
arms who hath declared that he hath even remembered the hairs of my head &
that He careth for me it has tended to drive my thoughts to other earthly objects
at a distance. I do want to have my feelings & affections disengaged but so vivid
so pleasing are the recollections of some dear friends at the North that their
images stand like the frontice piece in the next volume of my life & engage more
of my thoughts—desire & anticipations than I believe is good for me—to be able
to live one day, one hour at a time—& to leave the future without anxiety to Him
who has ["]yet & always will do all things well."

April 4   My mind has this morning felt the emotions of love & gratitude.
H[enry] & S[elina] unexpectedly returned yesterday & this morning when they
were about to set off I remembered the condemnation I had felt & said to him
smiling come let me have a kiss he very willingly complied & she said, to be sure
he means to give you one she is a sweet little woman & my heart at times craves

for her & more a knowledge of Him whom to know aright is life eternal—this little circumstance has felt very grateful to me & I am thankful for it—to be faithful I feel very much the necessity of having my name withdrawn in favor of the Master—it is hard to give up my friends there but I believe it must be done, & done quickly too—the time seems to have come for the sacrifice to be made. O Lord give me a willing mind, take all but thyself away. I do not say I am willing now to part with all Oh no! but I pray to be made willing in the day of thy power. The great enemy of souls tells me I have given up a great deal already & tempts me to charge thee O my Savior with requiring too much of me but I am praying against his will—help me to watch against them too & to say as thou didst "get thee behind me Satan." I desire to see clearly what is required of me here & to do it however difficult it may be. Lately I have been much troubled at finding so much of self in all I say. I think my actions are more disinterested than my words—but these do most sadly manifest a self seeking spirit—it seems to me I scarcely ever speak without sinning but I do sincerely desire whenever I sin to suffer for it.

April 5   Today have been to meeting twice but my mind was so filled with vain & wandering tho'ts as to conclude what was good & tho' I know this to be my state could not weep over it. This afternoon was sending to Mother "the assurance of Faith"[2] and made some remarks on the dreadful state of religion among professors here—as usual she did not like my strictures & seemed to elicit some proof of my assertions, this led me to remark on the state of our own family & observed that the description given by Paul of the Heathen would just suited us a few years back "without natural affection, hateful & hating one another" dear Mother seemed shocked at what she called my harshness & seemed to deny it, but when I brought to her remembrance how many of us at different times would not speak to each other she was silent this led me to look at our state now & to remark how very few were redeemed from the dreadful feelings & how much cold-heartedness & indifference still existed among us, that even now we had not natural affection for each other—she could not but allow all I said to be true. I wanted to tell her what I believed to be the state of her feeling towards her children & particularly to myself but it seemed as tho' I had said enough for the time & so I remained silent. E[liza] soon after coming in and beginning to speak on some indifferent subject I left the room—when alone felt tendered & some flowing of love towards B[enjamin] F[3] and a desire to write to him when permission was granted. Of late I feel the necessity of dear Mother's seeing the bitter fruit of her system of education. I want her instead of priding herself on the morality of her sons to see & acknowledge that tho' far from gross crimes they are not moral men that is they do not fill their respective stations in the domestic circle. I want her to see & feel that it is in a great measure her fault that we have always lived in strife & contention—caring too much to please ourselves to care for each other. Let every one do as they please has been her motto & we have been too willing to adopt & act upon it too.

April 6   Woke this morning with an impression on my mind that all difficulties in the minds of the Morris's[4] would soon be removed & that dear Sister [Sarah] would in a little time receive the promised reward "they who sow in tears shall reap in joy."[5] I expect to spend the whole day out having promised to assist the Rains[6] in their work. O! that I may be kept from putting my hand to any thing I disapprove of their wearing, & from saying any thing which I would be afraid of saying in the presence of the Master. My heart is cold & dead too cold for me to torment my sad & sinful state.

April 9   Yesterday I read part of the 119th Psalm—these words seemed to suit my situation "Remember the word unto thy Servant, upon which thou hast caused me to hope."[7] When coming from the North it seemed as tho' it was promised I should return in the Summer if I was faithful & upon this word or promise I have literally been hoping ever since I arrived here—how true the remark of dear Sister [Sarah] that after we have given up our own will & slain self in this respect it revives again in the hope of reward. I think I could a little adopt this language of the Psalmist also—"The proud have had me greatly in derision, yet have I not declined from thy law"[8]—this was when I was going to meeting but when I get to the corner of Society & Anson Street I felt that I ought to have kissed Sis & thanked her for a little act of kindness she did for me whilst dressing. I returned therefore & told her why I had come back, she seemed surprised & gratified & we parted in love. O that we could have each other more. When I returned at 1 for I had to go down to the R[ain]'s. Mother came in the room & read us a letter she had written to B[enjamin] F. I did not think such as it was that it would produce the desired effect & therefore said nothing at all for my opinion was not asked—so sometime after she said she intended sending it to the office & I ventured to say I tho't she had better think of it she seemed tried & said she had tho't of it for that she wd not have written such a letter without consideration & prayer & left the room—she went to ask S[ister] E[liza] what I meant who advised her to come to me about it—she did so & we had a trying conversation in which I not only remarked that B F had been driven from his Country & kindred by her unkindness but took occasion to speak of the coldness of her heart towards all her children & then mentioned how much I had been tried by it this winter reverting to the feelings of enmity which subsisted between us & the wonderful manner in which my feelings had been changed into love & tenderness Mother said I it seems sometimes at night when I lay upon thy bosom that a lump of ice could not be colder & this with tears—many things went very hard with dear Mother but she certainly bore it far better than I could have imagined—one thing she said which I am sure she felt was wrong in speaking of B F being driven away by her unkindness she said C[harles] had been forced to leave her house too on account of my unkindness. Mother said I God only witnessed my conversations with Charles & therefore I can appeal to no one but all of you were witnesses to my treatment of him generally which bore no marks at all of unkindness—for I did everything I could to oblige him, never mind she said he tho't you were very unkind—but said I there is a very great difference between what he tho't & the truth—before dinner E & myself conversed about what had passed & found one tho't very much alike about the letter—at dark I felt depressed, I knew Mother found it very hard to bear our disapproval about any thing because she had for so many years held herself so far above us, my heart was drawn to her & when alone I put my chair close to hers & leaned my head in her lap—my tears soon began to flow & she felt much also—putting her hand on my face she assured me she loved me very much but that it was not her way to show her love by outward caresses—you have been continued she a very affectionate & a good child since your return but never before—here we were interrupted by some one entering but when they left the room we continued for some time in silence & I believe for the first time I felt communion of spirit with dear Mother—when she went down to tea I went into E's room, she was going to leave me alone but I prevented her & we sat with our arms around each other & had some comfortable conversation & feeling together. I then said that so far from wishing to be alone at dark it would be very pleasant if she would when she felt she could sit with me in silence & that I believed the time had almost come for me to make a proposition to Mother. This morning I have felt that I had a great deal to be grateful for in the circumstances & feelings of yesterday—the language of my mind is "I will offer to thee the sacrifices of thanksgiving & will call upon the name of the Lord."[9] I may have that wisdom which cometh down from above which is first pure, then peaceable, gentle & easy to be entreated full of mercy & good fruits.

April 10   All yesterday morning I was at the Rains making out their accounts for them. I was very much tried about it & tried to get some one else to do them because I did not like even in the name of another to use the titles of the world & I felt released from this exercise when I got down there I felt it was a case of necessity, their health was too feeble to allow of their writing so much & it must be done yesterday & I think I did it without condemnation, if I sinned I do sincerely hope I may both see it & suffer for it. At dark I again seated myself by Dear Mother with my head in her lap after a little I told her I tho't if we sat in silence together every evening we would find it profitable & that it would be the means of forming a bond of union between us—she assented to what I said & with her arm round my neck we sat for some time my heart was full for I remembered the painful alienation which had once subsisted between us & the contrast between former feelings & those I believed we for the last two days were favored to feel—truly the time had now come when the lion & the lamb were lying down together—"how marvellous are thy works O Lord God Almighty["] I desired to feel this was His work in our hearts & it seemed refreshing to my soul to know that we were both drinking from the christian stream of sympathy & feeling. Dear Mother kissed me very tenderly several times & we parted in love, just as she was going down to tea E came in the room & taking the chair she had left vacant. I think we were also helped with some desires after good feeling. These little yet great events have tended to make me feel more reconciled to the idea of staying here this Summer than I ever did—so altered are my feelings that I really do believe I might be happy tho' I should have to give up going to the North. It has appeared to me lately as tho' I must be entirely reconciled to stay & yet that I be permitted to go if my will was entirely given up & a fear has prevailed in my mind that the hope of this reward would be my motive to resignation instead of the love of C[hrist] constraining me to say & feel "Thy will be done."[10]

April 11   Have been reading dear Sister's [Sarah] diary the two last days find she has suffered great conflict of mind particularly about her call to the ministry—& am led to look at the contrast between our feelings on the subject. I clearly saw winter before last that my having been appointed to this work was the great reason why I was called out of the Presbyterian Society—but I don't think my will has ever rebelled against it—perhaps the exercise & sufferings I passed thro' in giving that up absorbed my feelings too much to admit of any feeling much on any other account & since then I have enjoyed comparative rest. I have believed that in some instances where I was entrusted with a message of warning or admonition to different persons that it was very necessary I should be faithful in delivering them, as they were preparatory to the great work assigned me & that exact faithfulness in little things would very much lessen my suffering in the future performance of greater. I remember one day in meeting a message of this kind being given to me & it was plainly shown me I had no more right to keep it from the individual than if it were entrusted to my care for her to keep that back—neither were my own they were entrusted to me for her. So far from murmuring against the appointment I have felt exceedingly impatient at not being permitted to enter on my work at once—& this has been an evidence to me that I am not prepared for it—it is hard for me to be & to do nothing, my restless ambitious temper craves high duties & high attainments & I have at times tho't that this ambition was a motive to me to do my duty & submit my will— the hope of attaining to great eminence in the divine life has often prompted me to give up in little things to bond to existing circumstances, to be willing to be tempted upon—those are my temptations—for months it seemed to me every thing was from a hope of applause, I could not even write in my diary for whenever I did attempt to the accuser of the Brethren stood beside me to charge me with doing it in hopes that one day it might meet the eye of the public—but that winter I wrote more freely than ever in it & am still permitted to do so—very often when thinking of my useless state at present something of disappointment is felt that I am as nothing & the language has often been presented with force "Seekest thou great things for thyself—seek them not."[11] Lately I have felt troubled about Chas—he has left and gone into the country for the last two months no doubt on account of what I said to him a few weeks after I arrived. When I came back to C I think I had feelings of good will towards all my family and very much desired I might have nothing to say to them which might alienate us from each other. I soon felt however that I would have to speak to C about doing nothing & living on Mother as he did—one night he began the subject by saying how much he desired to get a place but could not & how much he was distressed at obliged to live on Mother. I felt a good deal agitated, I believed the time had come for me to tell him candidly & affectionately what I tho't. I did so with tears—but he took all I said as proceeding from great unkindness & accused me of taking an advantage of his misfortune & of being pleased to wound his feeling & was especially tried at my telling him I tho't he ought to live in the plainest manner as he paid no board & ventured to say that I at one time did not taste butter & drank water at breakfast because I was afraid I would not be able to pay the whole amt—a good deal passed & I think I was preserved thro the whole conversation—what vexed him very much was my frequently addressing him by the term dear Charles for my heart was full of love to him but he tho't this was hypocritical—the next day at the table I said something to him rather quickly from which he took occasion to treat me so rudely that Mother reproved him— he was very angry & said she did not know how I had treated him, she appeared surprised (not knowing to what he alluded) & said she was sure I had been very ~~un~~kind to every one since my return & old things ought to be forgotten, very kind he angrily replied, I don't know what you call kindness & left the room. I trembled with agitation & felt this was no time for me to speak—at night when he came home, being left alone again I took occasion to tell him that I had felt very much condemned for treating him rudely & believed it right to confess my fault to him (in tears) he abruptly replied that what I had said at table was of no consequence at all—he counted that nothing, but he could not forget my con- versation with him a few nights since & evidently wished me to retract what I had then said. Charles said I, I have carefully and prayerfully been thinking on all ~~I said~~ that passed & do not feel condemned for anything I said to thee, my opin- ions were based on principle & they are exactly the same now. I went on to say that I believed his situation was designed to humble him but that he would not submit to it, therefore his heart was hardened & he was miserable—he was exceedingly angry & asked whether I wanted to see him sit down at Mother's table & eat like a Negro he believed he said I would be very much gratified at it therefore he would not do it, but that to eat plain things would be no self-denial to him. I tried to show him that the love of eating was a natural propensity & that he did not know his own heart—he was even more angry & I said Dear C, if thou had not a swift witness in thy own bosom to the truth of all I said thou would not be so angry at this he left the room & slammed the door after him—when alone I gave full vent to my feelings in a flood of tears & was enabled to crave divine help & strength to do my duty & resignation to bear with the painful conse- quences—& an answer of peace was given—he always went into H[enry]'s room of an evening & told him all I had said making out that I had treated him very ill. I knew this was the case from H's manners became colder than ever to me & he threw out some hints about people's wounding the feelings of others & then call- ing them dear in order to hide their ill natured feelings—this hurt me very much but still I felt I was to say nothing, but to leave all to the blessed Master. "The Lord shall fight for you, & you shall hold your peace."[12] Several times they both treated me so harshly as to cause my tears to flow & my heart to bleed—but still I was & have been preserved in love towards them, and whenever I knew they wanted any thing done would do it willingly rejoicing that opportunity was granted me to show that I had nothing but love in my heart to them, tho' ~~they~~ C accused me of hating him & H of not caring at all about him. One night C came into Mother's room & said he wished to see her alone, I immediately offered to leave the room & did so—he told mother that I had taken such a hatred to him that I said all I could to wound his feelings & render his situation as painful as I could & much more to this effect. Mother as usual tried to comfort him saying he was always welcome to whatever she had, but at the same time professed her belief that what I had said was thro' kindness & a sense of duty—he then came into S[ister] M[ary]'s room for a candle & told her good night—& I said good night to thee Cha's—he took no notice of me & slammed the door—the next morning I felt a great deal at finding he tho't I hated him before breakfast we were thrown together alone & I was exercised to know whether I ought to assure him I had no such feeling my heart overflowed with love & I would have thrown my arms around him & told him how deeply I felt for him—but the language seemed to be "thou must be willing to see him suffer["] this was very hard ~~to me~~ but a sense of duty restrained me from saying any thing to him—dear Brother— I do not think he ever eat a meal afterward without feeling what I had said—he became very much depressed & it is now full ~~two~~ months since he went into the country I believe intending to remain there until I should return to the North which he seemed to think I would do & advised me to—but I don't think I am in my right place waiting here now & must go up & sit with dear Mother.

April 12   Last night at dark Mother went into S[ister] M[ary]'s room instead of sitting in her own. I felt tried at this & desired to know & do what was right & believing that they injured each very much & hearing loud talking determined to send her a message merely saying that I was alone in her chamber—she soon entered & placing my chair beside her she invited me to lay my head on her lap. I did so & my heart was again broken & contrited before the Lord for the tender mercies of his wonder working hand—no language can describe my feelings at the manifestations of that affection & approbation my precious Mother has lately evinced—my petition for her was that she might have a gentle spirit. I have lately so fully felt the value of the little I possess that it is the best blessing I can ask for others—a desire was granted that I might be enabled to feel with her and for her to have mine eye anointed to see & my heart tendered to feel her spiritual wants. O I did feel that it was a right thing for me to tell her how deeply I mourned over her coldness & the good effects which have been produced tended to make me think I did it in a right spirit—we parted with a kiss of love—when alone my heart overflowed with gratitude for the feelings I had enjoyed & it seemed as tho' all I had suffered or should suffer ought to be regarded as light afflictions when weighed against this blessed work of reconciliation wrought in my heart. This morning I have remembered how earnestly I prayed when I first returned that our evening together might be for the better, not for the worse. I fervently desired to be a blessing to my family & her in particular, but month after month elapsed & I had almost folded the arms of despair on my desolate bosom when these circumstances occurred & caused me to blush at my unbelief. O to be laid low very low at my Master's feet, for tho' he did appear after a great conflict one first day in meeting 8th 2 Month & promise to bless me, yet faith was alive but a very little while & it seemed as tho' the most I could do was to be resigned to be nothing.

About here there is the vertical margin note "First day."

April 12   I have just returned from meeting—a feeling of sweetness & tranquility clothed my mind—many circumstances which occurred last summer were again revived & the command was often repeated, "write those things which thou hast seen & heard"[13] but I am & have been very much afraid that earthly & selfish feelings are too prevalent to admit of my doing so in a right spirit. This morning I woke with dear Sister [Sarah] full on my mind and the trying circumstances under which she has for some months been placed—these words were lovingly brought before me "Stand still & see the salvation of God"[14] & I think an entire surrender was experienced. Yesterday I was favored to receive a long & precious letter from her but don't feel as if I could write just now—some reproofs were administered & received in love—she mentioned that in laying awake one night thinking of me, these words came impressively over her mind I will give her to thee, on reading this the tears started to my eyes & I exclaimed Lord it seems as tho' I could ask no greater earthly blessing.

April 14   Yesterday I spent the day at the Rains & as usual had to mourn over my aberation from the narrow path—spoke disrespectfully of a Professor believed it best to confess my fault—then do I desire to repair the breaches any unwatchfulness makes that ["]the path of peace may be restrained for me to dwell in." In the afternoon spent an hour with Sally Silsby. I hope I did not speak too much of my own experience, a fear was felt but no condemnation. This morning I am peaceful—have been led to look a little at the progress of the souls work. I think at first many gifts were bestowed upon me but little grace, now the gifts are taken away & I think I have more grace but often have I thought much would be required of me because an uncommon degree of light & knowledge has always been granted since I became serious tho' I am well aware that the light which was in me at first was darkness in comparison to that which I more enjoy. How transient our feelings of good are at times—they have appeared to me like the momentary darting of the sun's rays thro' the dark & broken clouds. It is said that when the Israelites passed over the Red Sea that the waters were a wall unto them on the right hand and on the left and O I have tho't that the soul is in seasons of deep trial favored to witness just as a miraculous an interposition for ~~that's~~ deliverance—the waters of tribulation which at one time lay before ~~them~~ it tossing their angry billows & threatening even to move out of their place to meet ~~them~~ it, are when ~~they~~ it is willing to "go forward," commanded to stand on an heap on either side, a way is not only made for it to pass over [unreadable] but an impassable barrier of defense is raised on either hand which effectually shields ~~him~~ it from the attacks of it's enemies.

April 15   Very much that is uncharitable & harsh ~~h~~ was ~~been~~ said against the Catholicks a few months back. Protestants exclaim against their keeping the Bible from the poor & ignorant but what are most owners doing to their poor & ignorant slaves—are they not depriving them of the Sacred Volume by not allowing them time & opportunity to learn to read, & do not a great majority urge the very same reason for their conduct that the Catholics do for theirs, vis—they are too ignorant to understand it—& are not Slave holders the more criminal of the two because they occupy the time of their servants in working for them & are clothed & fed by their industry. Again much horror has been expressed at the practice of Catholic priests receiving pay for praying for the dead—and what are Protestant ministers doing constantly are they not paid for their prayer for the living who are dead in trespasses & sins—are they not paid for preaching to their fellow man tho' their Master expressly says "freely ye have received, freely give.["]¹⁵ I want to be at peace, has often been the language of my heart of late. I want to be free from anxiety of every kind, to learn to bend to existing circumstances—"to be careful for nothing but in every thing give thanks."¹⁶ I want the North to be completely taken from my mind that I may not even think of it but this is hard—but I must be patient & be thankful for the measures of resignation which has been granted. Sally Silsby will probably sail in the L.C. in a fortnight time—this looks outwardly like a good opportunity for me to return, but it does not feel so at all & I think I do sincerely desire to be preserved from my own times & ways & to say with David "I will wait upon the Lord."¹⁷

April 16   How I do feel the importance of being quiet—this morning I think I can say I want to do what is right & do very much desire I may not be tempted beyond what I am able to bear—if it is my duty to stay here the

Summer I want to be willing to do it & to do it with so much sweetness that no one may know I do not want to do it. O to be the Lord's without any reserve at all. I know I ought to be willing to do his will not my own, & I do desire this most sincerely.

Night   Henry returned to day—we met affectionately—this afternoon. I felt as if I must go into his room again, found him lying on his bed & after tenderly inquiring how he left Selina & how he had been, helped him again & left the room. O Lord what shall I render unto thee, some times in looking at the trials thro' which I have passed this winter & have the feelings of some of my family have been changed towards me I am ready to exclaim ["]I am conqueror & more than conqueror thr'o Him that loved me & gave himself for me." O Love, divine love, O all powerful love, how my desolate heart has been made to be glad & rejoice. How gentle, how soft are thy influences, they come over the soul like sunlight warming & illuminating the deadest darkest prospects of life. Well may our Divine Redeemer be called our ["]Sun & shield & our exceeding great reward."[18] He has enlightened my path, he has shielded me whilst walking in it, & he has rewarded me for so doing.

April 19   This morning Mother woke me with a kiss. I do desire to be grateful for every little mark of her affection. I do not know whether my feelings are right but it appears to me that these things do not proceed from love in her heart but from a conviction of duty since I told her how very hard her coldness & indifference had been for me to bear, I believe dear Mother sees how solitary my allotment is here & that at times she does pity me, but I don't think she feels with me at all, nor do I think she ever has experienced that deep & tender affection for me which right to exist in a parents bosom. One thing wounds me much, she never consults me about any thing she means to do, no doubt one reason is because she knows I would disapprove of many things & that if my advice was asked of course I would feel it my duty to express an opinion, whereas when it is not my mouth is, as it were closed this winter she had the drawing room papered & painted & means to take it as a sitting room in Summer—this has tried & yet I have never felt as if the time had some for me to speak about it. I have never gone into it since & believe I will be exceedingly tried when I am obliged to. O Lord direct, support & bless me in this thing.

Charleston 4th Month 1829

"I will be to them, as a little sanctuary in the countries, where they shall come."[19] "Seek it thee great things for thyself, seek them not, but thy life will I give unto thee for a prey in all places whether thou goest."[20]

April 21   I have just received a letter from Dear Sister [Sarah] her mind has been released from exercise—she has taken her son, her only son Isaac & offered up unto the Lord & she feels the reward of peace. I saw this surrender must be made, tho' I do believe the staying arm of the Angel will be stretched to prevent the final stroke. I do not see any way at all by which her desires are to be accomplished but I do believe they will be. He will make a way where there is none for his faith is in the deep & his way in the clouds. The language to me seems to be "go then & do likewise" (the North).

April 23   Sometimes I think resignation has been attained to, that I have given up the North & am willing to stay here until the cloud is taken up & moves forward, but then again I fear I have not—this much I can say, that I do sincerely desire to give up my own will & submit unreservedly to the good pleasure of my Master. The impression still remains on my mind that I shall go this Summer tho' I see no way at all open for me to escape thro'. I crave for both of us that we may be like the wheels ~~of~~ in Ezekiel's vision entirely moved by the Spirit. Yesterday in going to & whilst in meeting a sweet calmness seemed to clothe my mind & these lines of Newton's rested with me O for a clear walk with God. A light to shine upon the road A solemn & heavenly home, That leads me to the Lamb. Whilst returning I queried with myself whether this was not resignation & my heart was lifted in earnest prayer that my will might be even more broken & subdued, when I saw before me a color'd woman who in much fear & vexation was vindicating herself to two white boys one about 18 & the other 15 who walked on each side of her—the dreadful apprehension that they were leading her to the Work House crossed my mind & I was on the point of turning down a Street near me but did not feel at liberty to do so—as I approached the younger said to her I will have you tied up my knees smote together & my heart sunk within me, as I passed them she exclaimed Misses, but I felt all I had to do was to suffer the pain of seeing her my lips were sealed & my soul earnestly craved a willingness to bear the exercise which was laid on me. How long O Lord how long wilt thou the foot of the oppressor to stand on the neck of the Slave. None but those who learn from experience what it is to live in a land of Bondage can form any idea of the weight of exercise which is endured by those whose eyes are open to the enormities of Slavery & whose hearts are tendered so as to feel for these miserable creatures. For two or three months after I arrived here it appeared to me all the cruelty & unkindness & oppression which I had from my infancy seen exercised towards these poor creatures came back to my mind with as much force as tho' it was only yesterday, & as to the House of correction in this city it seemed as tho' its doors were unbarred to me & the wretched lacerated inmates of its cold, dark cells were presented to my view—night & day they were before me & yet my hands seemed bound as with chains of iron, I could do nothing but weep over the scenes of horror which passed in review before my mind. Sometimes I felt as tho' I was willing to fly from Carolina, but the consequences be what they might, at times it seemed as tho' the very exercise I was suffering under, was preparing me for future usefulness to them & this hope, I can scarcely call it, for my very soul trembled at the solemn tho't of such a work being placed in my feeble & unworthy hands, the idea was the means of reconciling me to suffer & causing me to feel something of a willingness to pass thro' my trials if I could only be the means of expressing the cruelty & injustices which was practiced in the Institution of oppression & of ["]bringing to light the hidden things of darkness"[21] of revealing the secrets of iniquity & abolishing it's present regulations—above all of exposing the awful sin of profession of a meek & merciful Master who left as an example that we should walk in his steps who when he was reviled reviled not again & possitively commanded in "not to resist evil" of these very professors sending their slaves to such a place of cruelty & having them whipped so that when they can scarcely walk, or having their feet upon the tread mill until they are lamed for days after it. These are not things I have heard, no, my own eyes have looked upon them & wept over them. Such is this opinion I have formed of the Work House here that for many months whilst I was a teacher in the First day School having a Scholar in my class who was the daughter of the Master of it I had frequent occasion to go to it to mark her lessons & no one can imagine my feelings in walking down that Street it seemed as tho' I was walking on the very confines of hell & this winter being obliged to pass it to pay a visit to a friend I suffered so much that I could not get over it for days & only wondered how any real christian could live near such a place if my feelings were so harrowed by only passing it.

Night   This is the day [that a] year [ago] I spoke to Wm McDowell about leaving his Church—lately I have very much desired to feel something of that calm resignation which I was favored to enjoy at that time & I think my desire has been measureably granted. ["]The Lord requireth, let the earth rejoice, let his people be glad" & in childlike simplicity cast all their cares on ["]Him who careth for them."

April 25   How often has the fear of falling into sin proved a safeguard to me, if we see danger before us & fear it, we will be sure to watch against it & the more sensible we are of our own weakness the more earnestly will we seek divine strength, this it is said "blessed is he that feareth always" the truly humble, wasteful soul is always fearing, his humility will show him his own nothingness & insufficiency whilst by constant watching he will be made sensible of the danger which ~~constantly~~ encompass him. ["]Whether light or darkness, prosperity or adversity, fulness or completeness, trials or temptations be his allotment still he trembles before the Lord."[22]

April 26   This is the first day year since I began to attend Friends Meeting regularly. I have been thinking lately of the benefits of silent worship. I think it has tended to teach me patience—to show me my own nothing & emptiness & to infuse a degree of calmness & settleness in my manner & feelings & tho' the language of Pharaoh "what profit is there that we serve the Lord" & that this has often been bro't before me yet from time to time the resolution has been uttered "I will wait upon the Lord"[23] & at others I have been able to say "it is good to be here." I was at meeting this morning—at dinner time something was said which wounded me so deeply that I did not think my mind was in a fit state to go this afternoon. I felt willing to suffer. My daily prayer is that I may be willing to stay here this summer. I want to feel my will completely broken & subdued. I often experience the truth of what the Prophet says, ["]He hath set the solitary in families"[24] but words of comfort & encouragement are often spoken & strength is granted sufficient to my day—what more can I ask.

April 27   This month has been an important one in my life—it was the 8th of 4th month 1826 that I left the Episcopal Society how well I remember the night of that day—it rained very much & as I lay in bed I prayed the Lord if I had done what was pleasing in his sight that he would close the windows of Heaven & grant me the indulgence of going to the Presbyterian meeting all the next day which was First day, peace flowed into my soul like a river I fell asleep & think I never shall forget the delightful feelings which clothed my mind as I was in bed & my eye caught the glittering leaves of the wild orange tree waving with the gentle breeze in the Sun beams—I <u>felt</u> my prayer had been answered & was happy beyond expression—it seemed as tho' I might have said with David "he hath made my feet like hinds feet"[25] with nimble footsteps I took my way to the courts of the Lord's house, feeling that I was unworthy even to be a doorkeeper there & as the herd panteth after waterbrook so did my soul pant after instruction. This was the beginning of glorious dispensation to my soul in which "I rejoiced with joy unspeakable & <u>full</u> of glory."[26] For a year or 18 months I hung on the breast of consolation & was borne on the side & dawdled on "the knee." I was a little child folded in the arms of paternal fondness & enjoyed ["]the most undoubted evidence that I was born of God." I had many trials to contend with, many deep baptisms to pass thro,' but so near was "the beloved of souls" so rich & full & constant were the cups of consolation which were administered that I counted those these light afflictions as nothing when compared to the glory which should be revealed, of which I enjoyed so large a foretaste that at times I surely know whether I was in the body or out of this body. I desire not to glory in these things but to be low in the dust remembering I was & still am nothing but a woman—this was the infancy of the new born soul & times of such joy, but great ignorance, of fervent feeling but little experience it was the spring to the tender tree which had just been planted in the Lord's vineyard, the great Husbandsman watched & watered it daily lest it should wither & die—soon under His fostering care it put forth leaves & was decked with blossoms—but they soon withered & fell to the ground so that very little fruit & that in a very imperfect state was gathered—the root was not deep enough to bear the body of the tree & the time was come when its branches must be lopped off & the root itself cleared of the insects which it was now found had been preying on it. This was a time of nakedness & poverty, a time of deep heartaching, a time of humiliation & abasement—whilst walking in the wilderness Satan was permitted to tempt & try me—my mind was tossed to & fro for many months like a wretched vessel on the surging billows driven by the black tempest, still there were Seasons when I could say "Lord I believe, help then my unbelief,["] seasons when I felt I was still under the care of a Pilot who could bring me safe thro' the rocks & quicksand which lay beneath my shattered bark. Some scriptures were opened which had been sealed as with 7 seals. I remembered the time when like James & John I had stood on the mount of Transfiguration ~~and had stood~~ beneath that cloud of glory which overshadowed them & heard a voice saying "this is my beloved son hear him"[27] it had been my privilege like Abraham to speak with Him face to face & by doing the will of God to <u>know</u> for myself that the doctrine of the divinity of my Lord & Savior Jesus Christ was of <u>God</u> & not of man; how then I one day queried how then, if all I say & felt was true am I thus forsaken & left to doubt at times even the existence of a Supreme Being—& my own conversion—it was then shown me that tho' James & John did ascend ~~the~~ Mount Tabor with the adorable Redeemer & did see his glory of the only begotten of the Father, yet they too had to come down in the valley of humiliation & sorrow, they too had to follow him thro' the painful changes of his life, to the garden of agony, the hall of judgment & the place of Crucifixsion & I shall never forget the delightful feelings of encouragement & consolation which filled my mind when I remembered that he had not been sent down alone but that <u>he</u> descended <u>with</u> them. I tho't

of their reluctance to come down & of their desire to build there these taberna-
cles & of the transport of joy which so overwhelmed them that they exclaimed
"Master it is <u>good</u> for us to be here" & resist not what they said—all these feelings I had passed thro,' & now with the promise that "He never would forsake
me" I was willing to pass thro' any suffering he was pleased to lay upon me, for
now I knew that it was <u>His</u> hand which was chastening me & I could kiss the rod
for I felt he loved me & that it was for my good & in answer to my prayers for
purity of heart & humbleness of mind. Then came a time of great agony, for it
was plainly shown me I must leave the Presbyterian Society & unite myself with
Friends—this was to cast the idols I had been graciously permitted to carry this
far on my journey to the snakes & to the beasts—to give up the image I had bowed
before, to be ground to powder, to cut off the right hand & to pluck out the right
eye—there was an awful silence in the temple of my heart I trembled before
the Shechinah. I dared not refuse, for I remembered my vows in the days of
mine affliction & yet it seemed as tho' I had not strength to meet the requiring
—strength was promised & I was "made willing in the day of his <u>power</u>." I could
not speak of these things to any one, for it seemed as tho' it was said unto me
"tell the vision to no man." I waited daily to know & do his holy will my various
active employments were one after another taken from me the burdens dropped
from my hands & the way gradually but clearly opened for me to leave the Presbyterian Society—here another scripture was unsealed to me. I remembered
that day in which the Friend of Sinners submitted himself to the Baptism of John
that he might fulfil all righteousness—"when he was baptized, he went up out of
the water & the heavens were opened to him & lo a voice from heaven saying this
is my beloved Son in whom I am well pleased"[28] it appeared as tho' I had just been
baptised in the dark water of tribulation & as tho' the consolitary language was
applied to me "this is my beloved child with whom I am well pleased"[29]—I fear
that I am not recording the condescending mercy which was so signally displayed at that time with that darkness of spirit & that lowliness of mind which
becomes so poor & unworthy a creature as I am but these lines seemed to be
required of me just now, so I proceed. At this time I again enjoyed his favor
which is <u>life</u> & ["]his loving kindness." A deeper spring was opened in my heart
& my soul daily drank of these hidden waters & whilst many were saying that it
was impossible I could enjoy any but a false peace, I felt that <u>my</u> "<u>life</u> was <u>hid</u>
with Christ in God"[30] & that I enjoyed that true peace which ["]no stranger
intermeddleth with." Hosea spoke to my case when he said by the Holy Ghost
—I will allure her & bring her into the wilderness & speak confidently to her.

And I will give her her vineyards from thence, & the valley of Achain for a door of hope "<u>and she shall sing there as in the days of her youth, & as in the day when she came up out of the land of Egypt</u>"[31]—But it was shown me I must be very careful not to unfold my feelings to any, for none here could understand me, the case of Hezekiah was brought before me how he showed to the stranger of Babylon the house of his precious things, the silver & gold, the spices & precious ointment & all the house of his armour & all that was found in his treasures & how the Lord commissioned Isaiah to take him that in consequence of his doing so, he should be deprived of everything, nothing should be left. I think I was mercifully preserved from speaking to others about things. I knew they would either not believe or not understand & being brought into the banquetting house of my beloved. I experienced his banner over me to be <u>love</u> "then it was I felt the truth of his word <u>my flesh</u> is bread indeed, <u>my blood</u> is drink indeed"[32]—then I could say I understood the invitation "eat O friends, drink, yea <u>drink abundantly</u>, O beloved.["][33] I think I was very careful not to give to others the bread which was handed for my own sustenance, like the manna upon which Israel was fed it was sweet to my taste & I gathered it daily—now I know that it was "the willing & obedient who eat the good of the land"[34] & time was come when the Lord would satisfy his people with his goodness. After drinking the bitter waters of Marah ~~very much~~ and finding there was a virtue in the Cross which would make them palatable and even sweet a way was very unexpectedly opened for me to go to the North—this language seemed applicable "My presence shall go with thee & I will give thee rest."[35] For 6 months I was permitted to encamp at the waters of Elim—every outward circumstance seemed combined to render me happy— but little exercise was laid upon me & whilst at times I would be tried at the prosperity which surrounded me & fear I was cast off this language was spoken in reproof—"they despised the pleasant land, they believed not his word"[36] for of a truth the promise had been graciously given me "Because thou hast kept the word of my patience I also will keep thee in the hour of temptation."[37] Never did I feel more sensibly the need of divine strength—the necessity of obeying the command "watch & pray always."[38] I was aware of my danger then, but in looking back I have seen still more clearly that my feet were set in very slippery places & that nothing but Almighty power could have upheld me. O my heart is sometimes humbled within me when I am given to see the wonderful preservation which was then granted. The kindness of Friends I think I can never forget, they received me with open arms & I believe had some little assurance in their minds that I had been redeemed with the precious blood of the Atonement. Such was the happiness I experienced in Pennsylvania that this language was constantly before me, "take thy rest["] "I have given thee all things <u>richly</u> to enjoy"[39]—it was shown me that tho' many friends had been raised up for me, yet I must be very careful to see them exactly in the <u>place & way</u> designed, they were given as fathers & mothers, brothers & sisters & so long as I was willing to receive them as <u>such only</u>, I should fully enjoy them but no longer—& as preservation was graciously continued to the close of my stay there, I did enjoy my tenderly beloved friends to the last moment. In the midst of all these external enjoyments, the Lord of Glory was pleased to unveil the glory of his face from time to time & to pour out his spirit so abundantly upon me as to cause me feelingly to acknowledge that "a day in <u>his courts</u> was better than a thousand"[40] a day or an hour in the <u>spiritual</u> enjoyment of <u>His presence</u>, was far better than <u>any earthly</u> happiness which could be felt. But the greatest blessing which was given me was the close union & communion I felt with dear Sister [Sarah], it seemed as tho' we were joined together in the Lord & that we were one spirit—our hearts seemed to vibrate to the same touch, our feelings to flow in the same channel— our desires to same form & return to the same pure source of <u>all</u> good—we loved each other (I believe) with a pure heart fervently & with something of that ["]charity which seeketh not her own."[41] For many weeks after I arrived in Philadelphia I tho't I should not return to Carolina in the winter & indeed I could not bear the idea of doing so—it seemed however like great ingratitude in me not to be willing to return if the Master so pleased & the subject of the necessity of my being as willing to give up my enjoyments as I had been to receive them was brought before me for consideration—the question of Job would naturally arise, Shall I receive good at the hands of the Lord & not evil? Shall I drink the cup of pleasure when he presents it & yet turn away when the cup of sorrow is placed to my lips? O no! I did love him for himself & if I was not willing to suffer for him still the desire of my heart was, that He would make me willing, & this I had faith to believe he could & would do. One day I think late in the 9th Mo in passing a room where the first carpet had just been spread these words were spoken, the time of thy departure is at hand, I felt sad at this plain intimation that soon I should break up my encampments at Elim & set off again to traverse the desert, but I murmured not but prayed for resignation. A short time after as I was sitting in silence one evening at dark, the command seemed to be given "Return unto the land of thy fathers & to thy kindred & I will be with thee"[42] from this time I think I was certain of leaving Philadelphia & my willing was entirely subdued, so that when time of my departure did come, I was not only willing, but anxious to be gone feeling that Charleston was my right place for the winter at any rate & believing that if I refused obedience, ~~that~~ all my enjoyments would be marred & the work of grace in my heart hindered. I think I was mercifully strengthened to give up all my friends and to say with one of old "The Lord gave, & the Lord hath taken away, blessed be the name of the Lord["]—or tho' it might be into dangers & difficulties & I suffered myself to be led like a little child—a few days before I sailed it seemed as tho' this language was spoken, "Verily, verily, I say unto you that ye shall weep & lament, but the world shall rejoice, & ye shall be sorrowful but your sorrow shall be turned into joy!"[43] I know I was coming back to suffer—& to be nothing among those who had once caressed & loved me much—soon I was to be a stone in the steps of the Sanctuary, made to be trodden upon. I saw just what was before me & earnestly craved divine strength & wisdom to direct & enable me to tread the hidden but thorny path which lay before me—an impression was then made upon my mind that if I was faithful during the winter, my release from Carolina would be signed & I be permitted to return to Philadelphia in the Summer, this was somewhat confirmed by a Minister one night saying (in reference to my departure) "perhaps she departs for a reason that we may receive her forever" still I think I desired to obey without any reference to future rewards & advantages—it was harder for me to give up dear Sister [Sarah] on <u>her</u> account than my own, I mentioned this a dear Friend of [words missing] know all her trials when she came to bid me Farewell, but she marked that I need not be afraid to leave her for I left her in very good hands, this was a word in season. It was thus that I left Ph. being able measurably to say I had sought the spiritual good of some of my young friends when among them. Some tendering heart subduing manifestations were granted on the voyage & peace, sweet peace was mostly the clothing of my mind tho' some fear was felt during one of the storms the vessel encountered. Three weeks of unbroken rest was granted after my arrival & was happy tho' my situation was as I expected, a lonely one—after this, trials came upon me, & ~~in mercy~~ from time to time the Father of mercies has been pleased to bend my spirit under a weight of exercise, causing me to drink some bitter cups—but praise be his holy Name—he has given strength equal to my day; & I think an uncommon degree of cheerfulness considering the circumstances under which I have been placed has been experienced. My first intention in the beginning of this statement was merely to mention that it was on the 8th of the 4th M. 1826 that I left the Episcopal Society and on the 23rd of the same month 1828 that I left the Presbyterian—but I have been unconsciously led on to write of the different events of my religious life during the 3 years since I felt myself to be renewed in the spirit & temper of my mind.

4

Strengthening of Will

April 30, 1829–June 12, 1829

The spring of 1829 was one of great conflict for Angelina. The source of the conflict was her strong desire to leave South Carolina in the face of her declining prospects of actually doing so. She desperately wanted to go but had to reconcile herself to the reality that it was unlikely to happen any time soon. Apparently there was a question of living arrangements in Philadelphia, and questions pertaining to her transport there and that issue complicated her successful departure. As to her relocation to Philadelphia, she complains that while, at times, her "will has been subdued," she continued to be tormented by a reappearing longing like a "Phoenix it has arisen from its own ashes."

This inner turmoil led Angelina to view most of her life in Charleston with increasing frustration. She saw her dispute with William McDowell and the Third Presbyterian Church as a "painful & humbling" experience. Indeed, the dispute grew into a confrontation when the church's Session formally charged Angelina with neglect of worship, among other things. The interactions she had with her family were increasingly strained. She saw the family as hopelessly dysfunctional and repeatedly confronted them about her concerns. For example, she felt that her mother's refurbishing of their drawing room made it "too handsome for one who has professed to renounce the pomp & vanities of the world." Most importantly, she lived amidst the "depravity" of slavery only with great pain. It was during this period that Angelina seemed to strengthen her resolve to respond actively to slavery, as she apparently continued to confront her family, even her mother, about it.

In the face of these conflicts Grimké was determined to endure the turmoil and to accept the pain. She wrote extensively about the necessity of reflecting the virtue of Christian charity and concluded that she would leave Charleston when God, not she, was ready. As this section of the diary ends, Angelina had become resigned to wait as long as necessary, but her desire to leave South Carolina and her will to overcome her torment had never been stronger.

$$\infty$$

April 30   There is at times a heaviness of mind about me which I cannot attribute to anything but the noisy, talkative, turbulent spirits with which I am often in company. Much fear has lately been felt least I should lose even one inch of the ground I have gained in my family. All the sacred and enduring ties of christian fellowship which once bound one to Charleston seem to be entirely dissolved. I go out to pay visits merely because I think it right to do so, & I try to watch for every imposition of duty & in simplicity to go where & when I am bid, not that I expect to receive any satisfaction in the visits except that, derived from a consciousness of having done my duty. Here no one delights in me & I delight in no one. I feel like an isolated being in the midst of those with whom I have often take sweet counsel & in days past walked to the house of God in company but I never have murmured tho' this has at times been hard to bear, & now I think I am not only willing to be "as a thing of naught," but I am contented that I should be so. In wisdom it has been thus ordered—may this dispensation humble me in the dust.

May 1   I think my will has been subdued about going to the North, but self which has died in giving up the will, has revived again in the hope of reward— like the fabled Phoenix it has arisen from its own ashes. I despise this feeling of my heart, for I know that I ought to serve such a Master from a pure love to Him, a sincere ~~desire~~ desire to please Him alone, not myself but I am so selfish, this monstrous idol of my heart is like the Hydra, as soon as one head is cut off another instantly springs up in its place—as soon as one unholy or inordinate desire is slain, another grows up in my polluted and ungrateful heart.

May 2   Yesterday was a day of depression with me, for the first time I began to think that the resignation I had felt was the preparation given me for staying here, not as I had fondly hoped, that subjugation of the will which was necessary before ~~I~~ my release should be granted. I certainly see no probability of my removal this summer, and yet the words have often been bro't before my mind, I will make a way where there is no way—they were given me by Elizabeth Wing in a religious communication whilst I was in Phila. & whether they have been revived by the Comforter or the Tempter I know not. My allotment is solitary, & yet such as been the tender mercy of Israel's Shepard to me that mostly I have been enabled to say "I am alone, yet not I for the Father is with me["] & yesterday I thought much of this precious promise[1] "I will be to them as a little sanctuary in the countries where they shall come."[2]

May 3   The great reason why we find the want of humility in others so hard to bear, is because we have so little of it in our own hearts. First day. I have been much troubled by Mother's painting and papering the drawing room, I have never felt as if I would go into it & I know not what I shall do when it is expected we shall sit in it of an evening—it is from what I have seen by casually passing by the open door quite too handsome for one who has professed to renounce the pomp & vanities of the world. O how many of us are ruined by indulging "the lust of the flesh, the lust of the eye & the pride of life"[3] which the Apostle declares "is not of the Father, but is of the world.["][4] Sometimes I fear that the ease of mind I most enjoy proceeds more from torpor & spiritual stupidity than exact faithfulness, at others I am given to see that what is principally required of me now, is a willingness to be nothing here, & to bear patiently & thankfully the many deprivations I daily experience—patiently because it is the Master's will, thankfully, because it is designed for my good & because in this situation I am shielded from some temptations to which I am but too liable to yield. I still sit in silence with dear Mother but feel very sensibly that she takes no interest at all in it, still I am not easy to relinquish the habit, believing that it may yet be blessed. E[liza] came this evening as she has several times before—it was a time of great deadness & yet I am glad to do it together in silence—at these seasons a door of utterance is sometimes opened & where there is conversation there will be some union.

May 4   This morning I woke surprised with ~~this~~ a dream. I thought I was about to set off on a journey with two of my sisters & that just before we started we were conversing with Mother about it & that all at once I inquired whether some gentleman was to go with us, Mother immediate replied yes, & I eagerly asked who, desiring to have some human guide and protector, she looked very impressively in my face and said with deep solemnity Jesus Christ. I tho't I burst into tears: disappointment at finding there was no arm of flesh for me to lean on & shame & confusion of face at not being willing to trust myself implicitly with such a Guide so agitated me that I awoke.

May 7   Today my prospect of going to the North this Summer seems to have closed. I desire to be grateful for the calmness I feel under the disappointment, for it has been a very great one to me & to record my sense of the tenderness with which I have been dealt, for Oh! could I have seen last fall when I left Philadelphia that I was not to return in a few months I believe my soul would have sunk under the gloomy prospect. How kind then was it in the Father of Mercies to cover the future with his holy hand, and now that the time has come when I am required to give up this darling wish of my heart in condescending mercy He has granted submission to his blessed will O that he would take me & do with me just as he pleases, only save me for his mercy's sake. As to my situation in my family, I cannot be sufficiently grateful for the preservation which has been granted. I think I have experienced something of the feeling of that good man who said he felt a spirit within him which "takes the kingdom with entreaty not with contention" & earnestly do I desire to "keep it by lowliness of mind."[5] They love me, but 'tis said to me tho' there are professors of Religion there is not one whose heart is wholly set to serve the Lord in spirit and truth they have fled from the world but like Rachel have carried their idols along with them. I fear they are among the mixed multitudes who still leave spiritual Egypt with the true Israel but who though among them are not of them & must sooner or later separate from them.

May 10   Yesterday my mind was much tossed & tried by receiving a letter from Wm McDowell in answer to a note I wrote him two months ago, his long silence I felt was not only a breach of politeness but a positive neglect of duty & I tho't that he had trifled with my feelings—but I do very much desire to feel a spirit of love under the dealing of the Session with me. I want to remember that they never have been able to realise the suffering, thro which I ~~have~~ passed in leaving the P[resbyteria]n S[ociet]y last Spring, nor did they I am very sure know the anxiety I felt many times after their Committee had called & I had written to Wm McDowell on this subject last winter. To receive their certificate of dispensation tho' painful & humbling will still be a release to my mind O for preservation in replying to this letter.

May 11   How vivid the feelings thro' which we pass even in one day, this morning I felt my heart unburthened but soon began to feel that Earth was a tiresome place nothing existed to interest me, my spirit was weary & faint & there was no bosom for me to lean upon, no heart to sympathize with me. O He hath set the solitary in families. S arrived today she is very gay & my heart weakens at the heartless pleasures she seems to enjoy—the loud and boisterous mirth pains me—this is not the society my beloved Mother ought to have. I am sure it tends to keep her back. It is generally only cheerful.

May 13   Had a comforting time at meeting this morning the language seemed to be "I have sent thee for a sign to the people" not yet as a ["]defense of

the gospels"—& living desires were felt that I might be willing to "be still." & be
gazed upon as "wonder unto many." In thinking of the disappointment I had met
with in finding I was to spend the Summer here, I remembered the condescending language of Jehovah to Israel, "come let us reason together," and some things
were shewn me why it was best I should stay with the encouraging assurance "I
go to prepare a place for thee" among those who thou lovest. My stay here at this
time I believe will hasten not retard my final reward & I can adopt the words of
David "in faithfulness hast thou afflicted me but I pray thee thy merciful kindness
be for my comfort."[6] But what shall I render unto the Lord for the sweet resignation he has granted me, the solemn submission of my will, the entire confidence I feel in Him as having ordered this very thing for my good & his glory.
Painful as is & will be that abstinence which my soul ~~will~~ does and will experience in my solitary allotment, and yet I am constrained to say "it is good to be
here,"[7] just where Thou hast placed me; ["]it is good to wait upon the Lord" & to
know that "all my times are in his hands."[8] These disappointments & crosses teach
me the necessity of having no will of my own if my will was always (as it ought
to be) the Lord's will, how easy my path would be—like a little child I would
wait from day to day & from hour to hour the manifestations of His will & in
sweet simplicity would do it without murmuring or wishing it to be otherwise
than exactly what it is—this would be living no longer to myself but to Him who
died for me & rose again. Some ungrateful servants always resist the will of their
Masters, they are willing, they say, to be anywhere or do any thing but just what
is required of them, and are we not too much like them, how often do we say
to our blessed Master, Lord we will go any where but where thou requirest we
should, we will do any work but what thou hast assigned us—but this will not
do, such servants love themselves, not their Masters, under the pretext of serving him, they seek to gratify themselves, they are willing to follow him when he
feeds them with bread, but they forsake him when he is to be led into the wilderness—they are willing to cut down branches of palms & spread their garments in
the way whilst admiring multitudes exclaim "Hosannah to the King of David," but
they are not willing to follow him to Calvary or to bear his Cross for him. If a
young unmarried woman can give up admiration of men for Christ then she can
give up any thing, for I have no hesitation in saying it was easier for me to part
with every thing else than this, & I do believe we have daily evidence that the curse
is still fulfilled, "her desire should be to him" this is no less true than humbling.

   May 14   After two or three attempts I at last answered Wm McDowell's
letter today, but before I could send it Tho's Napier called to deliver another by

order of the session citing me to appear before them next second day evening. Very little passed between us & I gave him mine to carry & expressed my intention to comply with the summons. I was composed whilst he was here but as soon as he left me gave way to my distressed feelings in a flood of tears. How desolate the feeling under such trying circumstances to have no friend on whose bosom to repose, no human consoller, no sympathising heart to take my trials to, but "the Lord reigns, let the Earth rejoice"⁹—full well do I know it must be for my good that I am thus alone, in the midst of relatives, in the midst of those who were once the helpers of my joy. My full heart again pierced, why so much suffering?

Night I know not why, but I am mostly cheerful in my family, no one could tell from my conduct among them today, that I have suffered so much in mind & thus often have been the case since my return that after passing this much exercise whilst alone I will be able to go among them with cheerfulness the burden of my heart will be removed & like Ezekiel I will bind the ties on my hand & go forth. I desire to be truly thankful for this, for all things I do wish to manifest by my conduct tho' in solitary a situation, yet that I am happy for that there is a power in Religion which gives that Peace which outward circumstances cannot destroy, that true happiness which as the priest justly remarks "has no bolsters" that delightful feeling which Paul enjoyed when he said "I have learned in whatever state I am therewith to be content."¹⁰ O I want to show them (tho' deeply sensible of what a poor unworthy creature I am) something of "the beauty of holiness."¹¹

May 15 This morning I can feelingly say "The Lord is good to Israel & with the Psalmist testify that he is faithful" he is a very present help in times of trouble. Sometimes I have tho't whilst deprived of his sensible presence that he had forsaken me, but as soon as trials come upon me then I find "he is nigh upon all who call upon him."¹² He is my strength & shield, my rock & fortress, the high tower to which the righteous flee & are safe. Last Spring I remember it was said unto me one day when I was about leaving the Presbyterian Church "thou art a chosen vessel unto me, to bear my name before the gentiles & people of Israel, & thou shall be brought before governors & kings for my sake for a testimony against them but takes no tho't how or what thou shall speak; for it shall be given thee in that same hour what thou shalt speak. For it is not thee who speaketh, but the Spirit of thy Father who speaketh in thee." I had no idea at that time of being brought before the Session (ruling elders of the 3rd Pres Ch) even if I did leave it, but these things will now come to pass & that I may obey the injunction to "take no tho't what I shall speak." This morning I answered Wm McDowell's letter I have been much exercised in mind, but the encouraging language seems to [have] spoken "Fear not warm Jacob, I will be with thee."[13] I am certain my heart is fixed, ["]O God my heart is fixed," fixed to serve thee in any way thou pleasest. Only "forsake not the work of thy own hands."[14] Now mine eyes are opened to see why I never could feel as if I ought to apply for admission in Friends Society last Summer, there would have been an impropriety in my joining them before I was dismissed from the Psn Chh:—but I then had no idea of the manner of their proceeding against their members & tho't as I had spoken to Wm McDowell & told him I intended leaving his Chh that this was all that was necessary—but our Guide is infallible, O that I may follow him even to prison & unto death, if requested but I am a poor Creature, liable to temptation—& many times do I fear that instead of enduring unto the end that all my past experience will stand as a handwriting on the wall against me. I have just received another tender note from Wm McDowell, O that we may be preserved in love, pure love.

May 17   First day. Went to Meeting this morning, it was a time of exercise & much light seemed to be thrown on the emptiness of the charges to which I am cited by the Session to answer. The first is "A neglect of the public worship of God in his house" this charge I cannot admit first because I believe the Supreme Being to be a Spirit who is not worshipped by the multitude of wonder or the parade of ceremony, but in the Spirit & in truth no offering of the lips can be acceptable to Him (however good the words may be) unless it is offered in the Spirit, the Apostle tells us that even that pure & spotless sacrifice which was offered upon the Cross for the sins of the whole world was offered "thro' the Eternal Spirit" how much more necessary than our poor offerings of prayer and praise. If He is a Spirit & he is worshipped not by our Spirit, then this worship certainly may be performed without the intervention of wonder. Secondly, I do not regard the Pres place of worship any more the "house of God" than Friends meeting house. Paul tells us that the "house of God" is the Chh of the living God, ["]the pillar & ground of truth" again he says "that believers are builded together for an habitation of God thro' the Spirit," & Peter says that believers "as living stones, are built up—spiritual house," &c. I cannot find any place in the New Testament where any house built of wood & brick is called the "house of God" it is a spiritual house, where we may worship at any time & in any place for Ichabod is no longer worshipped either at Jerusalem nor in Mount Gerisim, for the sacrifices he accepts are as Peter tells us "spiritual sacrifices." And even under the old Dispensation Jacob found that spot in the wilderness where he wrestled with the Angel & attained the blessing to be the h "none other than the house of God, the very gate of heaven."[15] The second charge is "a neglect of the ordinance of the Lord's supper." I never promised specially to observe this—my promise was "to observe all the commandments & audiences of God in the Sanctuary in the family & in the closet" & as long as I regarded it as His ordinance I did strictly observe it, but had I continued to observe it after I ceased to regard it as such, & I looked upon "an ordinance of men" then ~~had I continued to observe it~~ instead of keeping my promise to observe ~~of~~ Gods ordinances I would have broken it by observing what I conscientiously believed "to be an ordinance of men." If it be said that I knew my will when I joined the Pres Chh that the ordinance was regarded as sacred & obligatory on all its members then I would say that in no part of the Covenant did I promise to adopt no other principles than those professed by them, nor did I promise to follow either their Minister nor their Elders in their religious faith, but most solemnly engage to "take the Lord Jesus Christ to be my prophet to instruct me, & the Holy Ghost to be my guide to whom alone. I was to look for light, holiness & peace." And what is the Lord's Supper & does not Paul himself say that in assembling themselves together & eating bread & drinking wine "was not to eat the Lord's Supper." Is the privilege of eating the Lord's Supper peculiar to believers or is his table opened for the ungodly and the profane also? I think not, I believe that Supper to which he invites is spiritual— ["]believers alone are taken in to his banqueting house," ["]believers alone open the door of their hearts to the heavenly guest when he stands & knocks, & they alone know what it is to sup with him & He with them" for it is with them alone ["]He takes up his stool." The 3rd Charge is couched in more general terms "A subject of the means of grace & audiences of God generally." As to the prayer meeting lectures & as long as I found them to be means of grace to my soul, I did regularly attend, but when I found that I had drunk to the very bottom of the well & drained the streams then I left off going to them, then it was shown me that ["]tho' the streams were all dry yet the fountain was full & that if I would cease from man whose breath is in his nostrils" that the sion of the tribe of Judah would unloose the souls which no human being had been found worthy to unloose. As to the ordinance I find none of any set form to be observed at any set time established by the Redeemer. The Apostle does expect us not to forsake the assembling of ourselves together but as to praying & preaching this is to be done "in the Spirit only["] & that Spirit we know is as uncertain as the wind that blows—therefore I must regard all forms of worship however good in themselves, to be contrary to the mind of Christ, as being established in the will of man.

May 20   I believe it best for thy satisfaction ~~of~~ in time to come to write down some little account of my appearance before the Session on the evening of the 18th. I felt anxious Mother & S[ister] E[liza] should know nothing of the Summons & therefore took tea at Rebecca Eaton's and requested Wm McD to come there for me when the Session were ready to receive me; my mind as might be supposed was greatly tried from 6th day when I received it to 2nd when I was to meet them, nevertheless I was enabled in a good degree to be cheerful when not alone, so that none suspected my real feelings. As the 8 O'Clock bell rang I heard my beloved friends footsteps in the passage & rose to put on my bonnet & shawl, as he entered he met me with a smile but my soul was too sad, too solemn to reciprocate it. Rebecca evidently perceived by my manner & tone that I was exceedingly tried & asked if I must go now. I simply said yes, she kissed me affectionately & I left the room, my feeble knees almost refusing to bear me along whilst I put my trembling arms in his, I hoped he would be silent for the few moments only but he soon began to speak, but my lips were sealed & I made no reply to his remarks on the mysterious dealings of providence. On entering the room, (to me it seemed almost like a judgment hall) I felt this feeling of love to all around & offered my hand in token of fellowship. I stared like a statue in the midst of them, speechless & almost trembling with agitation as they came forward one by one & took my hand—one or two smiled but "My soul was exceeding sorrowful"[16] & I believe my countenance was deeply solemn for I felt it was a solemn hour. I took my seat & lifting my eyes saw my 7 judges seated around the room (for I could but regard them as such) tho' I was well convinced they had none but feelings of tenderness & kindness towards me; a strange mixture of feelings filled my heart, & O how precious a season of silence would have been to my troubled mind, but the Moderator very soon addressed me by saying that he supposed it was unnecessary for him to explain why we had thus met together as the letter I had received from [him] had already informed me, he paused, but I had not the power of utterance, he continued & asked how I felt with regard to the charges brought against me, whether I did not feel I had neglected "the public worship of God" & how I felt about the Lord's Supper which I had also neglected for some time past he paused—& I remarked I did not think I would be doing myself justice if I admitted the first charge & made some observation on the spirituality of worship under the gospel dispensation. He then asked how I felt about the second charge. I readily admitted this but observed I did not think in neglecting it I had broken my Covenant, because in it I had perceived to "observe all the Ordinances & Commandments of God" that so long as I regarded the Lord's Supper (so called) his ordinance I did sacredly observe it, but when I ceased to believe it was, had I ~~had it~~ observed it, I would have broken my Covenant instead of keeping it—here I was much agitated. I felt I was disregarding what they deemed most sacred & remarked that tho' such were my views I wished it to be distinctly understood I blamed no man, judged no man, condemned no man for observing it. He then asked whether I did believe the Lord's Supper to be an ordinance of man, I replied, if I did not I should observe it. I was then asked to state my views distinctly as to what course I felt it my duty to pursue with regard to Preaching & that Ordinance. I did with a trembling voice & addressing them by the name of friends told them I could feel for them & did feel for them under these trying circumstances. The Moderator hoped I fully understood the feelings of the Session towards me to be those of kindness & good will whatever censure they feel it their duty to pass on me. I expressed my full belief that my judges were my friends. Some more passed as to the spirituality of worship & I again said I could not see how their first charge could with justice be bro't against me. The Session were then asked if they had anything to say. C McIntire remarked that were they to conceal their personal feelings of interest & affection for me, he believed the Session would willingly lay any one aside, but that as Officers of the Ch[urc]h of C[hrist] they felt it their duty to proceed —the Moderator rose & I left the room with him, he returned to the room & finding myself alone I gave vent to my conflicting feelings in a flood of tears. I tho't how the Lord had turned "this fruitful fodder of my enjoyments into a barren wilderness, I tho't as the days gone by & in my afflictions remembered all the pleasant things I had in the days of old" the scene thro' which I had just past was strangely mysterious & I felt it was humbling indeed thus to be brought before 7 men to give an account of Principals and Practices into which I believe nothing but the Spirit of all Truth had led me. After some time Wm McD came to inform me that I could not know at that time the decision of the Session as they had not come to any. After their meeting was over C McI entered & offered to see me home, but I expected the Carriage & declined his kind offer & soon after it came. And how I would record the deep sense of gratitude I have experienced in looking at the conduct of the Session toward me particularly at this time. The respect & delicacy, the tenderness & affection they manifested I hope will not easily be forgotten & I came away that night feeling a stronger bond of service with them than I had ever done even when a Presbyterian—a sweet savour of good still remains in the recollection of that meeting for which I desire to feel grateful, as I regard it as strong evidence that not only they but I was mercifully forced to keep in my right place. O for preservation even unto the end.

May 22   Yesterday I opened Wm McDowell's letter which I had received the day before but did not read as I was obliged to be a good deal out & my mind was kept on the stretch about intervals, so that I laid it by until I could read it entirely. I fully expected it to contain the final decision of the Session & hoped my mind would then be released from anxiety & trial, but to my great surprise they had determined to make trial of solemn & affectionate admonition thro' their moderator which was accordingly conveyed in the letter in which I am warned of the dangerous tendency of my erroneous principles & exhorted to examine the Bible with humility. His letter tried me almost to a hairs breadth. I wept abundantly over it & scarcely to know whether to answer it or not as my beloved friend said he had much more to say to me, but this morning I sent an answer written I think under feelings of much love & I hope such a one as will induce the Session to cast me off from Membership at once & release me from the great trial of mind I have lately suffered.

Night   I do not believe it would be right to wait recording the goodness of the Lord to me this afternoon; as usual at dusk I took my seat by Mother & was thinking what a comfort it would be if she would feel for me or with me; when she put her arm around my neck & placed my head on her bosom tears stole from my eyes and after a season of silence she said "let not your heart be troubled; neither be afraid, you will be brought thro' this trial as you have been thro' the others.["] I said nothing for my heart was full she kissed me affectionately & we parted, when left alone I enjoyed a season of tenderness & comfort. Mother knows nothing of this business but that a correspondence is carried on between Wm McDowell and myself, but does not suspect that I had to appear before the Session for she has not yet seen any of the letters.

May 24   We know that it is only when the Astronomer takes his position as it were in the center of the Sun that he is able to understand the order & beauty of the Solar System, it is only whilst here that he can see the planets rolling in harmony around their several spheres or at all account for their appearance & disappearance & the varied changes of their size & position as seen from our little Earth—to us all is confusion, we cannot even understand the waxing & waning of the Moon, nor could we tell why Venus at one time our Morning, at another our Evening Star—& this I have tho't it is with the Christian, so long as he stands within the pale of his own particular denomination & from that position looks on the Religious World, to him it will appear like a scene of perfect confusion—he will wonder why all do not think as he does, & when he comes in contact with another who views things from the ground of another Denomination & each will be surprised that the other cannot see just as they do, forgetting that they are standing in very different positions & of course can no more see alike than two persons standing in Jupiter & another in Venus; but if they would only come out of their own Churches & stand as it were on an conscience above then all I look at them in the light of the Sun of Righteousness, would they not both be struck with the order & beauty exhibited by the different Christian Societies, each filling its allotted place & moving in its own proper sphere of action, & all receiving light & life from the same great Source of all Creation; all formed & guided by the same Almighty hand. May it not be laid down as an axiom that that system must be radically wrong which cannot be supported best by transgressing the laws of God.

May 25 During the last fortnight I have been tried with a weariness of spirit which at times have been hard to bear. With Rebecca of old I have almost said "I am weary of my life" nothing seems to interest me or arouse the energies of my soul, & sometimes I wonder how I shall live thro' the Summer—well has a friend SM addressed these lines to me "O be not sad, altho' thy lot be cast No shepherd's tent within thy own appear, far from the flock & in a desert waste, But the chief shepherd is forever near." I dare not say I have not felt His life giving presence, O no! praised be his name, ["]he has upheld my sinking soul, he has fed me with food convenient for me," & could I think I was in the least degree advancing his glory. I think I would be satisfied, but I am doing nothing; "tho' the fields are white for harvest, yet I am standing idle in the market place"[17]—would not even suffering in his service be preferable to this lassitude, this indolence of mind & body—here I am like Diner "faring sumptuously every day"[18] but I am thankful it is against my inclination, against my principles—why! I am often tempted to ask why am I kept in such a situation, a poor unworthy worm feeding on luxuries my soul abhors, tended by slaves whom I would (I think) rather serve than be served by & whose bondage I deeply deplore O why am I kept in Carolina, but the answer seems to be "I have set thee as a sign to the people." ["]Lord give me patience to stand still" give me patience to wait until "thy arms bring the salvation" until the mountains of separation melt before thy presence until thou shalt say "it is enough," my times are in thy hands, strengthen me to say "thy will be done."[19] I feel too as tho' Wm. McDowell & his Session were trying my feelings more than they ought. I cannot but think my dismission ought to have been signed after my appearance before those this night week. I am sure they are depending too much on that cord of love which they evidently see binds my heart to theirs, O that they may not stretch it much more lest it break & this sweet bond of fellowship be destroyed.

May 26   Last evening I took tea at BT's. With a handsome house, an elegant garden, a prosperous family & an exalted reputation among the learned & religious world so called I could plainly feel there was no real happiness to be found there. I do not know that I ever felt more sensibly the vapidness of all human enjoyment—it is not like the soap bubble borne aloft by the fickle breeze & perfectly empty even whilst gilded by the rays of the Sun of the Prosperity & soon very soon to burst & sink into nothingness.

May 30   At times I have had my mind much exercised as to whether a Christian ought to wear gold in any way even in a watch. I thought the Bible forbid the "wearing of gold" but upon examining the exhortations of Paul & Peter upon this subject I find they forbid its being worn as an ornament just as they object to clothing, but not at all where utility or convenience alone are consulted therefore as I believe it is necessary to wear apparel (modest & plain) so I do not in the least doubt now but that a plain gold watch may be worn without sin because it is very useful & necessary & may be worn without being seen & therefore cannot be classed with broaches rings earrings &c. which are worn as ornamental not useful appendages to dress, they are worn expressly to be seen & to gratify the pride & vanity of the wearer without being of any use at all.

May 31   Last night for the first time the Drawing room was opened and several gay fashionable people came to take tea. I said nothing to Dear Mother about it but felt it incumbent for her to hear my silent testimony against these things by absenting myself from the room. I staid down stairs & read she has made no remark at all on my conduct & I want very much to keep the door—of my lips with all diligence, lest I be tempted to speak my own words in my own will & time.

June 2   This morning opportunity offering I wrote a few lines to C[harles] in E[liza]'s letter dear brother how little he can understand my feelings toward sin—when sewing up the bundle to go to him I felt my heart broken & a renewed desire to leave this and all my other concerns with him "who loved me & gave himself for me.["] My mind has of late again been exercised about going to the North. I am much tried & find it hard very hard to stay here, but I am praying for resignation & patience.

June 4   At times, Slavery is a heavy burden to my heart—last night I was led to speak on the subject, of all others I think, the sorest to touch a Carolinian on. This depravity was spoken of with contempt & it was said by one, they were fit to hold no other place than they did. I asked what had made them so depraved, was it not on account of their degraded situation, & was it not white people who had placed them & kept them in this situation & were they not to blame for it? Was it not a fact that the minds of slaves were totally uncultivated & their souls are no more cared for by their owners as if they had none. Was it not true that in order to restrain them from vice physical power was employed in order to supply the place of that moral restraint which had proper instruction been given them, proper principles been instilled into them, would have effectively guarded them against evil. Another remarked they wished I would never speak on the subject & why I inquired? because I spoke in such a way she replied. Truth will cut deep into the heart I said & this was no doubt the reason why no one liked to hear me express my sentiments, but that I did feel it to be my duty to bear a decided testimony against an allowed practice which I believed altogether con-trary to the spirit of the Gospel for it was a system which nourished the worse ~~feelings~~ professions of the human heart, a system which sanctioned the daily trampling under foot the feelings of our fellow creatures. But it was said it is exceedingly imprudent for you to speak as you do. I replied I did not think so. I was not speaking before servants, I was only speaking to owners whom I wished to know my sentiments—this wrong had long enough been covered up, & I was not afraid or ashamed of any one hearing my sentiments, they were drawn from the Bible. I also took occasion to speak very plainly & pointedly to SM about the bad feelings she had toward negroes & to tell her tho' she wished to get rid of them & would be glad to see them "shipped" as she called it; that this wish did not spring from gospel love, it was not the effect of pure Christian benevolence. My heart was heavy after this conversation, but I know not why, unless I dis-played too much zeal, or these words tho' true & good were not required, or I did not obey the injunction of the Apostle "speak the truth in love" but of this last I do not feel at all guilty, one proof that I did speak in love I tho't was that even SM had no bad feelings towards me after it, but treated me just as usual, whereas I have often seen her offended with E for two or three days for saying much less—indeed I never saw anyone feel the truth more than she does but she will not receive it. "the strong man armed still keeps the house." O how many there are who like the Devil "believe & tremble"[20] but how few have that "faith which

purifies the heart, works by love, & overcomes the world."[21] In a little season of
retirement before going to bed I desired to know wherein I had sinned & to be
able to discern between good & evil, the bitter & the sweet. Yesterday some
unguarded expression from me greatly offended Sister E & she treated me very
coldly—after dinner I asked her whether she tho't she had right feelings toward
me—some conversation ensued, I think I convinced her that tho' I had been the
offender I had no bad feelings towards her, but that she had very bad feelings
towards me. I wounded her unintentionally, but she resented it willfully—but
even if I had had improper feelings, was it right I asked for her to retaliate. I was
however careful not to say I had bad feelings because I had not, and by so doing
I would have injured, not helped her, besides departing from truth—for some
time she contended it was right for her to behave as she did, but remarked that
the way in which I tested my feelings was by love the instant I was from under
that covering & influence. I know I was from under the covering of the Lord's
Spirit & I sinned no matter what words I spoke or how I behaved, ["]everything
which is not of that faith which works by love is sin." I then appealed to the Light
within her whether that did not show her she had no feeling of love towards me,
or she could not have been so cold & unamiable—at last she was melted & we
kissed each other & I believe all is well now. At dark she came & sat with me &
remarked that a great while had elapsed since anything unpleasant had occurred
between us (about 18 months) & that we never ought to allow such a thing to
happen again. At dinner table yesterday I talked too much. I said nothing either
wrong or in a wrong spirit but I felt much condemnation & was not relieved until
I mentioned my feelings to E before I spoke to her about her conduct to me. I
felt grateful for these reproofs of conscience, ["]for whom the Lord loveth he
chasteneth" by the holy Spirit, for every sin, however small (comparatively)
whilst the sinners heart of stone remains impenetrable to the arrows of conviction even for those of much greater magnitude. Of late I have tho't much of that
Charity which Paul describes in the 13th of Cor. How few even know what it is,
how few possess it. It is not that Charity which whilst it unloads the purse,
inflates the heart with pride & self gratification for I may "give all my goods to
feed the poor,"[22] & yet not profess it—neither is it that charity which with sinful
weakness ascribe goodness of heart to those who live in sin, and as soon as death
cuts off a fellow being to say they have gone to Heaven tho' we never saw anything like the fear of God in their lives & conversations—there are also many
other things which the world & professors call Charity & Religion which are no
different from it as light is from darkness & which are empty, as their substitutes.

Charity say the inspired Apostles "suffereth long & is hard." He who professes it will not only endure contempt continually & persecution, but he will be kind to those very persons who scorn & oppress him, no feeling of revenge or hatred will be experienced, but he will be enabled to obey the divine command "love your enemies, bless them that curse you," do good to them that despitefully use you & entreat you. "Charity envieth not"[23] when he is in adversity & he sees others in prosperity he will not desire to deprive them of their enjoyments, but will be enabled to obey the command "to love his neighbor as himself" & so far from wishing to deprive of him of any pleasure will even add to his happiness if he can, thus his own experience will testify to the declaration "he that watereth others shall himself be watered" for such a disinterested effort will assuredly secure to him the smiles of ["]Him whose favor is life" & even whilst in the wilderness of sorrow will feel & taste the cold flowing waters gushing from the barren rock. "Charity vaunteth not itself."[24] He will never boast of the purity of his heart on the benevolence of his actions, for true Charity as it is wholly the work of the Holy Spirit, will humble him, will lay him low in the dust, so that whilst exalted in righteousness he will be crowned with humility. "Charity is not puffed up."[25] He will not only not boast of his own excellence to others & try to display his good qualities but when pressed & extolled by others his heart will not be lifted up with pride, he will reject the tributes of their praise & with the Psalmist exclaim "Not unto me, not unto me be the praise," for "by the grace of God I am what I am."[26] ["]His heart is fixed" & Prosperity cannot lift him up because his feet are planted on the Rock of Ages—he sees the emptiness of worldly honors & riches & so far from their lifting him up he feels they are his servants & possesses them as tho' he possessed them not "he holds them only as a Steward & employs them to glory of his Master in heaven.["] "Charity doth not behave itself unseemly."[27] There is a beautiful consistency of character about him, which is his daily covering thro' all the changing scenes of life, at all times & in all places— his example will shine even in the glare of prosperity & thro' the dark clouds of adversity. "Charity seeketh not her own."[28] There is a disinterested generosity in her possession which leads him to seek the real happiness of those around him & to obey the command "Let everyone of us please his neighbor for his good to edification"[29] neither does he seek his own honor for he becomes a "fool for Christ's sake"[30] & treading the narrow path of duty is willing to be trodden under foot by those whose faults he feels bound to reprove, nor will he seek to justify himself. "Charity is not easily provoked."[31] There is a settled calmness about her possesser which enabled him to resist the provocations to anger, hatred & other evil passions "the peace of God rules in his heart" so that he is not easily provoked by the faults of others. "Charity thinketh no evil."[32] He will not easily be persuaded that others intend to injure his feelings by unguarded expressions or hasty actions, nor will he wish or even think of retaliating & no evil feelings will be harboured in his bosom against any one. "Charity rejoiceth not in iniquity."[33] Amidst the glare of prosperity surrounded by the luxuries of life, his heart will be heavy, because he sees & feels these things to be inconsistent with the self denial enjoined upon the Cross bearing disciples of Jesus. Neither can he rejoice in such love & admiration from a human being however flattering to the pride of his heart which he feels is greater than that felt by the individual for his divine Master, this is a species of iniquity he abhors. There are some too, whom the Apostle describes as not only doing evil themselves but taking pleasure in them who do evil & then rejoicing in iniquity, but not so with him who possesses Charity he can neither enjoy sin in himself, or in others, he mourns over his own aberrations from the path of duty & his righteous soul is vexed from day to day with the unholy lives of those around him. "Charity rejoiceth in the truth."[34] There is an openness & frankness about him which shrinks from falsehood & will ingenuously confess a fault rather than cover it with false glasses & whilst condemning himself a secret satisfaction will be felt for he rejoices in the truth tho' it may be against him. No selfish circumscribed views are pursued by him, he rejoices not in individual prosperity half so much as in the vigor of Truth & he willingly relinquishes his own desires if he finds they will hinder the progress of "the Truth as it is in Jesus." "Charity beareth all things."[35] Ignominy, contempt poverty & affliction are alike borne with meekness & resignation, he bends under the weight of exercise for himself & others willingly, & seeks not to throw off any burdens which are laid upon him. He can bear too to be found fault with by anybody with weakness even tho' he may or may not be worthy of censure. ["Charity] believeth all things." He sees nothing in the Bible which he does not receive as the truth & under every dispensation thro' which he is called to pass he still believes this promise "all things shall work together for good to those who love God" & tho' often tempted let go the shield of faith can still say "Lord I believe, help then mine unbelief." ["Charity] hopeth all things. That hope which has been produced in his heart by the combined influence of patience & experience is as an anchor to his soul both sure & steadfast" & bears him up as he treads thro' the wilderness or traverses the deep of tribulation. ["Charity] endureth all things." Like "a good soldier of Jesus Christ he endures hardness." Wherever duty calls he will go leaning on the arm of his beloved—"he that endureth unto the end (& he only) shall be saved." "Charity never faileth."[36] Like the sun which fails not to enlighten our world with his shining beams & shines alike on the evil & the good—so Charity never fails to those around her possession a meekness and patience a gentleness and benevolence which is as plainly felt and seen as the light of the sun—he is courteous not only to those who are his superiors or equals in mark & edification, but she stoops to the lowest & "condescends to men of low estate"[37]—she is humble to the slave & ~~does~~ can not tread him beneath his feet merely because she has the power. He obeys the precept "all of you be subject one to another be clothed with humility" his daily conduct is a commentary on this text "love is the fulfilling of the law"[38] he professes that gentleness which David says makes great & when he bestows a favor "he giveth liberally & upbraideth not" as if called to reprove, he does it with all long suffering "speaking the truth in love."[39] There are also dispensations thro' which he passes when he feels that prophesies have failed tongues have ceased & knowledge has vanished away & yet "Charity never faileth"[40] his heart is still imbued with holy love to God & good will to men—& now abideth faith, hope & charity these ["]I but the greatest of these is Charity"[41]—"it is the bond of perfectness." "If ye know these things happy are ye if you do them."[42]

June 5   It was this day [a] year [ago] that I sailed for Philadelphia, this day year every burden was removed from my heart & every cord broken which bound me to Carolina at that time, it was the beginning of a dispensation of rest & pleasure to the weary traveller Zionward which continued until I returned. A very different Summer seems to be before me now & my heart is contented before the Lord when I think of the wonderful calmness which overspreads my mind under the ~~so~~ great disappointment of being detained here, the Summer at least. I feel very plainly that this is my right place & in reference to the North the language seems to be "all things are not now ready" but I will prepare a place for thee—indeed I would rather not go unless I can do so permanently & I am fully convinced that if I am faithful & willing to wait the Lord's time He will set an open door before me & carry me from this land of bondage. I received a letter from dear Sister she speaks the words of encouragement to me which I bless the Lord He has permitted me to receive—how my heart responds to the injunction "be thou faithful unto death."[43]

June 6   Have just written a farewell letter to Anna Braithwaite[44] believing it not only permitted but required. "Verily, verily I say unto you, you shall weep & lament, but the world shall rejoice," has returned with familiar force to my mind today, but not without the promise "your sorrow shall be turned into joy."[45]

June 7   Great condemnation fell again last night for speaking too much. I was asked whether there was any thing in the Bible to prove that the first day of the week in preference to any other was to be specially appropriated to the worship of God. I said no—a long argument ensued. I said I saw nothing that could prove that the Apostles had any reference to the Resurrection of their divine Master on that day in resting as is maintained on the first day of the week—that I believed that it would never have been altered but to show the Jews that the First Dispensation was ended & with it, all distinction between days as well as meats. I was accused of wishing to destroy the Sabbath. I said I fully believe not only that it was necessary to observe one day of the week as a cessation from our worldly employments & a rest to our hearts of burden, but that it was a great blessing to be permitted to set apart one day wholly to the worship of God, but that I believe that the 4th or 6th day would be as acceptable as the 1st were it not that in not keeping the latter we would be an offense to Christians & as Paul "became weak to those who were weak,"[46] as I tho't it the duty of believers to condescend to each other, and he gives a striking illustration of this when he says "if meat make my brother to offend, I will eat no flesh while the world ~~lasts~~ standeth, lest I make my brother to offend." "One man (says the Apostle) esteemeth one day above another, another esteemeth every day alike,"[47] & the conclusion he draws is this "he that regardeth the day, regardeth it to the Lord & giveth God thanks, & he that regardeth not the day to the Lord he regardeth it not & giveth God thanks,"[48] so that all that is needful is that "every man be fully persuaded in his own mind" & we are especially commanded not to despise each other, not to judge each other in such trifles, "for the kingdom of God consisteth not in meat & drink, but in righteousness & peace & joy in the holy Ghost."[49] I was asked whether I would work on the first day of the week. I said no, because in so doing, I would be an offense to others & we were warned "not to put stumbling blocks, or an occasion to fall in our brother's way." It was asked why the First day was called in Scripture ["]the Lord's day."[50] I denied that it was, for it was merely said that "John was in the Spirit on the Lord's day" but no one could prove that was First day—it was argued there was a propensity in keeping that particular day because our Lord rose on that day. I said the most acceptable way in which we could keep that event was daily & hourly to let his power to arise in our hearts over our evil propensities, for thousands kept it outwardly who know nothing at all of the "gospel of Christ being the power of God unto the Salvation of the souls from sin." ["]Blessed is he who hath part in the first resurrection." It was asked whether the fact of the Apostles assembling on that particular day did not prove that they regarded it as the most proper & whether the natural inference was not, that they kept that day because the Redeemer rose then? I said I did not think it did, because Paul laboured very much to do away the distinction of days (he told the Galatians he was afraid of them, because "they observed days & weeks &c.; & it had in so doing turned to the beggarly elements") & because I would not but believe that if it was necessary to observe that particular day for that particular reason, that a command would have been given & the reason assigned, just as under the Jewish Dispensation they were commanded to keep the 7th day because ["]the Lord rested on that day from all his work." Silent worship was looked upon & S[elina] asked whether I really believed it to be better than the worship among other denominations. I told her to say no more of it, at least it was not solemn mockery which I believed every form was more or less, for confessions & professions & promises were made in forms of prayer which were nothing more than solemn sounds on tho'tless tongues in most instances, she asked whether I tho't it best to sit in silence than to attend preaching, I said I tho't it far preferable to all preaching except that which flowed from the immediate influence of the Holy Spirit as no others could possibly be effectual or acceptable & made some remarks relative to the Apostle's preaching and speaking "as the Spirit gave them utterances" & the perfect emptiness of the best forms without the power—she did not appear to have tho't of these things before. I have tho't these arguments were permitted in order to initiate me into the practice of "contending for the faith once delivered to the saints," but they do at the same time manifest how little prepared I am as yet, for that awful work I believe to be before me, there is still too much of natural feeling excited when I argue, too much earnestness in my manner, tho' I gratefully acknowledge there is not as much impatience about me, nor do I feel the contempt or anger I once did towards my opponents, I can measurably obey the command to ["]speak the truth in love" and am willing others should differ if they do so conscientiously. I felt very much reproved too, for not speaking the exact truth, O how hard when with those who are gay & tho'tless & careless as to truth, to be always on the guard, always watching & praying; I wish to remember that such society is a net spread by the enemy to catch the unwary in & that instead of doing them good, I will be overthrown by them if I cease to "watch unto prayer with all perseverance."[51]

June 7 1st day. Have been to meeting—remembered that this time year I was on my voyage to Philadelphia, but was mercifully favored to feel entirely satisfied with my present allotment, it was shown me that the Lord gave all his blessings in season & that this was the reason they were so much enjoyed—the North came before my view it looked like a field thickly sown with seed which was just springing but which would not yield any grain until the harvest— it seemed as tho' by my visit there last Summer ~~I had soon~~ the seeds of future enjoyment had been sown that as it were they were just springing up in the tenderness of affection, the interest & respect felt by friends found there—at a distance I looked upon these things & they were beautiful to the spiritual eye as the field of wheat just springing out of the ground—particularly lovely because they were harbingers of an abundant harvest. I saw that at present I had nothing to do in the field, my efforts to increase the rapidity of the growth of these seeds would be as ineffectual as the planters to bring on the harvest sooner than the appointed time, & as he leaves his wheat to be watered by the rain of heaven & matured by the genial rays of the Sun, so I was to leave ~~this~~ all events entirely in the hands of Him who has all hearts in his hands & ["]turneth them whithersoever he will."[52]

June 11   Truly my spirit is weary within me & the oblivion of sleep is an inexpressible blessing to me. This listlessness left me in a great measure but it has returned, even the interesting books I am reading fail to rouse me & I would rather sleep than do anything else. I feel that nothing but great watchfulness & prayer will prevent my being a burden to those around me under those feelings, I want to be patient & resigned. I want to remember that these changes are designed for my good—the more easily & completely I bend to them, the sooner will the design of them be accomplished.

June 12   Believe it best to record the particulars of a conversation which passed two evenings ago with Mother. The Board of M. of SBS met here in the afternoon, Mother objected very much to let Stephen go to L.C. with my boxes, she said it was impossible. I mildly told her it certainly was not impossible for William under my direction could easily hand the fruit &c. to them—she seemed to think it very unreasonable I should ask such a thing tho' the vessel was to have sailed at 8 O'Clock the next morning & said she was always very willing to oblige me when she could. Dear Mother said I, thou art very willing, if it does not put thee out of the way, but does not this instance show that thou art not willing to do so if it inconveniences thee. She reluctantly consented to let him go after this & I undertook to see after W. (George was sick).

There is a margin note in the diary further explaining the issue with the boxes. It reads: "had the boxes not been sent at this time they could not have gone at all for it rained constantly."

At dark as usual I went to sit with her & the way seeming to open I spoke of how great a trial it was for me to see her living in the luxury she did & observed it was not (as she seemed to think) because I did not wish to see BT & SS that I was tried at their dining here every week (unless something prevented) but it was the parade & profession which was displayed when they did come. I spoke also of the drawing room & remarked it was as much my feelings about that which had prevented my coming into the room when M.A &c. drank tea here as my objection to fashionable company—it was very hard she said that she could not give her children what food she chose or paper a room without being found fault with, indeed she was weary of being continually blamed about every thing she did, she wished they would let her alone for she saw no sin in those things. Mother said I, I trust I do not speak to thee in the same spirit in which thou art speaking now—nothing but the conviction that I am bound to bear my testimony to the truth could induce me to find fault with thee, nor in doing so I am casting with Eternity in view, I am acting in reference to that awful hour when I believe thou wilt stand around my death bed or I by thine—thou sayest thou seest no harm in these things, but are they not "the lust of the eye, the lust of the flesh & the pride of life" "if the light which is in thee be darkness, how great is that darkness."[53] [unreadable] coming in, a silence followed it seemed as tho' I must lean my head on Mother's shoulder when [unreadable] went out I did so & said with tears Mother I never feel that I love thee less after these conversations & I have tho't if I spoke to thee in a wrong spirit that thy would certainly alienate me from thee, but it is not so, tho' thou speaks to me so unkindly. I am willing to suffer for thee interrupting me she said, if I was so constantly found fault with I could not bear it either for her part she was quite discouraged. O Mother said I there is something in thee so alienated from the love of Christ. Charity never fails us— if we have charity we can & will bear to be found fault with & not only this, we will not have unkind feelings to those who do, it can bear all things—yes she said Sally & yourself always say I speak in a wrong spirit, but you in a right one. I don't remember whether I replied to this. And this thing had rested on my mind about Mother & I told her I had often tho't how much better it would have been for her to have assisted Aunt Roger Smith with the money ($26) she had spent in doing up the drawing room—there now she said, there is another cause of finding fault with me, because I don't assist your Aunt. Mother said I, have wondered how thou could see an old widowed Sister in want of necessaries & do nothing for her—she did not feel it her duty she said for AM dressed very well & ought not to allow her Mother to want but said I we ought not to stumble at the faults of others—would thou not think if I went to Sister Sally or Sister Sophia's for an afternoon and found them dressed in clothes so patched & old that I could not wear such even as a coat, would thou not think as their Sister I was bound to assist them—she said nothing to this, but began to say how much I was changed for instance about Slavery—for when I was first serious I tho't it was right & now condemned it. I acted according to the light I had I replied—well then she continued you are not to expect everybody to think like Quakers. I remarked true believers had but <u>One</u> Leader who would <u>if</u> they followed him guide them into all truth and teach them the <u>same things,</u> yes she said she remembered I said in the winter nobody who wore a bow on their cap could go to heaven. I was very much surprised at this for I had no recollection of having said so & said I tho't she was mistaken. No, she said I did say it, but <u>I</u> never did any thing <u>wrong</u>. Mother said I should be sorry to think so for I know that I do sin & if I ever said what thou accuses me of I do condemn myself without hesitation & am very sorry I ever said it. I freely own my fault (this was said in tears but it did not seem to soften her, she seemed glad she had been able to fix one fault on me at last. She again very ungenerously (as she frequently does) alluded to my turning <u>Quaker</u> & it was because I was a <u>Quaker</u> that I disapproved of a great many things that no body but Quakers could see any harm in. I was a great deal roused at this & said with a good deal of energy dr Mother what but the <u>power</u> of God could ever have made <u>me</u> change my sentiments—my full heart forbid further utterance & a silence ensued. Some very painful conversation followed about Kitty and I was accused of saying a thing I am sure I could not have said because I had never heard of it. I did not hesitate to say that no one with <u>christian</u> feeling could have treated her as she had been treated before I took her—her condition said I was a disgrace to the name of any Christianity. I was tauntingly reminded that <u>I</u> had advised the very method which had been adopted with her, this stung me to the quick—not after I professed Christianity I eagerly replied (and that I should have done so before only proved the wretched manner of my education—but Mother is perfectly blind as to the miserable way in which she brought us up I did not retort here as I might have done). In The latter part of this conversation I was greatly excited for so acute have been my suffering on account of Slavery and so strong my feelings of indignation in looking upon their oppressed & degraded condition, that I cannot command my feelings in speaking of what my own eyes have seen of their suffering & thus I believe I lost the satisfaction I would otherwise have felt for "speaking the truth." A heaviness of spirit the next day was felt & I was almost afraid of the consequences of the conversation. I felt desirous of manifesting that no evil feelings had been felt towards her & yet was afraid lest any extra attention might be misconstrued into a consciousness on my part of having said what was too pointed, so I tried to keep in a straight line— my lying on her bosom that night (which I very seldom do now that it is so warm) & kissing her so affectionately ought to have convinced her of this. No breach seems to have been made between us. When alone after this conversation the language seemed to be, there is death, spiritual death there & the petition was uttered O Lord give her not over yet, but have patience with her yet a little while, I tho't of the rock from whence I had been hewn & the hole of the pit from whence I was digged, I felt the loneliness of my situation now & some comfort was experienced in the reflections tho' separated from Fds I was yet suffering affliction with them. I am very much afraid that my reading to E & S throws me too much into the society & under the influence of a worldly spirit. I am afraid this is not spread for my feet by the Adversary. O that the snare may be broken & I may escape. Lord then knowest all the circumstances of my situation, be pleased to throw around me thy preserving power, but I am afraid lest I have already fallen from my steadfastness in little things, many times have I felt condemned—O chasten me by the reproofs of thy holy spirit & suffer me not to become lukewarm & blind to the purity & humility which ought to clothe one who professes to love & to serve thee. Much cheerfulness has generally been granted to me, to manifest to others & myself too the power of the blessed Master to make me ~~solitary~~ happy in my solitary situation, but I have abused the blessings, I have turned it into lightness & I am condemned by the light within me. It seems as if tho' I have much to write against myself, much to mark me ashamed, that yet I can say with regard to staying here this Summer, the work of resignation is done. O to be kept resigned & humble. I remember about 3 months ago uttering the prayer "try me O God & search me & see what evil there is in me,"[54] I stopped as the tho't rushed into my mind, suppose He is pleased to try thee by keeping thee here, my soul shrunk from back at the tho't & the language of my heart was not so Lord but in any other way, I remembered however this was not a right feeling & was enabled to ask for resignation to any thing he was pleased to allot me & my present feelings testify that He is the Hearer & the Answer of Prayer.

5

Strengthening of Spirit

June 13, 1829–July 25, 1829

By early summer Angelina was more comfortable with public displays of her religious and social convictions than she had been. She willingly intervened in a personal dispute between two male members of the Friends Society in Charleston; she wrote at length about her opposition to ministers getting paid; and she confronted her mother about the family's extravagance. She also refused to help her sisters with their sewing or their shopping lest she would enable them to commit the sin of excessive ornamentation. In one entry she admits that the family's dinner-table bounty no longer tried her quite as much as it had. Perhaps her detention in South Carolina was no longer as frustrating for her as it once had been.

Although the prospect of going to Philadelphia was still a major focus for her, she seems to have become resigned to waiting for the opportunity to fulfill her desire. In her writings she seems assured that she will go and content to wait patiently for that time. Her recollections of conversations she had with others on the subject of slavery reveal almost an excitement about confrontations that earlier had much distressed her. In her 24 June diary entry she describes such an argument, and her reaction seems to be self-satisfaction that she had made a difference in another person's perception of slavery. Regarding arguments she later had with Henry's wife, Selina, Angelina wrote that Selina "readily admitted the truth of them." It seems that a few months made a difference in how she viewed these public disputes.

In June entries she admits that "the living must suffer" and her belief that "an awful eternity seems to hang on a few months." The same month she also wrote that "a state of peace & quiet is generally my allotment" and that "cheerfulness has returned." And in July she wrote: "My feelings about remaining in Carolina certainly are not the same now that they were a month ago, then I felt like a captive . . . but now the chains seem to have dropped from my limbs tho' the door is not yet open for me to escape thro'." So, not only had her resolve been strengthened to leave South Carolina, she did not agonize over the prospects as she once did.

∞

June 13   It is generally supposed those who embrace Friends Principles fall into their little peculiarities only from a desire to imitate them, but this has not been the case with me, for instance in the form of telling persons good morning it seems so strange that Fds will not do it, but I once had the lot to live with two persons who whilst very exact in telling me good morning always treated me with marked coldness & one of them with great rudeness—now I tho't, does not this show the emptiness of forms & are not forms in a great measure refuges of lies—both of these persons I believe would have tho't they were guilty of a breach of duty towards me had they neglected to tell me good morning, but they tho't nothing at all of the uniform system of coldness & neglect which they adopted towards me, as long as the form was kept up all was well again it seemed to me that in saying good morning, a desire was expressed that I might pass the day happily, but they could have had no such wish, therefore this was a falsehood & the Lord taught me that tho' I was to "do good unto all men"[1] yet that I was to make very free professions.

June 14   First day. Was less tried yesterday by the plenty of our table than for many months & this language seemed applicable from me to dear Mother "I have not shunned to declare unto you the whole counsel of God."[2] In reading the 4th of Eph. have been much struck with the words "but rather let him labour, working with his ~~own~~ hands the thing which is good; that he may have to give to him that needeth,"[3] how important the lesson taught here & how different the policy of the religious world—they think they may work handsome lace veils & collars & caps, provided they give the proceeds to some benevolent Institution, there they are constantly spreading mats for each others unwary feet for on the very same principle professors think they may purchase & wear handsome articles of dress—if reproved they are ready to say; I bought it from a Society the money expended in doing good. In the winter I spoke to one for working a handsome kerchief—she contended it was not sinful, because she was doing it for the Seaman's Society, I told her I did not think we had any right to induce another to wear what as christians we must condemn but the fact was like most others she was a great dresser herself. O how herself & her Mother try me whenever they come here, it seems to me, for "I judge no man,"[4] it seems to me their profession is so empty as a bubble, & yet they talk so much about Religion, my soul shrinks sometimes as I hear them so unconcernedly take the holy name of my Master in their lips. One morning they came here & were speaking of A. G. having danced at a ball a short time before (a professor). We were such poor creatures they said that we did not know what we would do if tried & ought to judge no man. Arthur was young, many young people & he was forced into it & great deal more to the same purpose. I sat for a long time under considerable exercise & at last looking Cousin A full in the face I said with a good deal of emphasis Paul felt the frailty of his nature & yet said "thru' Christ strengthening me I can do all things & our blessed Master's promise stands sure["] "with every temptation I will make a way for you to escape"⁵ she seemed confused & made no reply. ~~In her last visit she told of~~

Night   Every now & then some little thing happens which seems "to strengthen the things that are ready to die"⁶ & to revive their hopes of being useful here. When I went up to dress this morning E[liza] said she felt distressed about the states of the family something unpleasant had occurred between Mother & S[ister] M[ary]. I told her I was very glad she did feel on the subject for none but the dead would live here without mourning over it, for as SS remarks "the living must suffer" when I was going out of the room I kissed her and sd. I tho't it was a privilege to suffer then & that it was very necessary she should yield to the exercise & not throw it off such were not our natural feelings I remarked, they were given by the Spirit of God for our own good as well as the good of others if we sleep here I continued ["]we must sleep the sleep of death."⁷ It appears to me nothing can be done for SM until Mother sees herself as she is & is willing to be nothing for Christ's sake. O to be faithful unto him particularly here is my work. In going to Meeting I remembered that this precious promise had been given to dear Sister, "thou shalt see of the trevail of thy soul & be satisfied" & with disponding feelings I recollected it had not been given to me, I had to "hope against hope" when it was said to me & "thou shalt reap if thou faint not" but my soul replied ["]Lord I am fainting now" it was immediately said "I will strengthen thee with the strength from on high, in the Lord Jehovah is everlasting strength."⁸ Be thou faithful unto death I will give thee a crown of life "be not weary." In meeting it seemed to be shown me that I was not to return to the North until after my dear Mother's deceased & that if I was faithful to her I should in enter enter into dear Sisters labour and reap the precious seed she had sown. O God I beseech thee deeply impress upon my heart the awful responsibility of my situation here—tho' the day when permitted to approach the mercy seat on her behalf the parable of the unfruitful fig tree was vividly revived "let it alone this year also until I dig about it & dung it, if it bear fruit well, if not cut it down."[9] An awful eternity seems to hang on a few months.

June 15   "Let no corrupt communication proceed out of your mouth"[10] is a peculiarly necessary caution in the city where "iniquity abounds."[11] Some professors have tried me exceedingly on this point—there is one crime so exceedingly common here that it appears to me even professors think nothing of talking of it. Sally Silsby told me something of this kind one day—my heart was very heavy after it & I felt it best the last time I saw her to tell her in love how much she had marred my peace and how necessary I tho't it was for believers to be very careful how they handled such unclean things & particularly in speaking to an unmarried woman—she thanked me for my reproof. I said the fact was she had heard so many of these things since she came to Charleston that she was afraid her mind had become too familiar with them, & I have no doubt this was true. Feel it best to record something of the same kid against myself; lately I have been so cheerful that I have said things I ought not to have said. I heard it out & came home & told it when I know I ought not—how pure the christian should be, how careful that neither his tho'ts or his tongue be employed in uncleanness.

June 16   After reproving SM last evening for her unchristian feelings these words were remembered "reprove, rebuke, exhort with all long suffering"[12] in looking for it found these words in connection "for the time will come when they will not endure to hear sound doctrine"[13]—how lamentably true is this, how little of the meekness & humility of the gospel to be found in the age of many sounds & empty profession.

June 17   How often has the query arisen in my mind, Can any rightly anointed minister of the gospel take money for preaching? As soon as a word is said on this subject it is immediately replied "the workman is worthy of his hire"[14]—of late I have been exceedingly tried in hearing of the different salaries given in this city to Ministers from $100 to 200 it is lamentable to think there is not one here who preaches as Paul did "without charge." I have been examining this subject & am more than ever convinced that it is "a horrible thing" an abuse of power. Let us look at the examples of our adorable Redeemer "who left us an example that we should walk in his footsteps."[15] His life was one of suffering— "he had not where to lay his head"[16] & tho' he often wrought miracles to supply the wants of others he was never known to do it to relieve his own. When he sent his apostles to preach to the last sheep of the house of Israel he ~~sent them~~ expressly commanded them to provide ["]neither gold nor silver, nor brass in their purse, nor scrip for their journey, neither two coats, neither shoes, nor get stoves" (for added he the workman is worthy of his meat). It has occurred to my mind that the Master sent them out thus destitute in order to try their faith in his last declaration "the workman is worthy of his hire["] "they were workman hired into the Lord's vineyard & He not men were to pay them for their services,["] or how could he without a gross contradiction have in the first instance reminded them that they had freely received & ordered them freely to give. I would ask what had they freely received? was it not the teachings of the holy Spirit, the instructions of the Master himself & does it not follow then that this was what they were to give, not sell as Ministers now do for surely that man must be said to sell religious instruction who does not hesitate to take $2000 every year for preaching & yet if I were to say that they sold their sermons & prayers they would most positively deny it and think me most uncharitable. What I gather from this part of Scripture is tho' the Apostles were sent out freely to preach the gospel they were sent out without money, without even two coats to their backs & were told they had nothing to fear for he who had hired them into his vineyard would supply their wants, as I suppose by turning the hearts of the people to them & inclining them to supply necessary food &c. but suppose for an instant that these Apostles had taken advantage of the kindly feelings which their Lord had caused to fill the hearts of the people & instead of merely taking the necessaries of life had come back with their purse filled— ~~would~~ do not feelings of horror & holy indignation fill our minds at the bare tho't. There is another part of Scripture which is wrested from its true meaning. Paul it is readily allowed took nothing for preaching but labored with his own hands rather than make the gospel chargeable to any yet it is argued that he evidently proves in the 9th of Cor. that Ministers have the "power to live by the gospel & reap the carnal things of those to whom they preached.["][17] Undoubtedly they have the power & frequently receive an ample support from their people who give it willingly, but how can any one read this chap. & not see that the Apostle calls this an abuse of power that it, such a course in any minister would be taking advantage of the tender & generous feelings of those to whom he preached for Paul says ~~be~~ "it were better for me to die than to make my glorying void:[18] For tho' I preach the gospel, I have nothing to glory of for necessity is laid upon now; yea woe is unto me if I preach not the gospel. For if I do this thing willingly I have a reward, but if against my will a dispensation of the gospel is committed unto me, what is my reward then? Verily, that when I preach the gospel I may make the gospel of Christ without charge that I abuse not my powers in the gospel."[19] A. I understand

the Apostle he here affirms that a dispensation of the gospel had been committed unto him (we naturally conclude upon exactly the same principle it had been
to the other apostles "freely ye have received and freely give"[20]) & that in preaching the gospel he had nothing to glory of, for necessity was laid upon him yea,
woe would be with him if he did not preach it—he then says if I do this thing
willingly I have a reward or from a careful examination of the context I understand I have something to glory of he then asks, what is my reward, or what have
I to glory in "Verily that when I preach the gospel I make the gospel of Christ
without charge,["] in order that all may see I do it willingly & freely being "constrained by (no other motive than) the love of Christ["] & that I do not abuse the
power I have gained over the mind of the people by receiving any compensation
from them for my labor, for it were better for me to die than by receiving pay to
make my glory void. That Paul had a vast deal of power or influence over the
mind of his hearers is certain, for he tells the Galatians that if it had been possible they would have plucked out their eyes & given them to him, surely then he
could have enriched himself out of their property if he had chosen. Why then
does he so often tell us that for fear of hindering the gospel they suffered all
things rather than make it chargeable & wrought with their own hands rather
than receive even necessaries from the converts. Ministers of the present day tell
us they have not time for any employment by which to gain a living—have they
more to do than Paul had? (the great Apostle of the Gentiles) but the fact is he
preached ["]with the Holy Ghost sent down from heaven" & took no tho't what
he should speak, for it was not he who spoke but ["]the Holy Ghost which spoke
in him" whereas they reject the doctrine of inspiration & draw the substance of
their Sermons from books. But let us query if the Apostles were worthy of their
hires, how much do we understand they were to receive—in a parallel passage,
the word is rendered moot, that is, when sent into a strange land to preach they
were to receive their "meat" from those to whom they preached, this is very evident because they were commanded "in whatsoever city or town they entered to
inquire who in it was worthy & to abide in that house eating & drinking such
things as were set before them"—do we not learn also from the hire of the
labourers into the vineyard for only a penny a day that a barren subsistence was
all they ought to receive even tho' they might bear the burden & heat of the day.
Again Paul in speaking of this subject instances the one which when treading out
the corn was not to her muzzled, he was to be permitted when labouring in the
field to satisfy his hunger & to eat of the fruit of the field. How then can any
one from Scripture advocate the system of paying Ministers $1, 2 or 3,000 for

preaching or Can any rightly ordained Minister receive such compensation? I remember at the time I used to lead in family worship at home that this temptation to discontent was presented, one day Satan said to me, if it is right (which I did not doubt then for Ministers to receive money for preaching) then thou ought to live here free of expense for thou preaches night & day in this house, I felt surprised & wounded at such a tho't even crossing my mind, for I knew I was constrained to do this ["]by the love of Christ" & I was spending my strength for relatives & servants—therefore it would be unpardonable for me to receive any thing—but I do not remember it roused any enquiry about it as to Ministers doing so, which I think rather astonishing, for I am sure now it was designed to show me that the same horror I felt at such a suggestion ought to fill the mind of every one who had been called to & anointed for this awful work by the Lord himself. Is not conscience to the soul what sensation is to the body.

June 18   I hear much of the strength of natural affection, but when I look abroad in the world I see but little of it & am fully convinced that it is not affection but interest & a sense of duty which binds the members of most families together & when I look at home this opinion most sadly confirmed. I can testify from painful past experience that the bonds of natural affection can be totally dissolved. A very striking instance of its being interest not affection which kept persons together was presented to me last winter in the case of two Sisters who lived here without any other relatives in America, both suffering under ill health & both dependent on their united efforts for daily support & yet tho' so peculiarly circumstanced that one would suppose common sympathy would have bound them together in love, yet I do not hesitate to say they did not love each other & that nothing but interest & necessity kept them together. And why should one expect soft & tender feelings flow from hearts of stone, affection, true disinterested love for any one, is too noble a plant to find in a soil whose natural product is thorns and briars, she grows not in the natural heart of man —he is naturally selfish & what he loves, he loves from interest, he loves those around him just in proportion as they constitute to his happiness, not in proportion to the real weight & beauty of their characters. We meet with some individuals who possess very ardent attachments to particular persons, ~~but~~ they would even lay down their lives for them & in time of urgency will do great things, but let us follow them in their daily course & we will frequently find that from the indulgence of some darling propensity, some disagreeable trait of temper they will continually mar the ~~the~~ peace of those they profess to love & really fancy they do love—this then cannot be real love, it is only its' counterfeit for

"Love is watchful"[21] & ["]seeketh not her own" happiness in trifle any more than in great events, but the happiness & comfort of the individual loved. The love of the world like the light of the Moon is altogether reflected—that Luminary contains within itself no principle of light, it is altogether on account of its situation with regard to the Sun that it gives light & that only partially & faintly so with the worldling his love is regulated by existing circumstances & surrounding objects, it is faint & partial & as the Moon is always waxing & waning so the strength of his attachments is always fluctuating. But the love of the Christian like the light of the Sun is a settled, universal, powerful principle within he scatters his cheering beams over every planet within the sphere of his influence—the evil & the good are alike blessed with the light. So there is a beauty of holiness, or universal benevolence in the heart of the believer which every one around him sees & feels. Whilst he does "good to all men so much as in him lies," the light of his example like the light of the Sun serves "to bring to light the hidden things of darkness" & to manifest the deformity, "the exceeding sinfulness of sin" in others. But let us carefully remember that as the Sun was made by the Lord Almighty & is nothing of itself, so the believer is the ["]workmanship of the same power" nothing but an "earthen vessel" which when "filled with the Spirit" becomes a "light in the world." Believe it best to sleep no longer with mother on account of the extreme warmth of the weather. Fear I should also be compelled to give up sitting in silence with her at dark for this reason also & because the mosquitoes are so bad that it is impossible to enjoy any comfort without continual brushing which destroys the stillness & solemnity of this season of retirement. Have been a good deal tried at the servants having no nets & do not know how they can sleep at all.

June 19 A state of peace & quiet is generally my allotment—this morning have compared the work of the Spirit on my heart to the laying of the foundation of a building which must be allowed to settle before any thing more can be done—the Scriptures which have been opened to me lately & the instruction derived from looking at the work of providence & passing events, seem to be the material which by degree are collected round the foundation ready to be built up on it, when the right time comes.

Night A little thing tried me today. E begged me to help her work, I agreed to do so, she said she wanted me to whip some frills. I sincerely know what to do & at first wondered what dear sister would think of it. I felt instantly reproved for I knew I had an unerring Monitor within my own bosom, and as I felt uneasy at the tho't of doing the frills I tho't it best to tell E I could not do them, she smiled, this little thing tried me peculiarly because she was in a hurry for it & I should like to have obliged her, but we must be willing even to appear unamiable to our friends when in complying with their requests we must swerve from the narrow path of duty. Some time since, I refused to buy a pair of silk stockings for SM on the same principle in fact I never offer to work or shop for any body now without knowing what they want for I believe it right in me to be very careful not to help any one to do anything I conscientiously disapprove.

June 21   How often has the language of late occurred to my mind "be ye also ready"[22] & it is shown me that whilst enjoying ease & cheerfulness I must not forget to keep myself in readiness to bear any burden the Lord might be pleased to lay upon me. Yesterday was a day of suffering—my soul was exceeding sorrowful & out of the depths. I cried unto thee O Lord that thou wouldst make a way for me to escape from this land of Slavery. Is there any suffering so great as that of seeing the rights & feelings of our fellow creatures trodden under foot without being able to rescue them from bondage. How clear it is to my mind that Slaves can be controlled only by one of two principles fear or love, as to moral restraint they know nothing of it, for they are not instructed to act from principle, if the owners feed & clothe them it is all that is expected & when they have done that, they think they have done all & done well too. "Some men say Range Fox have the nature of lions to tear, devour, & destroy. Some have the nature of a horse to prance & vapour in their strength & to be swift in doing evil"—seems to combine all the qualities & such is the awful war of passion in his soul at times that I don't think he has any more controul over himself than the winds or waves.

Night   Feel as tho' I had nothing to do in this thing but by my manner to bear a decided testimony against such an abuse of power—the suffering of mind thro' which I have passed has necessarily rendered me silent & solemn, which is the more remarkable because I have been so very cheerful lately—the language seems to be "it behooves thee to suffer these things" & this morning I saw very plainly that this was a part of the preparation of the awful work of the Ministry. ["]O God make me willing to endure affections" for thee give me strength to "bear all these things & to endure unto the end"[23] suffer me not to throw off the burdens thou art pleased to lay upon me, but may I bend under every exercise & suffer thee to do the work of purification in my polluted heart just as thou sees best. I think I can say in looking at the different dispensations thro' which I have passed. "For all I thank thee, but most for the severe." Often was I tried by my own cheerfulness for when I looked upon our family I could not but feel that it was a dreadful state; I know this was cause of "lamentation & weeping & woe["]

& yet my heart was unburdened, & I must ever believe these feelings were given me to show to myself & others that the lonliness of my situation here could not destroy my comfort when the "God of all consolation" was pleased to say "Peace be unto thee." This night [a] year [ago] I was at peaceful Greenhill[24]—how well I remember the calm repose I felt when sitting in the piazza & looking at the loveliness of the prospect, but "it is well" this is my right place now & I am willing to "suffer affliction with the people of God." (Have been to meeting twice today).

June 23   The cause of my distress being temporarily removed, cheerfulness has returned. I am afraid my feelings are not right about this ease which I enjoy here, I think I would rather suffer, I tremble when exercise leaves my mind, for I find it very hard without the good of suffering to keep in my right place, how hard to obey the apostolic injunction "be sober, be vigilant. God thou knowest my down sittings & mine up risings, O watch over me & guide me with thine eyes & hold me by my right hand I know that I have fallen far short of thy glory["] but with Peter I can say "thou knowest all things thou knowest that I love thee" grant that I may ever prefer Jerusalem above my chief joy"; make us willing to give up every scheme of earthly happiness which is inconsistent with the inmations of duty to Him or to any human being.

June 24   Does not this no less possitive than comprehensive law under the Gospel Dispensation entirely exclude Slavery "Do unto others as you would they should do unto you." After arguing for some time on this subject one evening with an individual, I proposed this question "would thou be willing to be a slave thyself?["] She eagerly answered No! then said I thou hast no right to enslave a negroe for the Master expressly says "do unto others as thou wouldst they should do unto thee" again I put the query to her, suppose thou wast obliged to free thy slaves or to take their places, which wouldst thou do—of course she said she would free them, but why I asked, if thou really believest what thou contendest for, vis that their situation is as good as thine, but these questions were too close & pointed & she did not know what to say. Speaking to another person on this subject & alluding to the harshness with which they (Slaves) were often treated, she instanced a particular crime & asked whether I did not think a servant ought not to be whipped for it. I told her he certainly ought to be punished, but I remarked that the root of the evils of Slavery was in the fact that Owners seldom tho't of giving their servants moral instruction, therefore they had no right to expect them to act from principle, & nothing else could possibly keep them from such sins—they not only do not teach them themselves but do actually close the Bible (the fountain of moral instruction) to them by neither allowing them time or opportunity to learn to read. These seemed to be new ideas, but she readily admitted the truth of them—indeed I do not know how any man can have the conscience to punish a negro for doing what he has never told him is a flagrant breach of the law of God, not that I suppose the negroe to be ignorant as to what is right & wrong for I have lately had a very strong evidence (in an ignorant child from the field) that there is a light within which makes manifest what is sinful & reprove for it, but still the Owner is awfully culpable in the neglect of the Slave.

June 26   How needful it is for the believer to keep in mind that his "praise is not of man but of God."[25] Are we not to prone to ~~receive~~ wish to receive "honor of one another" instead of being satisfied with that "honor which cometh from God only" how hard it is to give up the world wholly, not only to forsake its sinful & pernicious amusements & vanities, but to be willing to be regarded as a fool by it & instead of its approbation to receive its contempt & reproach. It is said that Michal dispised David in her heart & this is just the feeling the worldling has towards the meek & lovely disciple of Jesus now. How directly contrary the maxims of the world are to the precepts of the Gospel. I was struck in reading the words "Behold I send you forth as sheep in the midst of wolves, be ye therefore wise as serpents & harmless as doves"[26] the very reason which is here is assigned why the disciples were to be harmless would be the very one which would prompt a worldling to violence & revenge—they were as ["]sheep among wolves."

June 29   Left the table today on account of a variety of unpleasant little things day after day & week after week am I tried in this way. There is such a spirit of finding fault, either the meal is given too late or things are too cold or they are badly cooked or if they are not found fault with, then they are crass & rude to each other or the servants—so that I have often remembered with feeling what Solomon says—"a dinner of herbs where love is, is better than a stalled ox & hatred therewith."[27] My daily experience causes me to say "Better is a little with the fear of the Lord, than great treasure & trouble therewith." So weary is my soul with the strife & contention that it seems to me I would willingly purchase peace, sweet peace, at the sacrifice of any earthly luxury or gratification.

June 30   In speaking of our natural feelings & propensities I think we ought carefully to distinguish between those which are incident to the fall & those incident to human nature—the former ought never to be indulged because they are radically evil, the latter may be without sin, in moderation—thus anger, hatred, revenge &c. are bad feelings & ought to be wholly subdued tho' they are natural to the fallen state of man's soul as the cravings of hunger or the desire of sleep when animal nature is exhausted with fatigue. I have been much tried at times by persons remarking that I did not visit among the poor as I used to do & sometimes have been ready to begin to do so, but believing that it is right at present for me to "be still"[28] & being very sensible that if I did go now it would be with a view to "justify myself to men." I have foreborne & hope I may be preserved from doing any thing unless commanded by my Master.

July 1   Have been to meeting this morning & compared my situation here to the appearance of a comet, my movements are equally eccentric & unaccountable, I am apparently as useless & like it I am a wonder. How poor our meetings are, often is the curse pronounced on the Mountains of Gilboa brought to remembrance while sitting in them "Ye Mountains of Gilboa, let there be no dew, neither rain, upon you, nor fields of offering, for there the shield of the mighty is vilely cast away."

July 2   Do not the spiritually like the naturally blind feel many things when they cannot see. Sometimes when I have been told by a person that they could not see any thing wrong in what they were doing I have asked if they did not feel it was sinful & they have not been able to answer me. This Apostles injunction has been revived today "owe no man any thing but to love one another"[29] & I have seen that very many sins are committed by professors in consequence of their laying themselves under obligations to those who have not the fear of God before their eyes—how necessary then that we should obey the command "come out from among them and be ye separate" for it is only to those who do, that the promise is given "and I will receive you: And will be a Father unto you & ye shall be my sons & daughters saith the Lord Almighty."[30]

July 3   This morning I have been ready to say "surely I have labour ed in vain I spent my strength for naught"—last night H[enry] had a wine party which did not break up until ¼ before one. When I look at dear Mother I am sad, & O how sensibly do I feel that tho' some of the branches of the tree have been lopped off yet the root of corruption is still in her heart—how could any real christian allow such a thing under her roof (for she not only gave her permission but her handsome glass & plate were all lent for the occasion & Stephen's services were entirely given up, tho' in the winter when F Bee sent to beg for him to wait at a ball Mother wrote her word that she could not conscientiously allow him to do it—now which is the worst of the two? Mother says she did not know they were going to stay so late literally carousing until past midnight but she does know that this has been repeatedly the case. H as usual is laid in his bed today for this is always the case after one of these parties—how horrible the tho't. I cannot tell how tried I have been thro' the whole to see her total insensitivity about it—last night she seemed to regret it only because they were in the room under her chamber & she could not sleep. O how hard to have right feelings towards any one who is grossly inconsistent, so selfish—but I have been praying for preservation. Lord grant that my heart may be filled with pity & love. This morning I have remembered the awful denunciation "If any man love not the Lord Jesus Christ let him be Anathema Maranatha."[31] Here is one of the evils resulting from H's living here & perhaps it is best they should be made manifest one by one when I have spoken to this effect dear Mother has always said she did not see why he should not. Two reasons I believe make it desirable to her, one is that it keeps up an extravagant style of living—another is that the arm of her power over her servants has been completely broken & she thinks if H was not here they would not behave even tolerably, for she knows they are not constrained by love or governed by principle, nor are they at all afraid of her. I sent at 12 O'Clock to ask if I would have some fruit, but I felt that all that was left from the party was forbidden to me & refused it. How necessary it is when we disapprove of any thing to bear an exact & consistent testimony against it, by neither helping in any way to promote it, & refusing to receive any advantage from it. I am often tried in this way & find that it is needful to be always on the watch against wiles of the Adversary—a few days ago E begged me for some silk but as soon as I found she wanted it to make up battiste dress, I told her I would not give it to her to make up a dress I did not think fit for anyone calling themselves a christian to wear— as usual she laughed & I left the room under much exercise. O that the Lord would be pleased to watch over me for good & to guide me with his eye—how narrow the road I have to travel in.

July 4   I have often been perplexed by the apparent contradiction in these texts, "Judge not, that ye be not judged"[32] "The tree is known by his fruit"[33]—but this morning in reading met with a text which to my mind removes all difficulty "The spiritual man (says Paul) judgeth all things, & yet is he judged by no man."[34] Now it seems manifest that by the first text is ment that we are to judge no man by apparent circumstances, nor under the influence of natural feeling—by the second we are taught to look at the spirit of individuals for the Apostle tells us that ["]the fruit of the Spirit is love, joy, peace, long suffering, gentleness, goodness, faith, meekness, temperance"[35] & ["]if none of these are manifested in the conduct it is evident they cannot have the Spirit of Christ, therefore they are none of his." But the third text opens to my understanding, who are competent to judge others & why the liberty is granted to some & denied to others. The spiritual man, that is he who hath willingly opened the door of his heart & received into it Him who "is made unto us Wisdom" ["]judgeth all things" because he has received of that "Spirit which leadeth unto all truth," [36] he walketh by that Word of God which is ["]a light to his feet & a lamp to his paths" & this Light reveals ["]the tho'ts of many hearts" & makes manifest both in himself & others the hidden things of darkness & reproves all sin as soon as it is brought to the Light. Hence the spiritual man is competent to judge of the actions of others, because he judgeth neither by false maxims of the world nor by appearances ~~by he~~ but as the Apostle says ["]he has the mind of Christ" [37] & under the guidance of this infallible teacher "he judgeth all things," whilst "himself is judged of no man," because his actions flow from principle entirely too high for the comprehension of the natural man which ["]receiveth not the things of the Spirit of God for they are foolishness unto him." The worldling would think this great presumption for a believer to tell him he had a right to judge of his actions & yet deny him the privilege of judging of his, but be it remembered that the one judge by the very same law by which the whole world is to be judged & under the influence of that "Spirit which searcheth all things even the deep things of God" whilst the other judges from his own finite capacity & false views of right & wrong, ~~putting bitter for sweet & sweet for bitter~~ calling ["]evil good, & good evil, putting darkness for light, & light for darkness, bitter for sweet, & sweet for bitter." [38]

Night   This afternoon, I related a little circumstance to E detrimental to dear Mother for which I felt severely reproved & it was plainly shewn me that if I ever desired to see them united I must be very careful never to tell either of them any thing to the disadvantage of the other, tho' I must be faithful to both in telling them their own faults. I hope I may be more watchful in future, & that at last I may learn to "speak evil of no man." [39]

July 8   When distressed & tossed in mind I believe it is best to try to be as quiet as possible—such feelings often prevail & we know not why, how necessary then that we bend under the exercise in quiet submission. I cannot tell why, but whenever I receive money which I have done today I suffer under a good deal of distress of mind. O that I may be kept from covetousness.

July 13   How strange does the declaration of the Apostle appear to those who are ignorant of the power of Religion. The law (says he) is not made for a righteous man, but for the lawless & disobedient &c. But they who have felt the "love of God shed abroad in their hearts by the Holy Ghost" know that like Paul they are ["]constrained by the love of Christ"—they need not the coercive power of the outward law to compel them to obedience, for they have a guide within them, which will "lead them into all truth"——the Laws of God are written on "the fleshly tables of their hearts" & having felt that "Love which is the fulfilling of the Law"[40] they are enabled measurably to obey the divine precept "to do unto others as they would others do unto them."[41] With such a principle within, they do not need to be told that they must not break any of the 10 Commandments, for if they had never seen them they would still revolt at the commission of the crimes thereby forbidden.

   Night   Received some of dear Sisters memorandums today, in one she says "Again has the promise been graciously vouchsafed in thinking of my beloved A.["] I will give her to thee this Summer & thus added I will bless you together. I cannot but think the impressions on our minds about my going to the North have been very singular——mine have long since worn away & so far from going this Summer, I see no end to my staying here. Is it not better to read books beyond our religious experience than below it, the first tend to be humble, but the last to exalt us. When I read I like to be in a teachable state of mind ready to receive instruction, for these reasons I do not read books written in other Societies, & because too I find it very unprofitable to read what I must often disapprove, I have been afraid it might cherish a spirit of finding fault. These remarks too will apply in some measure to our companions it is better to associate with those who are more experienced than ourselves, for this reason I seldom go out here, for the little knowledge in religion which I have gained by toiling & spinning is regarded as the effects of back sliding, so finding the mind of my former friends completely closed against my new opinions, I have thought it best to go but little among them & be willing to be "despised and rejected of man."[42] I have remembered the time of my childhood, when like the blessed Master I gain in knowledge & ["]in favor with God & man" & had believed as he had afterwards to pass thro' a dispensation similar to that I now experience, so it is right I Should do so too. In conversing with Presbyterians I have tho't & feared I was too anxious to keep my own sentiments out of view, for they seem to think it their duty to bear their testimony against my Sentiments & finding this to be the case & not being willing to enter into any dispute with them I have at different times allowed them to condemn me in silence. More than once have I been (I trust) sincerely engaged to know whether this course was right in me or not, & I think the Master has vouchsafed to show me that the time of my shewing forth to Israel has not yet come & that I must be willing to be in the back parts of the desert until the days of my preparation are accomplished, I must be willing to let others walk over my head, & think I cannot advocate my opinion or prove them from

Scriptures, all I have to do now is to live under their influence & be willing to be reduced to nothing in their eyes. It is a favor even to be permitted to be ["]a fool for Christs sake."[43] Of latter time the divine precept "do unto others as you would have them to do unto you," has rested much with me & I find myself continually recurring to it as a rule of action & have been greatly helped along by it in little things. Sometimes my friends seem surprized at my applying it to my conduct to servants as well as those on a footing with me, but "God is no respecter of persons" & expects his people to "be gentle unto all men"[44] & to fulfil the royal law of love to all. The more I feel of the precious influences of the Spirit on my heart & yield to its teachings, the more I am convinced that it will lead to Perfection, if humbly & patiently abide under & faithfully followed in childlike simplicity. What a beautifully consistent character it will form—how it ["]clothes with humility & beautifies with salvation." My attending meetings for some weeks past has been quite a trial to me on account of JR not speaking to DL—at times some exercise has been laid on me, on account of it, but I do not see my way to speak tho' it is hard to bear it in silence.

July 17   It is absolutely necessary that we should come under the teachings of Him who is emphatically called "the Truth" if before we can form correct ideas of right & wrong. The standards of the Bible is the only infallible one. It is very dangerous to allow ourselves to be in the daily habit of doing any thing, (let it be ever so trifling) in transgression of the divine precept "do unto others as you would have them do unto you," such a sin must blind the eyes and harden the heart.

July 18   Sometimes I almost feel discouraged about myself, so little spiritual sensibility & I profess the most I can say is, that I am content.

July 19   First day. How safe we are in the valley of humility—here the trees of righteousness flourish, whilst those on the Mountains are torn up by the roots. Have sat the meetings out with difficulty owing to the heat of the weather, the fatigue I felt after such long walks in the hot sun & the listless state of my mind. The thermometer was 96 in the shade.

July 20   We are told that all the Benjamites were left handed & does it not appear probable from the circumstance of the Ephraimites betraying themselves to the Goliadites at the passages of Jordan by not being able to pronounce the word Shibboleth, that this tribe was remarkable for a peculiarity in their dialect by which they were known wherever they went.

July 22   I have looked upon it quite as a favor that out of the 8 last weeks BT & SS have from some circumstance orther [or other] dined here only twice,

how good the Lord is to me & yet how cold this heart of mine—how insensible.
This morning after (I think) sincerely desiring to know the Lord's will, I sealed
my letter to Fd. R. & carried it to meeting, I did not like to give it to him before
Fd. L. & therefore had to drop it on the step as I went out supposing he would
see it. I have been careful to keep a copy of it, & am satisfied I did right in writing to him. During meeting was engaged to know how precious Sister's prophecy
about my being given to her this Summer could be fulfilled. BT may go to the
North on account of Sister's health but I do not see how this will be opening
a way for my going; and tho' I have of late felt that my labours here are quite
useless, yet I think I could not think of leaving Carolina before dear Mothers
decease, unless it became an evident duty for me to do so. I am quite sure that if
I am to return that I have no more to do with it than an infant. My will I think is
entirely given up, & as a little child is carried from place to place by its Father
without being consulted, so I feel in the arms of my Heavenly Father fully believing that "He will do what is best for me.["] On 2d day I had some conversation
with S M on the deplorable state of our family & today with E—they complain
very much of the servants being so rude & doing so much as they please—but I
tried to convince them that our servants were just what the family was that they
were not at all more rude & selfish & disabling than they were & gave one or two
instances of the manner they treated Mother & each other, and asked how they
could expect the servants to behave in any other way when they had such examples continually before them, & queried in which such conduct was most culpable. E always admits what I say to be true, but as I tell her she never profits by it,
ever since I came home she has [been] telling me she knew she had bad feelings
towards Mother & SM but so far from her temper improving it is evidently much
worse than when I first arrived & so I felt it my duty to tell her this morning. SM
is somewhat different she will not condemn herself & yet profess to admire principles & conduct entirely different from her own, she will acknowledge the sad
state of the family, but seems to think Mother's altogether to blame. And dear
Mother seems to me to resist all I say, she will neither acknowledge the state of
the family, nor her own faults & always is angry when I speak to her, but the other
two bear with me wonderfully. Sometimes when I look back to the first years
of my religious life & remember unremittingly I labour ed with Mother tho' in
a very wrong spirit, being alienated from her & destitute of the spirit of love &
forbearance, & then again remember how precious Sister came to her not "with
a rod" as I did, but "in love, & in the spirit of meekness["];[45] and when I look
at how the Lord has brought me back to her & laid me as a lamb in her bosom.

having brought love in my poor heart what had exalted itself against Him & against her too—when I think of all these things, the language which of old has spoken against Israel seems to be awfully applicable to her. "Ye uncircumcised in heart & ears, ye always resisted the Holy Ghost."[46] My feelings about remaining in Carolina certainly are not the same now that they were a month ago, then I felt like a captive who was not only shut up in prison but blind with fetters of brass—my way to return to the N[orth] was not only completely closed but I felt "bound in spirit" here, but now the chains seem to have dropped from my limbs tho' the door is not yet open for me to escape thro'. Lord I have given myself away to thee in an everlasting covenant, never to be forgotten let me be as clay in thy hands, do with me whatsoever thou will only make me "a vessel ment for the Master's use."

July 23 Fd. T drank tea here last night. It seems to me that whenever Mother thinks she can get any body to argue with her on the subject of Slavery she always introduces ~~the subject~~ it, but last night she was mistaken, for Fd. T fully acknowledged that notwithstanding all that could be said for it, there was something in her heart which told her it was wrong & she admitted all I said. Since my last argument on this point it had appeared to me in another light, & I remarked that a Carolina Mistress was literally a Slave driver & that I tho't it degrading to the female character. They are as great slaves to their servants in one respect as they are to them. Another thing was the little comfort which could be enjoyed on account of the constant orders that are given, really when I go into Mothers room to read to her I am continually annoyed by a variety of orders which might easily be avoided were it not for the domineering disposition which seems to me to be inherent in a Carolinian & they are such fine ladies that if a shutter is to be hooked, or a chain moved, or the bell rung or the work handed, a servant must be called to do it for them. O I do very much desire to cultivate a feeling of forbearance, but I feel at the same time that it is my duty to bear an open & decided testimony against so flagrant a breach of the great command of my Master "Do unto others as you would they should do unto you." I make it a rule never to broach any subject upon which I hold opinions opposite to those generally received, but if others do in my presence introduce any subject of this kind, knowing that I differ from them I believe it would be wrong for me to withhold the truth.

July 24 Yesterday evening I received a rude unfeeling letter from JH it seems to be written in that Spirit which says "Stand off, I am holier than thou."[47] I still feel that it was right for me to have written tho' the consequences have been so painful—he seems to have taken great exception to my leaving it on the step but why, I know not, for I have left Tracts for him in the same way, because I thought it would be indelicate to follow him round the meeting house to give it to him. The language seems to be spoken "Son of Man, be not afraid of their words, nor be dismayed at their looks."

July 25   How many there are who regard the Light within as nothing more than Conscience, whereas they appear as distinct to me as the Sun and the atmosphere. Conscience being the medium thro' which the divine influence is conveyed to the heart, just as the atmosphere is the conducting medium thro' which the eyes of the Sun are conveyed to the Earth. I have seen as much self-will & unamiability displayed by a persons refusing to receive a favor, as in their refusing to do one. I can scarcely say I have received the declaration of my precious Sister [Sarah] as to "all the days of my appointed time being fulfilled in this land" and yet there is an anxiety about me to have every thing in readiness to take my departure as soon as the door is set open before me, believing that it will be done in haste, under these impressions I have set to altering my dresses, mending my clothes & doing up my muslin. I am quite blind & see no way by which I am to escape, this language continually rests upon my mind "be ye also ready for in such an hour as think <u>not</u> the Son of man cometh."[48] ["]Wait patiently upon the Lord."[49]

The City of Charleston, South Carolina, engraved by Wm. Keenan. Courtesy of the South Caroliniana Library, University of South Carolina, Columbia.

View of the Battery opposite Meeting Street, Charleston, South Carolina, c. 1860 by Osborn and Durbec. Courtesy of the South Caroliniana Library, University of South Carolina, Columbia.

Arch Street Meeting House, Philadelphia, Pennsylvania. Courtesy of the Philadelphia Yearly Meeting of the Religious Society of Friends.

The Grimké Home on East Bay Street, Charleston, South Carolina. From the Collections of the South Carolina Historical Society, Charleston.

St. Philip's Episcopal Church, Charleston, South Carolina. From the Collections of the South Carolina Historical Society, Charleston.

The Slave Market, Chalmers Street, Charleston, South Carolina.
From the Collections of the South Carolina Historical Society,
Charleston.

6

Out of Charleston
July 26, 1829–October 10, 1829

On 2 August 1829 Angelina wrote, "The prospect of my going North was revived this evening with more clearness & fulness than hitherto." Moving to Philadelphia became an object of Grimké's concern even more as the summer progressed. She mentioned it more frequently in the diary, and her attitude about it grew more confident, yet more patient. She no longer doubted that before long she would be sailing from Charleston, and she was confident that "the Lord will bring thee out."

She also became somewhat more reflective of her motivation for leaving Charleston. Although she admitted in the diary that she looked to the North as "the promised land," she insisted that she did not expect to be "released from trial" by going there. She explained, "It is sin not sorrow that I groan to be delivered from." The atmosphere of bondage and the conditions that slaves were forced to endure wore heavily on her heart. Even though she maintained that her motive for departure was not her pain but rather the oppression of seeing those around her in a state of sin, her distress was palpable.

Angelina continued to look at Charleston with a critical eye. For example, she complained that families there lacked "natural affection." Referring to slavery with more frequency, she argued her case against the institution more solidly than before. On 20 August, for example, she laid out a thorough and rather sophisticated argument against a biblical sanction of slavery that foretold of the more substantial antislavery statements she would soon offer in print. It is clear that by autumn 1829 Grimké expected to leave Carolina soon and, in so doing, leave the burdens and the turmoil behind, perhaps forever.

∞

July 26   It is noble to acknowledge our faults to our friends, but still more so to our enemies. Perhaps there is not a greater proof of christian humility—if it be done in a right spirit.

Night Was much tried this morning at the prospect of meeting JH at meeting, & found he would not speak to me, but he treated me as usual. I think I see very plainly that I shall have to answer his letter & feel as tho' I could do so in love.

July 28 I have just finished writing to JH & have been led to see that when the Lord requires us to reprove sin in others, He either inclines their hearts to receive our words, or He does most wonderfully prepare us to bear & forbear with them in the spirit of meekness & love. So far I think I have enjoyed "the testimony of a good conscience towards God" in this thing & am willing to suffer the consequences of obedience. It seems this morning too as if this language was spoken with regard to dear Mother, thy work is done, my mind has been sweetly released from exercise & it seems as tho' I had nothing to do now, but to bear & forbear with her. I can truly say "I have not shunned to declare unto her the whole counsel of God, (but) she would none of my reproof." I stretched out my hands to her speaking the truth in love, ["]but she has not regarded"—perhaps He has seen fit not to work by me lest I should be exalted above measure.

July 29 Have felt much exercised in mind this morning & believed it right to offer BT to go to the North with Sister [Sarah] if she wished it. O Lord be pleased to order this thing to thy glory if the lot fall upon me instead of E[liza]. O do thou strengthen me to do my duty & bless me in my feeble efforts to do thy will not my own, O preserve me for thy mercy's sake. I sent my answer to JH yesterday.

July 30 Whenever I think of whether I shall go to the North or not, this language is consistently spoken, thou hast nothing at all to do with it now. I still believe I did right yesterday in offering to go with Sister.

July 31 This morning after some exercise of mind felt it right to go & see Fd. N & to try again to impress on her mind that she must live by faith, a great deal passed between us & tho' it was painful to do it, yet I felt I must tell her some of her faults between her & me alone. Some things seemed hard for her to receive but when coming away she melted into tears & begged me still to tell her her faults & said she knew she was even now nothing but a babe in grace. How prone I am after doing any thing of this kind in the spirit of love & meekness, to look for a reward, in the comfortable feelings I always expect to experience afterwards, but I think my Master has shown me that He withholds this reward, ["]lest I should be exalted by it, & think of myself more highly than I ought to think." When coming home it occurred to my mind that if I found it so trying to wound a friend by telling her her faults—surely it must give the Savior of Sinners pain to afflict & grieve us as he often does in order to accomplish the salvation of our souls from sin & wickedness.

August 2   First day. Have passed through some pretty close exercises in consequence of receiving another unkind letter from JH. If as he says, I am "a busy body about other men's business" I think I can truly say I desire to know it & to repent of it, but can I be said to have no concern in what has almost entirely destroyed the comfort of attending meeting, because I am not an outward member of Friend's Society is no reason why I may not be a suffering member of the body of Christ, but may the Lord's will be done in this thing, & if I have done what was not required may I see it clearly, & learn by painful humbling experience to be more careful how I step along in future. JH sent me Job Scott's Journal to read, it is a precious book & my soul has been encouraged in reading this & Fon's Journal to meet here & there with a passage of Scripture which has been opened to them just as it was to me, & their experience tho' far deeper, I think in kind corresponds with mine, so that I can say, this is my people, tho' when I set my feet on the print of their footsteps I find theirs is the print of the full grown traveller Zionward, whilst mine are those of a little child in grace.

Night   The prospect of my going to the North was revived this evening with more clearness & fulness than hitherto. Sister was attacked again this morning & two objections to her going have been removed—it seems as tho' this language was spoken—this is the way appointed for thy deliverance, but still thou hast nothing to do with it. I the Lord will bring thee out. Nothing at all has been said about Sisters & my going, but if my feelings deceive me not it must be so.

August 3   I think I never joke in any way that I do not feel condemnation neither do I ever speak evil of any one that I do not feel the same believe from today. I will begin & record every transgression—before dinner I dropt some unkind insinuations which tho' deserved I think yet still it was not right in me to say any thing about it. I also jested with Mother.

August 5   All that righteousness of which we are proud is literally filthy rags. I feel quite tried at not hearing from dear Sister [Sarah] again & am continually disappointed by hearing there is no letter. Dr. Simon dined here today & I felt something of a trial to take my seat & sit in silence whilst the family stood round the table; in these things are we not tried just in proportion as our love of the world's honor is subdued, if entirely willing to be a fool for Christ's sake, then I believe we will be unaffected by the idea of doing what is thought singular & foolish then again, it certainly is painful to the delicacy of young women to be remarkable in any way, if I know my heart, it was this that tried me to day, not the fear of being thought a fool.

August 6   Today has been one of much trial of mind & my soul has groaned under the burden of slavery.

August 7   When once we come to know the comfort of dwelling in the quiet habitation of Jerusalem, how exceedingly trying is every unkind look or word or action of those around us. Well may it be said of this house "there is no king in Israel & every man does that which is right in his own eyes."[1] Is it too harsh to say that a person must be destitute of christian feelings who is willing to be served by slaves who are actuated by no principle but that of fear. Are not the unfortunate creatures expected to act on principle directly opposite to our natural feelings & daily experience, they are required to do more for others than for themselves & all without either thanks or reward.

August 8   All prospect as to my going to the N has been again closed. I have drank the cup of disappointment once more, but can testify that the Lord is good & greatly to be praised—when he takes away our will & gives us his own, then do we know that "godliness with contentment is great gain."[2]

August 9   Experience has taught me that every thing above & beyond what is requisite to real comfort & convenience, whether it be in food or raiment, furniture or attendants is a vanity & vexation of spirit just in proportion as we depart from that "simplicity which is in Christ"[3] do we entangle ourselves with the world & ["]imbibe its carnal mindedness & lose that spiritual mindedness which is life & peace." Many give much in charity & go much among the poor to relieve their wants, but how few do it according to the Apostolic injunction "He that giveth let him do it with simplicity, he that showeth mercy with cheerfulness."[4] Have felt much tried at not going to meeting this afternoon, the weather was so threatening at the time I ought to have gone that I tho't it best not to venture as getting my feet wet would probably have injured me, but it has cleared off beautifully. I have however felt it right to sit in silence that tho' absent in body I might be present in mind. This morning went & returned in heaviness of spirit, still groaning under the burden of Slavery.

August 10   I am now reading Paxton's S.J.[5] & find it truly valuable work, & yet it has convinced me of the danger of imbibing erroneous opinions from Authors of talent & merit. Thus I cannot agree with him in his sentiments on dress.[6] He undertakes to alter this verse in Peters Epistle by inserting the word chiefly very unwarrantably. ["]When adorning, let it not be (chiefly) that outward adorning of plaiting the hair, & wearing of ~~of putting on of gold~~ or of putting on of apparel," ["]but let it be the hidden man of the heart, in that which is not corruptible, even in the ornament of a meek & quiet Spirit which in the sight of God is of great price." He says that if we understand Peter as positively prohibiting females from plaiting their hair & wearing gold, we must also suppose that he forbids their wearing clothes which would be indecent & absurd, but it has appeared to my mind very clear that the Apostle meant just what he said & that no one has a right to take away ought from the sacred text or add ought to it, lest he incur the curse pronounced in Revelations 22c: 18th & 19th vs. When adorning, (mark the word) let it not be "& that is, women must not either plait their hair, or wear gold, or put on apparel, in order to adorn themselves, but rather let them remember that the only ornaments worth their wearing as disciples of a Crucified Master are the incorruptible virtues of the spiritual man hidden in the heart & a meek & quiet spirit which he tells them is in the sight of God of great price["]—the words let it not be is certainly a preemptory command not to be gainsayed or resisted, this is confirmed first by his telling them what they must not wear as ornamental, then by directing them what they must regard as true ornaments, & must wear for he says "let it be the hidden man of the heart &c." Some writers by their altering one text involve themselves in much difficulty as to parallel passages, thus Paxton says "as one inspired apostle cannot, in reality, contradict another the command of Paul must be explained in the same way, not as an absolute, but comparative prohibition" but what right has he to misinterpret Scripture in such a way & by so doing open a door of communication between the Church & the world & issue a license with the counterfeit Seal of Jehovah upon it, for the indulgence of the vain & extravagant dress of professors & their sinful conformity to the trifling fashions of a world which ought to be beneath their feet & to which they pretend they have been crucified & yet would be afraid to wear a dress, or bonnet which was not ["]a la mode." In Revelations we find that it was the false church which was represented under the figure of a "woman clothed with scarlet & purple ~~cloth~~ colors, & decked with gold & precious stones & pearls, having a golden cup in her hand full of abominations" & so I fully believe it is in this day. But the true Church which consisted of "a great multitude which no man could number were clothed in white robes with palms in their hands."[7] But let us turn over the leaves of the sacred volumes & enquire further into the matter. When the Israelites were about to leave the land of Egypt they by divine permission "borrowed jewels of gold, & jewels & silver & raiment"[8] from the Egyptians—these we soon find became a snare to them, for they were converted into a calf which they bowed down to & worshipped; (& here the query naturally arises—may not all persons who wear jewels of silver & gold as ornaments, be said to worship them, in as much as they love them too much to part with them notwithstanding the positive prohibitions of Paul & Peter?) In following the children of Israel a little further in their journey we find that when brought to mourn over this idolatry that "no man did put on his ornaments"[9]—and that the Lord never intended these jewels to be worn as ornaments is very certain for he says unto them as a people "put off thy ornaments from thee that I may know what to do unto thee."[10] ["]And the children of Israel stripped themselves of their ornaments by the Mount Horeb"[11] after which a reconciliation was affected, Moses was permitted to see the goodness of the Lord pass before him, he reascended the Mountain & again received the 10 Commandments & particular directions as to the building of the Tabernacle in which the Holy One of Israel condescended to dwell & it appears that "they came both men & women, as many as were willing hearted & brought bracelets, & earrings, & rings & tablets of jewels of gold &c.["][12] and gave them to Moses as an offering unto the Lord with which to build & ornament his Tabernacle, and this undoubtedly was what they were originally designed for, for tho' the Egyptians or people of their world might wear such things to gratify "the vanity of their minds," still it cannot be supposed that the true Israel of God ever received the sanction of divine authority for such extravagance & pride of apparel. These circumstances have tended more than any thing to convince me of the sinfulness of all ornamental dress, for I tho't it very remarkable that as soon as the Israelites came to right feelings they not only put away their ornaments but gave them as an offering to the Lord & so experience has taught me everyone will do whose "heart is fully set to serve Him.["][13] Our outward ornaments must be put away from us, before we can "be clothed with humility"[14] & the Lord say "I will beautify the meek with salvation." ["]Gideon & Zachariah were clothed with the spirit of the Lord" & Job says "I put on righteousness & it clothed me.["] The Master also charged his disciples "to take no tho't wherewithal they should be clothed" remarking at the same time, that ["]after all these things did the Gentiles seek" leaving (as I understand it) a careful attention to the fashion & decoration of dress, as a mark of a gentile, that is an unconverted person. It cannot be disputed but that Isaiah severely reprobated the ornaments worn by Jewish females, many of which are worn at this very day by professors & approbated even by those who stand for the defence of the gospel, & are the leaders of the people, tho' the Prophet was divinely commissioned to pronounce this awful curse of Jehovah on that denoted nation in consequence of these very sins. Isaiah 3d chapter. This query I will also add before I close these strictures. Is it not a fact that the worst females are the most devoted to ornamental dress. Jesabel painted her face & tired her hair, "& experience daily proves that in proportion as we rise above the world,["] & "seek those things which are above, at the right hand of God"[15] do we see the littleness & sinfulness of all earthly vanities & extravagance whether it be in dress, furniture or food. Paxtons has also some remarks on the King of Babylon's worshipping Daniel and Cornelius Peter & John the Angel in Revelations, he seems to me to have darkened these passages instead of elucidating them 2d v. P412. He readily admits that it was & is a common custom in the East for an inferior to fall down at the feet of a superior & that the word worship is made use of in Scriptures sometimes to denote mere civil respect, as in the case of the servant who owed his Lord 10,000 talents, it is said, "he fell down & worshipped him saying, Lord, have patience with me & I will pay thee all & also of his fellow servant who appears to have been of inferior rank["] & "fell down at his feet,"[16] here there can be no doubt that that nothing but civil respect was intended & yet when used in reference to that respect which was paid the Savior or his apostle Peter or the Angel Or Daniel he supposes it was divine honor which was paid them and he labours hard to prove that Daniel must have rejected this homage from Nebuchadnezzar tho' there is no intimation that he did, but on the contrary it appears certain that he accepted it. Now it appears clear to my mind that the circumstances tend to throw considerable light on the difference between the Old & New Dispensations. Under the former I believe such honor from man to man was admissable, & that Daniel received the Monarchs lowly salutation & the adulation & odours which were offered him as nothing more than a common mark of that respect which was due to him as an eminent prophet of the Lord. In reading the New Testament we find the Redeemer of men never rejected these salutations & yet we cannot suppose that any of them were paid him as divine honors, because it is very certain that even his own disciples (the 12) who followed him day after day & were most intimately acquainted with him, were extremely ignorant during his life as to the true nature of his character as "God manifest in the flesh"[17] even after his resurrection all of them did not seek to know who he really was; it was not until the day of Pentecost that their eyes were completely open, yet as he knew who he was, he received every mark of homage for unto Him it was due, except in circumstances when he asked the young lawyer, why he called him good, ["]for there was none good but one, that is God" just as tho' he had said, if thou dost not believe me to be God, "why calleth then me good,["][18] thereby offering a pointed reproof to the Scribes & Pharisees who as men allowed themselves to be constantly addressed by the title of good Master, or Master, we often find him labouring to expose the vanity & sinfulness of all that kind of homage which was practiced among the Jews & which was no doubt allowable under the Dispensation of the Law, but which must be entirely excluded from the Gospel Dispensation. Thus he addresses the multitude & his disciples in speaking of the Pharisees, they "love greetings in the Markets,["]¹⁹ & to be called of Men Rabbi Rabbi. But be ye not called Rabbi for one is your Master, even Christ, & all ye are brethren, And call no man your Father upon the Earth for one is "your Father which ~~Christ~~ is in heaven.["] Neither be ye called Master "for one is your Master even Christ.²⁰ But he that is greatest among you" shall be your servant. ["]And whosoever exalteth himself shall be abased & he that humbleth himself shall be exalted."²¹ At another time when he found the 12 had been disputing by the way which should be greatest, he said unto them "if any man desire to be first, the same shall be last of all," "he that is least among you shall be the greatest."²² And again he queries "how can ye believe which receive honour one of another." From all these passages & circumstances I have tho't we may fairly conclude that the honors paid to Daniel and our Savior, to Peter & the Angel were all of the same kind, Daniel did not reject it because under the Dispensation in which he lived, it was allowable, the Master did not reject this homage for he knows he was God, tho' those who paid him the usual marks of Eastern courtesy looked upon him as a human being; that he did not receive their homage in his human character is certain for he says "I receive not honour from men"²³ & yet as a divine being he required that honor & worship which was due to God only Peter I look upon to stand on the same ground with Daniel as to the reverence which was done him, with this difference that the former rejected it because he had learned from his Master that tho' such homage from man to man was permitted under the Old Dis[pensatio]n. that it was not under the New. As to John's falling before the Angel being construed into a desire on his part to pay the Angel divine honors, it surprizes me how any one can suppose such a thing— is it not more reasonable to suppose that the Apostle did not fully understand that great marks of respect or homage were now exploded by the bringing in of a pure dispensation & that he merely wished to pay the Angel human honor (if I may so speak) which was rejected by the Angel because tho' of higher rank than John as an immortal spirit still such homage was not his due because ["]he was his fellow servant & of his brethren the prophets."²⁴ In reading the 23d of Matthew I have also felt instructed as to why the Savior in three verses twice charges his disciples not to be called of men Master. In the first charge, I think he alluded to the practice among the Scribes & Pharisees but in the second, it appears to me he intended a caution against Slavery for none can own Slaves without disobeying the command here given. Again he censures the Pharisees for making "broad their phylacteries & enlarging the borders of their garments["]²⁵—does not this expose the pride of Ministers at this day wearing long white & black gowns as the badges of their Office. He also says "they love the chief seats in the synagogues"[26] this has staggered me as to Ministers being seated above all the people in the Meeting, of not rightly engaged in the work would not this distinction have a tendency to exalt the creaturely spirit in them but I only say, my opinion is staggerd.

August 12   It appears to me there is a real want of natural affection among many families in Carolina, & I have tho't that one great cause of it is the independence which the members of families here feel—instead of being taught to do for themselves & each other, they are brought up to be waited on by slaves, and then an unamiable, proud, selfish spirit is cherished. I have many times felt exceedingly tried when in the flowings of love towards Mother I have offered to do little things for her & she has refused to allow me by saying that it was Stephen, or Williams duty & she preferred their doing it; the other night of tea being refused in this way I said, being hurt by it, Mother it seems to me thou would at any time rather have a Servant to do little things for thee than me; she replied, it was their business. Well said I Mother, I do not think, it ever was designed that parents & children should be so independent of each other, our Heavenly Father intended that we should do for others & be dependent on each other, not on Servants (none of them were in the room). From time to time ability is granted for me to labour against Slavery. I may be mistaken, but I do not think it is any longer without sin in Mother, for I think she feels no way sensibly, now that it is not right, tho' she never will acknowledge it.

August 13   Favoured with calmness & contentment, having no will of my own. Often of late whilst in social circles have I involuntarily exclaimed to myself ["]this people is not my people, neither is their God my God"[27] but my Heavenly Father has put the language also in my heart, "It is the Lord, let him do what seemeth him good, let him work my deliverance in his own way.["] How precious to feel that He is my Father, & that I am here in the ordering of his providence.

Night   Left the parlour after tea on account of some unpleasant occurrence & retired to weep in solitude over the evils of Slavery, the language was forcibly revived, "woe unto you, for you bind burdens, grievous to be borne on men's shoulders & will not move them yourselves with one of your fingers."[28] I do not think I pass a single day without apprehension as to something painful about the servants.

August 14   Of late I have desired that it may fall to my lot at some future day to bring up a child from infancy. I am well convinced that the Light within, that precious gift from God to man, is unaccountably neglected in children, and

I do want to see the effect of very early turning a childs attention to it & causing them to look unto this divine principle in their hearts to direct them even in the little concerns of life, being careful at the same time to avoid every thing like familiarity on so sacred a subject. I once tho't the heart was totally depraved without one ray of divine light to guide the poor wanderer to heaven, if this is true which many now believe, why is the countenance of a babe so placid, so innocent, in looking at their sweet little faces do we not see something of heaven there, & is it not true that for many weeks their countenances are changed not by evil feelings but by pain or pleasure.

August 15   Had a long conversation with S[elina] last evening about servants & expressed very freely my opinion of H[enry]'s feelings towards them & his treatment of John.[29] She admitted all I said & seemed to feel for slaves until I said I believed they had as much right to freedom as I had (in the sight of God) of course she would not admit my arguments on this point, but I was glad an opportunity was offered for me to tell her, that my life was one of such continual & painful anxiety that were it not for Mother I would not stay a day longer in Carolina. E[liza] & myself both said that were it not from a belief that H would treat his servant worse, were we not in the house, that we could not be reconciled to live with him, Dear girl she seemed to feel a good deal & yet bore with us with great good nature & kissed us when we parted for the night. How can any one advocate Slavery from the Bible & yet this is constantly done, it is said that the Jews were expressly allowed to keep Slaves, but let us examine the matter. It is true that they were permitted to enslave those Nations who had filled up the measure of their crimes & drawn down the vengeance of Heaven, these were sold & bought & entailed from generation to generation as slaves. But of their brethren the Israelites they were forbidden to hold any except as hired servants if these were sold because they had become poor, they themselves were to receive the money & were at liberty to redeem themselves at any time before the year of Jubilee, & could not on any account be detained after that period except by their own free consent, besides which particular commands were given that they should not rule over them with rigour. Let us now bring to mind the fact that many things were undoubtedly allowed under the Jewish Dispensation which are positively forbidden under the New, & altogether inconsistent with the spirit of Christianity. In the first place a broad line of distinction was drawn between the Jews & Heathen then, the former were quite justifiable therefore in regarding other nations as greatly inferior to them, for they were taught to look upon no one but a Jew as their brother or neighbor or equal in any way but under the glorious dispensation of the Gospel—all distinctions of this kind are done away, & every man is bound to view his fellow man as his neighbor & his brethren—if therefore the Jews were forbidden to hold their brethren even as hired servants after the year of Jubilee (or longer than 7 years) without their free choice, how can we for a moment believe that under a dispensation so much more glorious than theirs, that men, christian men, are sanctioned in buying & selling their brethren (for color cannot break the cords of union which now subsist in the human family) not for 7 or 14 or 21 years but for life & not only enslaving them, but their children after them from generation to generation & with this aggravation too, that the poor slaves did not receive the money of their purchase, but those who call themselves their Masters. When I say that all men are brothers, I am far from desiring to level the wall of separation which exist between different ranks of society, for I believe these distinctions are right, & tend to the happiness & advantage of the human family at large. Experience has abundantly taught me that so far from its being best to abolish these, that a person of high rank cannot put themselves on an equality with one of low life, without injuring both, and vice versa, & yet I fully approve the exhortations of the Apostle, ["]condescend to men of low estate"[30] & "in lowliness of mind let each esteem other better than himself,"[31] all this is perfectly consistent with a dignified standing without rank in life which the Creator has assigned to the great & mighty of the Earth. There is a beautiful order in the arrangements of Providence which cannot be disturbed without occasioning confusion. But tho' it is right that such a class should exist as servants, yet let us remember what Paul says, "Masters give unto your servants that which is just & equal,"[32] equal to what? I would ask, equal to the services rendered is undoubtedly the answer, but can that Master be said to give his servant what is equal to his labour, who only feeds & clothes him, I think not.

August 17   Today I feel quite depressed in consequence of the eruption having again broken out on my hand. It would not be so trying if my physician was kind, but ever since I became serious B[enjamin]. F. has treated me with such uniform coldness & neglect that it is certainly painful for me to apply to him for medical advice & yet as he is my brother I do not feel any liberty to send for anyone else. Dependence in any way upon one who scarcely deigns to speak to me at times is galling indeed, but My Heavenly Father seeth all my trials, for he sees in secret & knows all I have to suffer in this land of my birth where I am as a stranger, with not one heart to feel for me & with me, but may His holy will be done, I can say no more, for my heart is sorrowful. This day 4 weeks [ago] I got dear Sisters last letter, my not hearing from feels quite like a trial—today I have believed it would not be required of me to stay here next winter, but I see no way of escape.

August 18   O Lord grant that my going forth out of this land may be in such a time & such a way that let what ~~may~~ happen after I leave my Mothers house I may never have to reproach myself for doing so.

August 20   Of late my mind has been much engrossed with the subject of Slavery, I have felt the necessity not only of feeling that it was sinful but of being able to prove from Scriptures that it is not warranted by God. The advocates of the wretched system are very fond of this argument which they think quite irresistible. On account of Ham's laughing at Noah the curse of Slavery was pronounced upon his posterity & as Ham settled in Africa of course Negroes ought to be slaves. But a little enquiry into this matter will convince the candid inquirer that the argument is altogether futile. In reading the portion of Scriptures from which the conclusion is drawn, it appears that so far from the curse of slavery being pronounced upon all Ham's descendants that Canaan was the only one who was cursed whilst, on the contrary, his brothers were abundantly blessed & exalted over him, the text runs thus, "Cursed be Canaan, a servant of servants shall he be unto his brethren,[33] Blessed be the Lord God of Shem, & Canaan shall be his servant. God shall enlarge Japhet, & he shall dwell in the tents of Shem; & Canaan shall be his servant.["] From this it appears very clear that none but the descendants of Canaan were to be enslaved, hence we find the Lord commissioned Israel not to enslave those of their own nation but tells them expressly that "Both their bond men & bond women were to be of the heathen which were round about them."[34] This I take to be a special command to Israel as the commission they received to dispossess the Canaanites of their country & to take it for themselves—and as it universally allowed that no Nation would now have a right to rob another Nation of their possessions by force of arms without any provocation, & then justify themselves by adducing the example of Israel for such an outrage, so no nation can claim the privilege of enslaving another nation upon the same ground—unless they can like the Jews of old produce the divine command for so doing. Feel uneasy about my hands. Mother sent for the Dr. this morning, he says, that he is no judge of what the disease is, for that I have been using Carrosine Sublimate a great deal too severe & he wonders my hands are not even worse than they are, but it looks more like itch than any thing else, the sores he says must be healed by sugar of lead before he can determine—this disorder

I have always dreaded but my bowed spirit says "it is the Lord, let Him do what seemeth him good."[35]

August 21   Many weeks ago I might have written in my journal, ["]that which was weary has died" now & then it revives a little, but as my mind has gradually become more & more resigned, the weariness of spirit has less frequently been my companion & I am often led to bless the Lord for his sustaining & preserving mercy.

August 23   First day night. The weather has been so stormy & rainy that I could not go to meeting at all—on the whole it has been a comfortable day, have been much interested in reading Samuel Scotts Diary, & fell a little encouraged to find Friends Journals so deeply interesting to me now. Felt condemned this evening because in speaking of myself I said "when I was first religious," O how careful we ought to be not to assume any thing of piety in speaking of ourselves, tho' we cannot be careful by the consistency of our lives to show that we possess what multitudes only profess.

August 24   Great condemnation for throwing out a very unkind insinuation, about S[ister] M[ary] at dinner table, for tho' deserved, still it was very sinful in me.

August 26   Feel very low this morning & not free from condemnation for minor offences. Sat with but little sense of any thing but my own unworthiness until I remembered the Lords mercy in healing my hands & gratitude sweet gratitude filled my heart. O that my spiritual eye may be opened to see the bait of the great Enemy.

August 29   It is better for us never to find fault with any one if we can not do it in that spirit which wishes good to the individual; He who labors in the Masters vineyard must labour in his spirit, the fruits of which are "love, joy, peace, long suffering, gentleness, goodness, faith, meekness, temperance."[36] If we find it no cross to reprove others, it is a very bad sign & ought to alarm us. Sometimes I think that the children of Israel could not have looked towards the land of Canaan with feelings of keener sensibility than I do to the North. I do not expect to go there & be exempt from trial, far from it, yet it looks like a promised land; a pleasant land, because it is a land of Freedom & it seems to me that I would rather bear much deeper spiritual exercise, than day after day & month after month to endure the countless evils which incessantly flow from Slavery. "O to grace how great a debtor"[37] for my sentiments on this subject surely I may measurably adopt the language of Paul when with holy triumph I may he exclaimed "by the grace of God I am what I am."[38] How wonderful that Professors can be reconciled to close the Bible to their slaves, what right have they to take the inspired volume out of their hands & then say that it is best they should not have it, because they cannot understand it & may make a bad use of it; from day to day I am grieved to see the total ignorance in which Slaves are allowed to grow up, literally taught nothing but what will minister to the comfort & convenience of the selfish owners. "These things ought not so to be" ["]I have not so learned Christ."[39] As to poor dear Mother she seems to have found another resting place. I still feel as if I have nothing to do with her, & have compared my feelings to those of a person watching by the death bed of a friend without any power of alleviating the transient struggles or rousing the deep & fatal slumbers of one whose recovery is past hopes. These are awful feelings, but at times, I can still look towards the hills ["]from whence help cometh"[40] & have not altogether forgotten the reproof (administered to Abraham, "Is any thing too hard for the Lord?["]"[41]) Condemnation again for an unkind insinuation at dinner table.

August 30   Have attended meeting twice today & remembered this time last year I was at Frankfort. Great poverty & deadness prevailed and the enquiry arose, tho' with but a little life, Why O Lord are the heavens brass over our heads & the ground iron under our feet? Walked homewards with D. Lathum & in so doing expect I irritated JH for in one of his letters to me he says he would not be seen walking in the street with him. I have all along felt the necessity of being very grounded in my conduct being careful it should not extend beyond politeness & respect. In the winter I often walked with him, but it was to avoid DH who I found would join me if I went down King Street, so in this way I was compelled to walk with the Lathums, but since he went away I have with only two exceptions always gone down King Street preferring to be alone. I confess I see no impropriety in my being seen with the old man or would constantly avoid, but politeness & a little attention I think is due to his age. In reading S. Scotts diary this afternoon was so much struck with this remark for it is & has been the substance of my feelings about JH & DL. He says "I verily believe self-preference, & the despising of others, are detestable as more open immoralities, in the sight of Him, who seeth not as man seeth, but who searcheth the heart."[42] JH seems to me as guilty of the first as D.L. is of the last.

Night   John Woolman suffered much on account of Slavery, but he does not appear to have seen the great source of all the evils resulting from it. I mean the neglect of their educations, Were they taught to read & to value the instructions conveyed by books instead of passing their spare hours in the Street they might be usefully & pleasantly engaged in reading—but in consequence of their ignorance they have no resourses in themselves & eagerly fly to the Street for amusement where the ends of idleness & vice are sown in their hearts, those are the roots of other evils & often cause much unhappiness. Some are taught to read but no pain is ever taken to improve their minds, the Bible is given to them, but little or no effect is used to render it interesting or comprehensible. Slavery is a system of abject selfishness & yet I believe I have seen some of the best of it. In its worst form, tyranny is added to it & power cruelly treads under foot the rights of man & trammels not only the body but the mental faculties of the poor Negro. Experience has convinced me that a person may own a Slave with a single eye to the glory of God, but as the eye is kept single it will soon become full of light on the momentous subject—the arm of power will be broken, the voice of authority will tremble, and strength will be granted to obey the command "Touch not the unclean thing."[43]

August 31   ["]Charity suffereth long & is kind," O that I may have this charity whilst I suffer under the daily contentions which pass before me in the family. I cannot say that I individually have to bear much of this, for My heavenly Father does hide me from ["]the strife of tongues in the hollow of his hand,"[44] & often am I led to praise that goodness whh so wonderfully preserves me especially from S.M. for she is excessively ill-natured even to Selina who it appears to me gives her no provocation but if she can say an unkind thing about H[enry] or S[elina] or their servants, she is sure to do it, & in fact she continually reminds me of the Psalmists Declaration "the poison of the asps is under their tongues"[45] & yet she is never ill natured to me tho' she is unamiable at times. She is just as harsh to E. & nearly so to Mother & people generally. O Lord thou only knowest how much longer I am to live in this perpetual turmoil, thou only knowest the number of my days—grant that patience may have its perfect work & if consistent with thy will, cut short the work in righteousness for often is my "soul weary because of the way."[46] I fully believe this dispensation (which feels like the tedious & painful operation of grinding to powder) is necessary to my purification, but it is now 9 months since I have endured it & tho' my heart condemns me (& God is greater than my heart) for very many aberrations from the path of strict purity in tho't, word & deed, yet on the whole, blessed be the name of the Lord. I cannot charge myself with anything of consequence by which the work of grace may have been hindered but in sincerity can say I have tried to do the will of my Master as manifested from day to day & can join with David in saying "He is the preserver of all who put their trust in Him."[47]

August 31   Last night a distressing accident occurred to one of our horses, S.M. & myself had drank tea at B.T.'s & when coming home a chair run against us & the shaft was driven deep into the breast of the poor animal we were obliged to get out & walk home—the horse is not dead yet, but there is little hope of his recovery—he was immediately taken to a stable & attended to by a very good horse doctor. Fear I have not sufficiently viewed this circumstance as coming from the hand of the Lord—this morning feel tried & distressed in mind. There is some talk of prosecuting the man who was on his wrong hand & therefore to blame, but I feel no unity in such procedure for the Spirit of all Truth has led me into the paths of peace & good will to all men.

September 2   A circumstance occurred tonight which has several times since my return given me exquisite pain, but I did not this evening feel that deep exercise which had before covered my mind, whether my heart has become callow from familiarity, with evil I know not, or whether my days of suffering are over about this thing, but O my Father do not leave me or forsake me, but hold me by right hand, guide my weary footsteps & preserve me for thy mercy's sake.

September 5   Under some trial of mind this morning have been led to query whether the desire I feel to be one day released from Carolina proceeds from the belief that I shall thereby be released from trial or whether it proceeds from a belief that the simplicity in which I would live at the North is purer in the eyes of my Master whose I am & whom I desire to serve; if my heart deceives me not, it is the latter, & it appears to me my motives are less selfish on the subject than they ever have been. It is sin not sorrow that I groan to be delivered from.

September 6   Have been to meeting twice today and Sat as usual in lifeless stupidity. Went this afternoon to see S. Lathum who lies very ill, but nothing seems to rouse me. I live in a dry & barren land & whilst surrounded by earthly comforts find them totally inadequate to satisfy the desires of my soul.

September 7   Some feeble aspirations that patience might have its perfect work.

September 8   Last night was favored to receive a letter from Dear Sister [Sarah], soon after which I was thrown into great suffering of mind by Sally[48] getting into a fray in the Street & coming in with her head & hand streaming with blood. Every circumstance seems of late to lead me to look at the root of the evil I daily endure from Slavery, the total neglect of the education & moral improvement of Negroes, the vacancy of their mind & depravity of their hearts naturally lead them to the Street in their leisure hours where they learn nothing that is good, for of course it is the worst characters who parade the Streets at night.

September 11   Of late have had my mind at times much exercised about leaving Carolina, not being able to leave this subject as entirely as when I first received dear Sisters letter saying that "all the days of my appointed time were fulfilled in this land."⁴⁹ Yesterday very unexpectedly another letter from her was handed me saying that our dear Catherine's house was open to me & that the language to her seemed to be "take this child & nurse it for me & I will pay thee thy wages." Much as I have suffered here, yet I find the very idea of leaving dear Mother extremely painful. I think I can truly say it is so painful as to counterbalance the satisfaction felt at the prospect of leaving a land of Slavery. The only thing which seems to turn the balance in favor of my going is the consideration that if there is a human being to whose happiness I may contribute, it is my beloved Sister, & when I remember all she has done for me, from childhood, & look at the deep trials thro' which she has for years been passing, & the comfort I believe (under the divine blessing) I might be to her, it seems as tho' I had no right to refuse to walk in that path which has been so evidently set before me. I feel very sensibly that last Spring was my time for going but now is the Lord's time—then my views were altogether selfish, it was my release from suffering I anxiously craved, my enjoyment I contemplated & great has been the mercy and power manifested in gradually subduing these feelings until a willingness was wrought in my heart to say "Thy will be done"⁵⁰ tho' all prospect as to my release for many years was entirely closed & I felt myself a captive in the Desert surrounded by impassable barriers. If I could believe that I contributed to dear Mothers happiness, surely duty, yea inclination would lead me to continue here, but I do not. Yesterday morning I read her newspapers on Slavery which had come by the L[angston] C[heeves] greatly against her will, but it seemed to me I must do it & that this was the last effort which would be required of me. She was really angry but I did not feel condemned.

Night   Have sought a season of retirement in order to ponder all these things in my heart for I feel greatly burdened & think I must open this subject to dear Mother, tomorrow perhaps. I earnestly desire to do the Lord's will.

September 12   This morning I read parts of dear Sister's letter to Mother on the subject of my going to the North, she did not oppose tho' she regretted it. My mind is in a calm, almost an indifferent state about it, simply acquiescing in what I believe to be the divine will concerning me. The prospect of a voyage at this time of the year is rather disagreeable, particularly as it may so happen that no female may be on board, in which case, I am extremely doubtful whether it would be proper for me to go, but I don't feel as tho' I had any thing to do with these things, they neither disturb me, nor do they alter the impression that I shall have to go in the next trip of the L. C. When I mentioned it to E she made these very objections. I had some time before told her in confidence that I did not think I should remain here this winter tho' I did not see how I was to go away for I had no idea then that Catherine had at all desired my return to her house. It has been cause of secret satisfaction to find in overlooking my wardrobe that there is not a single thing I've worn in Carolina, that I cannot go to Philadelphia & wear amoungst Friends with their approbation. Some may say this is only a form of goodness, true, but if this outward form is maintained with a single eye to the glory of God, it becomes strength to the inner man & yields the peaceable fruit of righteousness to the rightly exercised mind.

September 15   This morning felt in very good spirits on two of my old friends calling in, I indulged in too much conversation, I feel that condemnation which necessarily follows an experimental evidence that ["]in the multitude of words there wanteth not sin."

September 17   Since I spoke to Mother & Sisters on 7th day & wrote to dearest Sister [Sarah] on 2d day my mind has been entirely released from exercise about my going away, until to night when I feel distressed & tried.

September 19   My mind has mostly been perfectly quiescent, being merely impressed with the belief that I was to go in the next trip of the LC without any feeling of pain or pleasure. Today I received another letter from dearest Sister & the way seems to be more open than ever, there does indeed seem to be an open door set before me ["]which no man can shut."[51]

September 20   This language of the Lord to the children of Israel of old seems strikingly applicable to my present situation. "And it shall be, when the Lord thy God shall have brought thee into the land which he swore unto thy fathers, to Abraham, to Isaac & to Jacob, to give thee great & goodly cities which thou buildeth not, and houses full of all good things, which thou fillest not, & wells digged which thou diggest not, vineyards and olive trees which thou plantedst not; when thou shalt have eaten & be full: Then beware, lest thou forget the Lord which bro't thee forth out of the land of Egypt from the house of bondage."[52]—but so low is all feeling with me now that tho' I can see the applicability of the passage & fully believe in going to Philadelphia that I shall be exposed to many temptations to which there will be great danger of my yielding, yet I cannot feel these things, nor have I the power to raise the petition "Preserve me O God"[53] but remain stupid & insensible. Well may I say that I have been in this land "in weakness & in fear & in much trembling."[54]

September 23   C[harles] arrived on second day, he had been very ill on the Sea shore. I have felt thankful I did not go in the LC. because by being here I shall have the opportunity of seeing him before I leave Carolina. Some conversation occurred between H & E last night about him & I was surprised to find they both tho't exactly as I did about his living on others, the only difference in opinion was this, they sd. it was useless to tell him what they tho't because it would injure his feelings & produce no effect. I contended that the family had but one voice in this thing & whilst they boldly told him what his duty was, were still to treat him with uniform kindness, it would I believe have an effect. they both agreed that were his eyes ever opened to see things correctly that he would feel that I had spoken to him last winter in real kindness & for his own good, but that whilst he was blind, he would take every thing that was said on this subject very unkindly. I expressed the satisfaction I felt in having done my duty to him tho' it had exposed me to much that was painful. E said it was useless to speak to him as I had done for it would only drive him out the house as it had done then & seemed to derive much satisfaction from the reflection that she had never done anything to make him feel his dependence & that he never should have to say that she did. She complained very much that his brothers did not get a place for him. H said he had made every exertion to do so but that he could not a genteel place which he was competent to fill & queried whether she would like him to get a place in King Street. O no she said. I then said I believed C would be a far happier man if he had a place in King Street & that it was nothing but pride in the family which induced them to wish to see him idle rather than in such a place; to my great astonishment H fully assented to what I said & remarked that a man ought to do any thing rather than be dependent & that such a place if it did nothing else would give him a habit of industry & fit him for a higher place.[55] E somewhat reluctantly came down to this point also, but said it was impossible to make C understand the right distinction between right & wrong for that he was naturally deficient, both H & myself said we did not think he was naturally deficient but that his mind from being undisciplined had run to waste, & queried then, what was to be done, & whether it was not our duty to teach him like a little child. E said this was impossible. I impressed my full belief that C's family would get tired of supporting him sooner or later, & that it was much better for them to deal candidly tho' tenderly with him at once, & to urge him to do any thing rather than nothing. H & E said it was a pity to hurt his feelings. This is the substance of what passed & it was an evidence to my mind that if we were willing to do our duty without seeking to justify ourselves before men, but in simple obedience to the manifestations of the Light within, that the Lord will so order events as to do this for us in His own time for it was very plain that H & E really tho't I was right, tho' they had not candour to say what I did to C. O how pleasant it is for me to feel that I have done my duty in this thing. Lord give me a grateful heart for all thy mercies. Have been to meeting, my mind was turned on the subject of my leaving Carolina. Since my return home have had some exercise of mind about it & tho' I'm favored to feel this is the right time for me to go, yet I cannot but feel pain at the thoughts of leaving dear Mother for I am sure I shall leave her to suffer—it has appeared very plain to me that I never would have been taken from her again if she had been willing to listen to my remonstrances & to yield to the requisitions of duty as shown her by the Light within & I do not think dear Sister or myself will ever see her again until he is made willing to give up Slavery for I fully believe there is a considerable struggle in her mind about it & that this is the sacrifice required of her—it seems to me her happiness will be completely destroyed by it & that it will become so great a burthen that at last, thro' suffering she will be made willing to give it up—it will also be her painful experience that she has no child here on whose bosom to lay her aching head—so great will be her suffering that I believe she will rather die than live, but it will not be her life that the Lord will require but her will & this she must surrender.

September 25   Have suffered very much from Slavery within the last 3 days & today my soul is bowed in the dust—going away seems an awfully solemn act, & doubts & fears have arisen, & yet there is no ability felt to go to "the Counseller" for direction.

September 26   Ability was mercifully granted this morning to raise the petition O Lord grant that I may bend under this weight of exercise which thou hast been pleased to lay upon me, & it was immediately shown me that it was the necessary preparation to my going away. My soul sometimes faints at the idea of going only under the Captain's care if there should be no female on board, but this language seems to be "the Lord will provide" this I have scarcely faith enough to believe, & the inquiry was raised, will I feel any condemnation if I allow the LC to sail without me? I immediately felt that I would feel greatly condemned, for that this was no longer a thing of choice with me, but that I must go. This text was brought before me, "How long stand ye idle in the Market place." "Wait ye not I must be about my Father's business."[56] It was also said, "I will show thee my evidence in taking thee away just at this time.["]

September 29   Continue to much exercised about going away, but am generally enabled to work & anoint so that I appear not unto men to fast. Sometimes when I think of leaving poor Mother I feel as tho' I cannot do it & yet when I remember how steadily she has always refused to listen to my advice I cannot hope to be of any service to her, but think the great work will be affected by some other means than my living here & admonishing & reproving with all long suffering—it appears to me so plain that nothing but her refusing to listen to me has caused this separation that I am sure I shall have to tell her so & yet it seems as tho' I cannot speak on so painful a subject; perhaps I shall have to write. Tonight the petition was fully offered that the Lord would be pleased to raise some obstacles to my going & prevent it if it was not right for me to go at this time. O I do want to walk in the way He casts up for me & in no other.

October 2   Yesterday I visited the Infant School & enjoyed the Masters presence while seated among a good member of gay professors. I felt that the peculiarity of my dress rendered me a speckled bird among them & these words seemed to be graciously spoken "I have chosen you out of the world"[57] my heart and eyes were full & I was thankful that I was alone in the midst of a crowd with no one to disturb the sweet emotions of love which flowed towards the little infants before me. The Savior's name printed on some cards which hung round the room caught my eye too & awakened some delightful feeling. "O there is magic in a name." In the evening paid my long promised visit to L's where I heard the L.C. was not to sail until between the 1st & 6th of this month. A feeling came over my mind similar to that experienced last year in Phila. when waiting to sail for C. an impatience to be gone as tho' the time for me to remove was come. There is now little or no doubt in my mind as to my going though I have not heard what Friends say to my doing so, if there should be no other female on board.

October 3   Yesterday I received a short but very satisfactory letter from dear Sister [Sarah]. Friends approve of my going & the way to do so continues perfectly open in my mind.

October 4   Last night E.T. took tea here—as soon as she began to extol the North & speak against Slavery Mother left the room, for she cannot bear these two subjects. E & myself joined with her heartily, but S found it very hard to hear & was I believe glad of an excuse to leave the room also, tho' not until she heard a good deal of our conversation. My mind continues distressingly exercised & anxious that Mothers eyes should be open to all the iniquity and evils of Slavery.

Much hope has lately been experienced & it seems as tho' the language to me was, "thou hast done what was given thee to do, now go & leave the rest to Me.["]

October 5   This morning when I spoke to C. I observed he did not answer me but upon my going into the room a second time & making some remark to him to my great surprise he said he wondered I was so fond of talking to him, for his part "he wished I never would speak to him for it would be far pleasanter to live on terms of silence with me.["] I've ventured to ask what was the matter with him & in what way I had unconsciencely offended him, he merely replied that I was always making remarks about him & were it not that I was so soon going away he certainly never should speak to me. I again expressed my ignorance as to what I had said to offend him & begged to be told, saying I tho't it was but just when a person was accused that they should know of what they were accused, but he remained silent & so did I. After some minutes of reflection I remembered that yesterday morning when I met him on the steps I said how art thou C. so thou wast sick again last night—he replied yes. I then said that was drinking wine I suppose & passed on—& had entirely forgotten the circumstance—but truth sticks fast on a guilty conscience for surely he must know that a man who spends his time in idleness & is from day to day eating the bread of dependence has no right to be drinking anothers wine who is working hard, & entertaining a friend at H's expense—besides which it was not 10 ~~days~~ nights since he rousted the whole family & even sent for B. F. from being attacked with cramp in the stomach & therefore it was the more inexcusable that he should indulge himself in eating & drinking freely. I did not however say anything to him about it this morning but could not help thinking that the time would come when the poor boy would find that I was not alone in my opinion about him (which he evidently thinks) but tho' all the others think the same I am the only one who will tell him the truth fearlessly—how often has the text occurred in reference to him "Ye count me your enemy because I tell you the truth."

Night   This morning I had a very satisfactory conversation with dear Mother on several different subjects & feel considerably relieved from painful exercise. I found her views far more correct than I had supposed & do believe that thro' suffering the great work will yet be accomplished. She remarked that tho' she had found it very hard to bear many things which Sister & myself had from time to time said to her, yet she had believed that the Lord had raised us up to teach her & that her fervent prayer was that if we were right & she was wrong that she might see it, remarked that if she was willing I was very sure she would see still more than she now did & drew a contrast between what she once approved

& now believed right—yes she said I see very differently, for when I look back & remember what I used to do & think nothing of, I shrink back with horror at the tho't. Much more passed and we parted in love. O God I thank thee for what thou hast done, forget not the work of thy hands but perfect that which concerns her for thy dear Sons sake. Amen.

October 7   Feel exceedingly tried by C's conduct. O that I may be preserved in pure love unto the end of all my trials here I ask not to be spared from suffering but to be delivered from all evil feelings.

October 10   Yesterday had another short but close conversation with C. on the uselessness & idleness with which he spent his time &c. he found it as hard as ever to bear, but of late I have been so impressed with the belief that unless he got some employment he would soon be a ruined man that I believed it duty to speak to him again if occasion offered—this occurred before Mother & I was glad it did.

7

A New Life

Finally the waiting was over; Angelina Grimké sailed from the land of her birth. She left her family, her fortune, and the prestige and privilege of high social standing. She also left the conflicts that had tormented her for two years or more. The battles with her family were behind her, and the painful relationships with former friends and church congregants would no longer torment her. Most importantly to Angelina, she no longer had to live amidst the "depravity of slavery."

The diary entry of 17 November, her first since leaving Charleston, is reflective of deep emotional conflict. Despite their past difficulties, Angelina clearly regretted the separation from her mother, although not so much that she regretted leaving Charleston. In fact, she wrote, "When I arrived I was quite calm" and that "I was just in my right place has mostly been the covering of my mind since." She was clearly satisfied and believed that "my home now is just what I asked for 'a quiet retreat.'"

She immediately began to consider membership in the Society of Friends. She met and greatly admired Jane Bettle, who was from a leading family of the Arch Street Meeting and someone who would figure in Angelina's life dramatically. Angelina made formal application for membership in January 1830. In July she was visited by representatives of the Overseers and told that the "neglect" of her aging mother, left behind in Charleston, would make it difficult to justify favorable action on her application. Once again turmoil and confrontation rushed in to upset Angelina's quiet retreat. After this, Angelina often entertained, with varying degrees of seriousness and intensity, the possibility of returning to Charleston. By the end of the summer, however, it was becoming clear that Grimké was not going to return. She never would.

⚭

Philadelphia, 1829

November 17   It has been on my mind from time to time to begin to regi-
ster my religious feelings, but I have been so circumstanced since my arrival here
as to render it almost impossible as I feel it best first to state something concerning my departure from the land of my nativity. Very unexpectedly it proved
to be a truly afflictive event to my beloved Mother who after suppressing her
feelings before me for three weeks was no longer able to do so after the vessel
arrived, in which I was to sail; the conflict of feeling became too powerful, her
heart was as it were been broken open by violence and it was seldom without
tears in her eyes until I left her. The first day before I sailed as I was leaning my
head on her lap (as usual at dark) being given to feel the grief of her soul I said,
Mother hast thou ever felt I was going to do a wrong thing in leaving thee. My
child said she don't talk to me about it, I don't know when I have ever been so
tried about any thing, her sobs prevented further utterances and silence ensued.
At this E[liza] & myself both had to leave the room on account of an overflow of
feeling and I have tho't that could all the family have understood what silent communion of spirit was, how precious it would have been to sit down together at
that time & enjoy the tendering inviting instances of that spirit which 3 of us at
least experienced to be a dew upon the tender pearl. The evening before I sailed
as we were sitting together Mother said something of her trials & she would be
enabled to bear them seeming to think she would never be released from them
but by death. With tears of emotion & pity I told her I did not believe that these
family trials were to last always, but if she was faithful these burthens would be
removed & I believed that a happy old age was before her, a period in which she
would enjoy far more real solid happiness than she had ever done before—thou
seemest to think I continued that necessity is laid upon thee to live just where &
as thou hast been accustomed to & that will have to drag out an exercise of continual trial, but it is not so—she made no reply & silence followed. E & myself
were soon after left alone & I opened to her my belief that Mother would in time
feel it to be right to leave Carolina & that it had appeared to me that my going
away would be the means of breaking some of the cords which bound her there
& that this change would contribute greatly to her happiness &c. A few hours
before I sailed I went into dear Mother's room & being alone sat down beside her
& leaned my head on her—fresh tears began to flow from our eyes & much
passed between us under the covering of love some of which I believe it right for

me to record—she spoke with great emotion of the prospect of our separation —it is in vain for me to reason about my feelings she said, why I am so afflicted I know not, I have parted with other of my children but never felt as I now do, sometimes I think I should never see you again, but it is in vain to reason. I expressed my belief that it was designed that she should feel it deeply, yes she said she did not doubt it but My Dear Child you must excuse me for having harrowed up your feelings in the way I have done by exposing my own; I have struggled to suppress them before you & did for some weeks, but now it is impossible, my weakness will show itself. My beloved Mother, I said, call it not weakness— these feelings were the most precious we have ever felt, & the pain we are suffering is not to be compared to the sweet satisfaction of being permitted to feel so near & so dear to each other—you are very dear to me she replied pressing me to her bosom & sometimes it seems mysterious that you should be taken from me just as you had become so dear & I was looking forward with so much pleasure to your reading to me this winter; I felt that a change had passed over me & that my mind was gradually becoming more & more congenial to yours— but it is all right, I feel that you are called of the Lord & would not say a word to keep you tho' I know that I shall miss you so much. Our feelings at this time cannot be described. I then felt it right to open my views more fully & said as near as I can remember as follows. Mother there is a part of Scripture which in thinking of thee has been forcibly revived & I believe it will be right for us to have it with thee. I mean the history of Jacob. I believe in the bitterness of thy soul thou hast been ready to exclaim as he did, "Joseph is not & Simeon is not, & ye will take Benjamin away also, all these things are against me"[1] but they are not against thee any more than they were against him. Jacob's children are taken from him to prepare a place for him in a strange land so I believe it is with thine it seems as tho' the constant language of my heart to thee was "I go to prepare a place for thee, that where I am there thou mayest be also."[2] Thou art not to end thy days in Charleston but in Philadelphia. To my surprise she testified her entire willingness to do what was right & if it was the will of the Lord that she should remove, tho' much opposed to it at one time yet his will was now given up. I then mentioned another text which had been given me in thinking of these things, it was what David said when his child was taken from him, "I will go to him, but he shall not return to me["]—is it not strange she said that my text has dwelt so much on my mind lately—if continued she I tho't should ever see you again I should not suffer so much in parting with you. Soon after I left her hoping that we might be favored with calmness when the solemn moment of separation comes. That moment soon came & we parted; after a voyage of 9 days I reached Philadelphia when coming up the Delaware I remembered what I had passed thro' in Carolina & it seemed as tho' I had left not a cloud behind me & could see none in my clear calm sky. If I could have arrived in one or two days after I left dear Mother I believe that I should have fainted under the violent conflicting emotions of my heart—for some days after I sailed it seemed too much for me either to look backward or forward on my situation but when I arrived I was quite calm & this feeling accompanied with an evidence that I was just in my right place has mostly been the covering of my mind since. It seems as tho' I have had no will of my own believing that my situation was just what was best for me, & receiving what occurred from my Heavenly Father's hand. When here before I was caressed by many among us whom I plainly see I am to be nothing new this was a surprise at first, but I have seen the goodness of my Master in this thing & I would not have it otherwise. Again & again I travel forward in my journey am I constrained to say "He hath endured all things well." These dispensations of nothingness are needful for me, for I am prone to "think of myself more highly than I ought to think" & they so serve very much to teach me what a poor creature I am, & how much secret pride lives in my heart not that I am discontented under them but did not the Lord see that Prosperity would exalt perhaps he would bestow it at least so I have tho't. My home now is just what I asked for "a quiet retreat."[3] I feel like a hidden one tho' in the city & exposed to much company, still my lips are mostly sealed when among strangers & I think they know me not.

November 22   Had a greatly favored time at meeting this morning & many hearts were melted under the ministry of E. P. much encouragement was offered to the hidden ones & a firm belief expressed, there were still a living remnant left among Friends. This evening in my season of silence felt that Jerusalem is indeed a quiet habitation her gates are praise & her walls salvation, there "every man may set under his own vine & his own fig tree,"[4] I think of the ["]waters of that river which maketh glad the city of our God."

November 24   I find it hard to keep right towards the M's sometimes there is a spirit within me that would throw almost all of them from me, then again there are occasions when I can take them in the arms of affection & pray for them. Have been poised this morning to seek after preservation particularly tomorrow when a good many of them are to dine here.

November 30   On the 26th J K paid me a visit & preached me a remark-able sermon, he began with this text "keep thine eyes single & thy whole body will be full of light,"[5] he said there is a circumstance to which I was looking forward

& waiting for, but that I must be careful how I put my hand to the work for all I had to do was "patiently to wait & quietly to hope"[6] trusting in the Lord &c. Sister [Sarah] returned from the Country on 7th day & I feel very sensibly that nothing but divine grace can preserve C[atherine Morris][7] & ourselves in the bonds of harmony & love, the constant language to man is "you are in great danger of separating each other; Satan envies the happiness you might enjoy together & if he possibly can he will destroy your peace & comfort.["]

December 20   Have passed thro' some trying feelings of late about becoming a member of Friends SY—was soon favored to see that Satan was doing all he could to prevent my doing so, by showing me the inconsistency of the people & persuading me I was too good to be one of them. I was led to doubt whether it was right for me ever to have worn the dress of a Quaker & I despised the very form in my heart & tho't it a disgrace to have adopted it so empty did the people seem. Sometimes it seemed impossible that I should ever be willing to join SY. I felt my heart was full of rebellion & I even dared to think it hard I should have to bear the burdens of a people I did not, could not love, but my Holy Redeemer was pleased to show me that I was thus refusing to enter into His service, to do His will, & to fill up the measure of his sufferings, it was Him with whom I had to do & it was awful presumption in me not to obey. "Scarcely for a righteous man would one be found to die, yet peradventure for a good man some would even dare to die, but God commended his love towards us in that whilst we were yet insincere Christ died for us."[8]

February 21, 1830   Perhaps it hasn't been right in me to omit writing in this book for two months at any rate I at last feel constrained now to resume my pen. Yesterday was my 25th birthday & I had tho't I would begin to wear caps, but when the time came my soul was humbled within me & fear & trembling took hold upon me lest I should be going before my guide & moving in my own will & adopting a dress (longeared caps) which indicated a further evidence in true piety than I had attained, but after some conflict & looking for divine counsel & I felt most easy to put them on, as in so doing I also enjoyed the approbation of my dear Catherine's Sister Elizabeth & Rebecca. In writing these names my heart overflows with gratitude to my Heavenly Father for the gift of such 4 friends all of whom I believe feel united to me in the bonds of gospel love. On the 17th of last Month I gave up to make application to become a Member of Society. I went to dear J[ane] B[ettle] who I believe feels much for me—from that time I enjoyed an almost uninterruptible season of silence, tho' at times brought into pretty close exercise on dear Sisters [Sarah] account particularly the evening she unfolded to C. her prospect of leaving her to reside at Radnor the loss of her Society would be inexpressibly great but I felt the necessity of giving her up cheerfully for "God loveth a cheerful giver" "only & it is the desire of my heart to bring all my offering with a willingly heart,["] "not grudgingly nor of necessity."[9] I want it to be as much my will, to give as it is my Masters to demand.

March 7   This night [a] week [ago] drank the cup of bitterness because I had offended a dear friend the day before, who tho' she sd. she forgave me when I in tears expressed my sorrow did nevertheless manifest a very different spirit in her conduct. I felt bound faithfully to tell her what I believed to be christian forgiveness. O how beautifully did this open on my mind from the remembrances of many passages of Scripture added to my past experience of how my gracious Master had forgiven me my transgressions & blotted out my iniquities as a thick cloud remembering them no more forever. A reconciliation was effected & the breach healed. This evening I have drunk the cup of shame and confusion—dear C was so kind, so true a friend to me as to tell me why she believed I had such poor meetings. The faithful witness testifies the truth of what she said & in tears leaving my head upon her bosom after a considerable silence I said, Catherine I am sincerely obliged to thee for what time hath told me, thou hast done me many acts of kindness but this is by far the greatest & I want thee to be unassuaged to tell me my faults. She took me in her arms & kissed me with all the affection of a Mother & said she was truly glad I had received what she had said with the love which dictated it. Dear Sister revived this text as one which had arisen in her mind before I came as being practicaly applicable to C & myself. "Take this child & nurse it for me & I will give thee thy wages"[10]—saying she believed this was the kind of nursing I needed. Our little meeting closed sweetly with the fresh arising of the spring of life & love.

March 10   Attended 12th St. Meeting with E. & R. & having dear J[ane]. B[ettle]. much on my mind went to pay a visit. I tried to go expecting nothing but still my mind was prepared to receive the words of consolation whh. she was enabled to speak without my telling her in what way my mind was tried &c. I returned home much encouraged.

March 25   Great leanness & barrenness with distressing fears & doubts as to the Lords remembrance of me for good & little ability to pray that he would not forsake the work of his own hands, ["]leave me not, neither forsake me O God of my Salvation." Lately have been led to query why I am so useless a member of the Church if I am a member at all—the activity of nature finds it very hard to wait, yet dares not lift an unbidden hand to the work. I think E. P. spoke to my state today in meeting; but I greatly desire to be preserved from "putting forth a hand to steal" that bread which is not designed for me, tho' I may feel that I am a hungry soul. "Wait at Jerusalem, (the quiet habitation) until you be endowed with power from on high."[11]

April 1   Pd. a visit to G. H. last week & was enabled to enter into feeling with dear I[srael] M[orris]—last night wrote him a letter under much exercise of mind & the flowing of Gospel love, but hope I may be constrained from giving it to him if it is right to withhold it. Lately have felt more of the quickening influences of the Holy Spirit than before. This afternoon met the Overseers of Arch Street Meeting for the first time it was somewhat a broken session & yet I believe an unsatisfactory visit to them.

April 7   Yesterday Dear R. called for me to go to N. Meeting. I went with a sorrowful spirit & sat under a heart searching sermon from A J. and a truly consolatory one from E. P. I felt unworthy of the invitation intended to the few to draw nigh to the table of communion or partake the living bread there dispersed by the Master—my mind was turned inward, sincerely desiring to see where I had missed my way & know how I should return. My heart was bent upon finding out the sense of my trials at home & was made willing to make any acknowledgment, but I would see nothing to acknowledge, & it appears that I must be willing to bear them in silent patience. O that I may be enabled to feel for C. in the trying state of her mind. Paid 3 visits with my friends & then returned home with the answer of grace, this was a favored day to my soul.

April 10   O God let thy favours unto me (the least of all saints, if ment to be called a disciple at all) be graven on my rocky heart with an iron pen. I had almost tho't I was forgotten but thou hast once more broken in upon my soul. This morning was tried & was enabled to bow before thy awful presence & crave ability, to see that the evil & the good do both come from a Father ["]whose right hand is full of righteousness." Paid a satisfactory visit to Burlington—have been favored within 2 weeks to sit under the preaching of E. Bates & W. Evans—the former seemed to come in the fulness of the blessing of the gospel of peace "to strengthen the feeble knees & lift up the hands that hung down" the latter seemed to go down with ["]lighted candles into the heart bringing to light the hidden things of darkness."

July 20   How often has the language of my heart been, Lord I am tried beyond what I am able to bear with patience and resignation—great have been the struggles of my rebellious soul which finds it so hard to submit to the thrashing instrument & the fan. In the beginning of last month E. T. & M. C. paid me a visit as Overseers. Much freedom of expression was used & I found it a satis-factory one—but yesterday they called again to inform me they could not see their way in taking my case to the Monthly Meeting & wished to know whether I still wished it left with them or was willing to make a fresh application when my mind was drawn so to do. I told them as near as I could judge I had applied at the right time & having done what I believed required of me I preferred it being left entirely with them as I did not think I had any more to do in it, adding I was very sure I had not made application in my own will. A great deal passed which was exceedingly trying & which I scarcely knew how to bear. M. C. fur-ther said that one of the tendencies the Society had always supported was duties of children to parents that the fact of my having embraced different opinions did not release me from my obligations as a child. I told her I did not understand her (for truly I am totally at a loss to know why she should speak thus as I was uncon-scious of any dereliction of duty). She went on to query whether we were in the path of duty whilst separated from our aged Mother & whether having found new associations & friendships there was not reason to fear we would inexorably lose that affection for her whh. we ought to cherish & a good deal more to the same purport. My tears which had before only stolen down my cheeks now flowed torrents. I sobbed aloud & E. T. seeing my great agitation proposed call-ing Sister as M's concern seemed to be with her also—but she would not allow her to. As soon as I could command myself I remarked that it felt deeply hum-bling & wounding to me that M should think we had committed a breach of duty in leaving Mother—that she was in excellent health & had other daughters with her & that I believed that circumstances must be very peculiar which would ren-der it binding on anyone who had embraced the principles of Friends to live in Slave country—& that I could not feel it my duty to subject myself to the suf-fering of mind necessarily occasioned by it—that if we were walking in the path of duty I did not believe our affections would be withdrawn from her as I tho't the more Religion gained an influence over the mind the more we should feel the world obligations we owed to our relatives & added that it was not only with her consent we had left C[harleston]. but that knowing how much we suffered there she did not wish to see us live there. M C said she did not wish to judge of the case but felt easiest to leave it for my consideration.

August 19   Seldom if ever have I set thru' a more baptizing sermon than the one preached by E[lizabeth] Evans this morning from these words of Paul "Remember them that art in bonds or bound with them, & those which suffer adversity, as being yourselves also in the body."[12] It is indeed with fear & trembling

I put forth my hand now to take any of the bread which is taken unto the hungry for by sorrowful experience. I know that the cravings of the spiritual man are not less keen & impatient than those of the natural appetite but this morning I dared not refuse what seemed to be ~~seemed to~~ given me for the words of encouragement & counsel were sealed upon my heart with the King's seal. She entered deeply into feeling with those states described by the Apostles (spiritually—for some such she believed were present & tho' far from wishing to sew pillows under armholes or to try peace, peace where there is no peace—yet she would not but speak a word of encouragement to the captive and the afflicted. And truly her pathetic sympathy flowed like oil over my tried heart some she said were there who were not over ready to wear the sack cloth on the outside, but who wore it within, who were ready to cast away the shield of faith as tho' ["]it hath not been anointed with oil"[13] to conclude from the barren state in which they were with scarcely any sense left of good, that they never had known many things of the Lord altho' from under examination of their hearts alone they knew better for all they had known, must have come from him, who had been pleased in his mercy to touch their hearts—that nothing could teach us so well as experience & that whether our sufferings were for our own sake or for the body's sake which is the Church—she wanted us to be willing to bear them—to cleave close to the Lord whom she felt assured would be near us & if we were faithful, would grant us better times—in our present state of captivity, she said, we must hold fast our confidence & crave the everlasting patience of the saints, & thus we would be enabled to sing the praises of him as one who sticketh closer than any brother. Some were ready to conclude in despair that they had brought their afflictions upon themselves, but the Lord who had meted out the heavens with a span & measured the waters in the hollow of his hand would not be unmindful of them for even the littlest sparrows were under his care; & he would bring them out; for he was able to remove all those barriers which encompassed them, all those difficulties that distressed them. She touched heartfully on the state of the Society & expressed her unshaken belief that its members would yet arise & shake themselves from the dust & lift up a standard for the sanctions. Much more did she say to the edifying of the Church and the building up of the saints but I cannot distinctly recall more of her communications except her concluding address to an individual who was turning their face Zionward & whose secret sighs and groans had gone up to heaven—she cared not she said, how secretly the work was done, but she encouraged such a one by the mercies of a Savior, to come; for there was bread enough to spare in their Heavenly Father's house. In sitting under her preaching I tho't how much I was like Hagar when who, driven into the wilderness by despair, sat down by the fountain & there to her surprise was met by the angel of the Lord who commanded her to return to submit herself under the hands of her mistress & at the same time meted out to her some precious promises. My place has long been in the wilderness and sometimes when favored sincerely to desire to abide unto the fountain of living waters. I too have been visited by the Angel of God his messengers of peace & comfort to my weary soul. Such a one was E. Evans to me this morning & such was Ann Jones last first day morning for altho' a friend remarked she preached to the Ministers yet I felt tho', little & unworthy that I had received a portion of meat from her hands. This is my gracious Master pleased in due season to find me with the bread of consolation & encouragement & to manifest himself unto me as he doth not unto the world.

August 20   I have been thinking of the opinion of some christians that were it not for our sins we should always enjoy the light of our Masters countenance they cite this passage of Scripture "your sins have separated between you & your God's & your sins have hid his face from you that he will not hear" but surely the context plainly shows that the wicked, not the righteous are here intended, for the prophet goes on to say "Your hands are defiled with blood & your fingers with iniquity your lips have spoken lies &c.["][14] But supposing it was the righteous never are separated from the Great Head of the Church, they abide in the true vine & continually derive their sustenance from the root tho' in the winter season the sap retires to the root & leaves the branches without even the appearance of life stripped of its fruit & leaves—as in the natural so in the spiritual world the Lord of Heaven & of Earth hath ordained "that seed time & harvest summer & winter (cold & heat) day & night shall not cease;[15] & as in a dark night when walking with a friend we cannot see him yet he is still as really present to protect & assist us as tho' we saw every feature in his face, yea & is more watchful over us knowing that we walk in darkness & are more liable to fall without his supporting arms than if we had the bright light of the Sun and it is not so with the true believer when introduced into a state of spiritual darkness is not his master as really present as tho' they saw him, look at the disciple going to Emau, will anyone say their Lord was not with them, merely because their eyes were hidden that they could not see him." Look at the deep baptism described by the afflicted prophet in the 3d chapter of Lamentations, will anyone say his heart was not right then. Read the pathetic wailings of the afflicted Job shall we take upon ourselves to censure him whom the Almighty pronounced to be "perfect." That when he came out of the furnace of affliction he was a more deeply experienced christian I readily allow, but shall we say a child is not perfect because it has not the strength or the intellect of a man—surely not—it is perfect according to its measure, & so was God. If his heart failed under the deep suffering which was laid upon him yet his trembling spirit could exclaim "tho' he slay me yet will I trust in him"[16] & tho' he feared his way was hidden from the Lord & he could not find him, yet his faith was strong for he says I know that my Redeemer liveth & that at the latter day he shall stand upon the earth &c. Again in this state of darkness the believer is not less watchful, humble & holy, how then can he be said to be separated from God when it is the influence of his Spirit only which can impart those graces he is so plainly manifesting to others, tho' deprived of any comfort. Under these feelings he does not like the worldling take refuge in earthly enjoyments & created objects—No! like the dove he finds no rest for the sole of his foot but in the true ark. What too did the Prophet mean when he queried "Who is among you that feareth the Lord, that obeyeth the voice of his servant, that walketh in darkness, & hath no light? let him trust in the name of the Lord & stay upon his God."[17] Here we find that there are some who tho' they fear & obey the Lord, do still walk in darkness & have no light & those the inspired Prophet so far from telling them their sins have introduced them in this state, does hold out the language of encouragement to such, telling them to trust in the Lord & to stay upon their God.

August 21 Sat two lifeless meetings today. J[ane] B[ettle] walked home with us this afternoon her parting words were Farewell dear friends every feeling of my mind is engaged for your welfare & taking my hand affectionately said feelingly, may the Lord bless thee & sanctify to thee all that may happen. O my Heavenly Father I thank thee for such a friend. I am unworthy of her sympathy & affectionate interest in my behalf—but how much more unworthy of thy holy care & the least of all thy mercies—surely "I am a worm & no man."[18]

August 23 When strengthened this morning to write dear Mother a letter offering to return home this fall, upon conditions altogether in her power. Attended North Meeting, it was literally a silent meeting to me, my soul was prostrated low before the mercy seat with the language How O God art the Potter & the clay—do with me what seemeth me good, only glorify thy own great name—my mind was utterly given up to go back to Carolina if it was my blessed Masters will. Remembered instinctively the declaration of Paul "Ye are not your own" & sincerely desired to act under a feeling & realizing sense of its truth. O how much I desire all the sacrifices I offer to be offered with a willing mind.

August 26   My prospect of my returning home has only been a few days standing & was occasioned by letters received on 2d day—it seems overwhelming & perhaps I might also say when it rushed on my mind last evening when setting in silence with Sister that "a horror of great darkness fell upon me" with a faltering tongue & fainting heart & said "Thy will be done" [19] but O! how my soul sunk down at the prospect & I felt as if my natural life could scarcely sustain the trials before me. This seems something like being "led down into the depths of the Sea."

September 2   This morning attended Meeting where S[amuel] B[ettle] spoke from these words "Study to be quiet & do your own business." [20] My mind had been greatly tossed & truly it was a word in season—he seemed to run thro' the course of my experience & offered the most encouraging counsel to the poor who were traveling thro' a dry & barren land—our progress he said was sometimes imperceptible to us so slowly did the plant of grace grow, but this was the very best growth, it was these exercises which made polished shafts for the quiver of the Lord & refined the golden vessels for his use.

Night   Whilst sitting in silence home was again brought before me. Have been enabled to view the prospect of my return with more composure, indeed so much do I dread the very idea of failing in my duty to my beloved Mother that tho' bonds & afflictions await me there yet my earnest prayer is that I may go, if it is my Masters will—his grace always has been sufficient for me & ever will be if I trust in him. O I know in whom I have believed.

September 4   Have remembered with comfort O A's prayer for preservation for "those who should be led down as it were into the depths of the Sea." [21] Surely this petition was offered for me for my poor soul has been plunging among the wave of anxious uncertainty & I have queried, what will become of me O Lord? Sometimes a momentary calm has succeeded, such as I have felt in a storm at sea when the wind & the waves have spent their fury for a moment & seems to cease their howling & foaming only to renew their strength & plunge the vessel in a still deeper gulf when the billows stand round her like a wall on every side & seem even to steady her in the depths. Such is my state of mind, last night it seemed as tho' trials were so peculiar, so complicated that as they assailed me on all sides I was like the vessel in the deep my conflicting feelings produced actual despair as to my own efforts being able to deliver me & I sunk down in quiet stillness committing my little bark into the hands of the Captain of my Salvation—but this morning she is again driven before the wind & tossed on the angry billows floating on the surface & therefore almost upset. O these waters of

affliction when we are willing to sink down into them to centre deep in holy stillness & resignation then are they indeed a wall of defense on the right hand & on
the left & actually support & preserve that vessel from destruction, which would
be completely overthrown if exposed to the wind on the surface of the waves.

September 5   I cannot describe the relief my mind experienced yesterday
morning after going to my dear J B & unfolding to her my intention of returning to Carolina the report in circulation, the part I had in it, & the letter I wrote
to J[ames] M[ott] & some other things—she took the first under consideration
& approved of the letter &c. My mind was unburthened completely & a new
song was first into my mouth even praise to the Lord for his directing & preserving power. But this morning I am again pressed down with exercise for I
am about telling Sister about what concerns her & every new duty requires a
renewed exercise in order to prepare for it. O that I may be preserved even unto
the end. Told dear sister who received it just as she ought saying she felt no more
concern about it than if she was not an interested person & that she had nothing
to do but to study & ["]be quiet" & let others do what their hands found to do.
Attended Meeting where S B preached with power & T H very sweetly, as soon
as he had sat down S B fell upon his knees & offered a fervent prayer in whh. he
pled for some present who had been deeply tried & that of latter time, (the Lord
knew who these were for unto him all hearts were open)—that when the work
was done he would be pleased to say to the raging waves, "be still" so that they
should not overwhelm & to quench the flame that it might not kindle upon them.
What an unspeakable privilege to enjoy as we have the tender sympathy of such
friends as S & J B & to have our case presented before the throne of grace even
in the great congregation. As I stood by the door after meeting dear Jane took
my hand with tears in her eyes & seemed to say, you see how deeply we both feel
for you in this hour of extremity R C also held out her hand to me almost for
the first time & seemed to do so in sympathy—my eyes filled with tears of gratitude for such kindness from a stranger when M C was standing by appeared to
catch the feeling & offered his also. Ah. how much our dear Catherine has lost by
not being able to feel for us on the subject—she has always said she could not see
it & of course all our trials on this account have been borne without uttering a
word to him & that bosom which I verily believe was the very one upon which
we ought to have bowed our heads in conflict & trial has been the last into which
we could pour our sorrow—she could not see it, I believe, because she never has
been willing to bend under that exercise which is as the clay with which the blind
man's eyes were anointed & which must he submitted to before sight can be

given. In consequence of this we have unavoidably from time to time felt separated from her in spirit, for whilst travelling under heavy burdens we have been compelled to shut up our exercises in our own bosoms & where there does not exist that confidence which ought to subsist between individuals—there cannot be that flowing of affection & feeling which would otherwise be experienced to the tendering & uniting of their hearts. We were designed I have no doubt, as blessings to her, but not being a Mother to us in these sore trials she has marred the design of best wisdom, & many has been the time that she has treated us with such studied coldness & perfect politeness that it has been overwhelming particularly to dear S[arah] who did not begin to pay her board until two months since. I think we were both sincerely engaged in searching after the cause of the treatment in ourselves, but truly I would not find it there but was hd. to believe it was a peculiarity in C's disposition—& many times of late have I been made willing (in looking at the defects of her character) to drink the cup of suffering now, & bear my masters yoke in my youth, if by so doing Ɨ my heart might be purified & I be prepared to be a mother in Israel to the Lords little ones. In the bitterness of sorrow have we known "the heart of a stranger" here, & I trust those trials will enable us to sympathise with the suffering soul hereafter. O! I do believe, even whilst in the depths of trial that He hath ordered all things well & in the language of David I can exclaim "Why art thou cast down O my soul, & why art thou disquieted within me hope thou in God, for I shall yet praise him who is the help of my countenance & my God." But it is not always so—there are seasons when the rebellious vessel exclaims under the forming hand of the Potter, "Why hast thou made me thus"[22]—but it dares not resist—no, never.

September 6   We certainly had very remarkable meetings yesterday. In the afternoon T. H. rose with words "He hath trodden the wine press alone & of the people there was none with him,["] "he insisted on the necessity of every believer treading the path of solitary suffering in order to be comfortable to the blessed Pattern—some he said were ready to say, if this cup was given me by my Master to drink I could drink it, but human beings are the authors of my trials, but such should remember that Jesus Christ was persecuted marked & crucified by human beings too, & yet he drank the cup of suffering with meek submission.["] He seem'd to promise such sufferers a change of dispensation when they would be enabled to rejoice in that which God alone creates. Many of his expressions were just what he had made use of to me on 6th day night & I felt so sure that we had been preached to & prayed for in both meetings, that I was afraid other people would know it. Restless anxiety still covers my mind at times as to the result of my letter to I[srael] M[orris] & the report—at others I can fearlessly commit my little vessel to the Captain of my Salvation and say in simple faith

> Rage on ye billows of the deep
> Blow on ye winds of Heaven
> Jesus will my vessel keep
> And love, tho' by the storm 'tis driven

September 9   I have been passing thro' too much to commit to paper since second day. The tempest has spent its fury but the roaring of the billows & the tossing of my vessel still indicates what I have been exposed to. I seldom dream, but last night I thought I had a child which tho' only two or three days old could yet speak & was as long in stature as myself. I dreamed that I bared my bosom to it whilst it lay in my arms & that after a little effort the milk flowed abundantly from my full breasts & it was satisfied. What is thy name I queried Abby it replied. No said I <u>Abigail</u> & I thought it repeated it after me & called me Mother. This morning I have been led to think whether it would not bear a spiritual interpretation—the name Abigail means "the father's joy" now the church is the Father's joy, emphatically & If I am ever a nursing mother in Israel it will doubt-less lie in my arms & perhaps I may feed the babes with milk as Paul did. In con-nexion I have remembered the text of Scripture from the 9th to the 14th verses of the last Chapter of Isaiah.

8

Discovery and Renewal

July 4, 1831–July 28, 1831

After 9 September 1830 Grimké did not write in her diary for ten months. During that time she contemplated what activity would occupy her life, now that she had successfully made a new home in the North. Not surprisingly, she considered becoming a teacher. Not only was teaching one of the few professions open to educated women in antebellum America, but Angelina had enjoyed her brief experience with that profession. When she taught first day classes at Third Presbyterian Church in Charleston she had felt a sense of accomplishment and wrote of it in her diary, and she was troubled when compelled to give up the classes. It is clear that Grimké felt she was suited to teaching young people.

On 4 July 1831 she left on a trip with friends John and Sarah Whitall that took them through New York, Massachusetts, and Connecticut. Her eventual destination was Hartford, where Catharine Beecher ran a school for girls. Beecher's reputation as an educator was established, and Angelina wanted to observe her pedagogical techniques and teaching philosophy in practice. While Catharine Beecher became a good friend, she and Angelina would, in just a few years, become embroiled in a public dispute over women's rights and abolition methods. On this trip she would also meet future literary figures Harriet Beecher and Lydia Sigourney.

This "excursion" was restful for Angelina, and the diary entries reveal that she clearly enjoyed herself. The fact that visits to prisons and a wool-carding factory were on her travel agenda is evidence that sightseeing was not the sole purpose of the trip. Moreover, the time she spent away from Philadelphia gave her an opportunity to see firsthand some women engaged in the profession she had been considering for herself. As she would eventually recognize and record in her diary, the time away from the Friends in Philadelphia, especially the Bettles, would allow an important opportunity for her to contemplate her future.

July 4, 1831   Left Phila. this morning in the Steam boat Preston & had the company of T. H. & J[ohn] W[hitall] as far as Burlington here as well as Bristol we dropped many of our passengers & this added to our comfort as we had been very much crowded. Passing Borderstown we proceeded to Trenton 7 miles further & 25 from Phila. where we landed & found many of the Stages & horses handsomely decorated with flowers in honor of the day. To my surprise I found the carriages delightfully easy instead of jolting vehicles I had expected to travel in. Over a level road we pursued our journey to Princeton 10 miles off—here some of the horses were ornamented of both garlands of flowers & bushes, a place of worship was open where no doubt an oration was delivered. We saw the College (a Theological Seminary) in passing thro' & going on to Kingston 4 miles further changed horses from thence to Brunswick where alighting from our coaches we entered the Steam boat Swan & enjoyed a comfortable meal after a rapid ride of 32 miles. The first place we saw on the banks of the Raritan was Amboy 13 miles from Elizabeth Town Point where after landing & receiving passengers we continued on our way & on entering the harbour of New York a delightful breeze sprung up & we approached the great city under very favorable circumstances the weather being clear and cool. This harbour is one of the finest in the world. Staten & Long Island make a beautiful appearance on the right with Fort Lafayette situated between them. Castle William on Governor's Island is an imposing object—on a nearer approach was seen the celebrated Castle Garden once a military fortress but now a place of public resort, having been converted into a promenade—on the top was flying the U S Flag of Stars—below which was arranged some theatrical scenery prepared I presume for the exhibition of fireworks to greater advantage in the evening. The Battery lies immediately behind & presented a moving mass of gayity & fashion. But notwithstanding all this and great quantity of shipping in the harbour with streaming flags &c. the main spires which proudly lifted their heads above the lofty houses around, I was sadly disappointed in the appearance of the harbour, for I had heard so much of it that instead of hills which skirt the surrounding shores I had expected to see lofty mountains & towering rocks—& instead of the artificial Promenade of Castle Garden I tho't I should have seen a wilderness of bounty. The wharves are far inferior to those of Phila, & but ill accord with the splendour of this metropolis. We had a pleasant ride up Broadway as far as the Park opposite to whh. we lodged & had a fine view of this public resort where hundreds were enjoying the cool air of a Summer afternoon. Boothes were erected on each side where water was sold & liquor was given away in consequence of a law prohibiting the sale of the latter. About dark NY seemed to have poured out its inhabitants into Broadway such was the crowd which were going towards the Battery & Castle Garden. We tho't it quite a favor not only to be above the giddy throng but to have been mercifully brought so far out the world as to feel no inclination to go to the fireworks to which they were pressing so eagerly, but rather preferred retiring to our own apartment before nine. The Museum & some other buildings near the Park were handsomely illuminated & transparences of Washington and Lafayette exhibited at the windows. So great was the noise & confusion in the City that it was difficult to sleep & in addition to this there was a huge fire about 12.

July 5 At 6 O'Clock found ourselves on board the Steam Boat Superior on our way to New Haven. The Morning was cloudy in consequence of which we were able to ascend the upper deck & enjoy the beautiful scenery on the Sound, this I had heard nothing of & perhaps was the more interested in it on that account. Brooklyn heights made a handsome appearance & the constant succession of handsome country seats, & rural cottages with sloping banks & verdant trees & here & there a little island presented a pleasing variety to a young traveller. The State Penitentiary was seen on our left about ____ miles from the city, it is a very large stone building but as yet unfinished, & could not inspire some melancholy reflections at the tho't of its one day becoming the habitation of guilt & misery, particularly if it is to be conducted on the arbitrary & severe system of the Auburn Prison in this State, which tho' celebrated for its order and discipline is I am inclined to think rather a system of vindictive tyranny than a system of mercy where the delinquent is punished with the benevolent view of winning time to virtue & true repentance. In passing up the Sound I was much struck with the beautiful appearance of the water the clouds began to break away & sometimes we would see little spots of light on the peaceful bosom of the waves which reminded me of those sunny spots in our lives which the mind loves so dearly to contemplate both in prospect & retrospect. I was soon recognised by N. Chauncy who introduced us to his sister after breakfast & they with Wm. & Harriet Norris from Lancaster Penn. proved to be very agreeable companions on the way. About 12 we approached the ~~harbour~~ town of New Haven—the Light House stands on the eastern point of the harbour. East & West Rock are situated 2 or 3 miles from the town & between them rises the Bluff of Mount Carmel still more distant. The white & dark stone steeples seen among the green trees & white houses have an interesting appearance, the wharf at which we landed is one mile long—over this we rode & thro' a part of the city admiring as we passed along the neatness & taste displayed in the buildings each of which has a lot attached to it ornamented with trees & grass plats. We put up at Tontine an extensive & agreeable establishment opposite the Green, round which is a white railing & a very beautiful row of Elm trees. After dinner we retired to our apartment in the 3d story where after a short repose we seated ourselves to write to our dear friend. N. C. called about 4 but before I could get down to see him he had gone having been told that we meant to sleep until 5 but this was a mistake for we were not quite so lazy. After tea went to call N. Smith & Noah Webster—the former was out riding, & the latter on a journey, but his wife received us very kindly & offered to take us to the burying ground which is large square divided into smaller compartments railed round, all of these had some monuments of the dead in them—long avenues of poplar trees led tro' them & these were carpetted with green grass—the tombstones displayed a great variety in taste, design & execution, one erected over a young man whose talents & prospects had been equally promising represented a broken column of white marble emblematical of the suddenness with which his prospects had been broken off by the hand of death. After spending some time in this cemetery we left it & continued our walk in which we crossed over one of the many neat bridges thrown across the canal. In returning home we met N. S. wife & daughters who had just been to call on my friend at the Tontine & returned home with them, we received a sincere welcome & after half an hour of sociable chat we rose to return home & received a kind invitation to spend the day, dine or take tea, as should best suit us, but intending to leave the next day, we declined doing so, & being somewhat fatigued with our travelling & walking were glad to retire for the night. N[oah] W[ebster]'s wife had also extended to us a hospitable invitation to tea for the following day.

July 6   At 5 O'Clock we joined our kind friends W & H. Norris in a walk thro' the town & gained some useful information by the queries he put to individuals as we passed along—from these we learned that the city was composed of 7 squares that the houses were built on lots from ¼ of an acre to one acre in extent—that a comfortable dwelling of 2 stories might be put up for $1500 & the lot purchased for $200 or 300 that 500 young females were then in seminaries in the town from different States in the Union besides the children of natives & that many families from abroad became transient visitors for the summer months & others had taken up their abode here for some years until the education of their families should be finally completed. Had encouraged us to visit Ethan Andrews School which we did after breakfast & were kindly received by himself & wife, he having been in College with two of my brothers. We were

conducted thro' the house into the Apartments devoted to the use of the pupils
—the first was where they studied & wrote—those below were Recitation
rooms—in one of them we stopped to hear a lesson from Worcester's History
with a chart, the pupils answered very well & appeared interested in their stud-
ies, but there was not that respect manifested in their conduct towards the
teacher which I think so essential in a well regulated school—they were rather
disorderly when they rose from their seats. After this there was an interval in
which the Principal of the School gave us some interesting views on the subject
of Education. The importance & pleasure of learning was the great stimulus
employed & this only because it is the only motive which would exert equal
power after School education is over as while it continued—no punishment was
employed excepting compelling them to leave their seats in the class if they
behaved improperly, these stimulants were found sufficient to produce the
desired effect in them even on the idle & indifferent pupil, together with the
respect manifested towards those who had made great attainments in learning.
The delinquent was also argued with & the impropriety of their fault set in
proper light before them. Latin Greek French & Spanish Languages were taught,
the two latter were spoken by the Scholars. Chemistry, Philosophy Botany,
Trigonometry &c. and a thorough an education given as at College, excepting
in those branches which wd. be useless to a female, (i.e. if the parents would
allow their children to remain at the Seminary long enough). Lessons in music &
drawing were given in the afternoon & in all 9 Teachers employed. The rooms
were furnished with chairs instead of benches. I saw no globe but many maps &
no Philosophical & Chemistry Aparatus. Lectures were delivered on Botany. At
the end of each year an examination was held at which the Parents & Guardians
& a few men of distinguished talents were invited to attend, but it was not a public exhibition & no prizes were distributed for it was held entirely in condescension to the wishes of the parents who were anxious to know what improvements
their children were making. After having received this information we were
invited to the top of the house where we enjoyed a beautiful view of the adjacent
hills, the tall steeples neat dwellings inbosomed in trees which were scattered all
over the City & the harbour—this edifice was a 3 story one with wings & was a
boarding as well as a day School; only 40 Scholars were at present in the Seminary. On returning home we passed a Presn: Bap: & Episl place of worship, the
latter had two steeples & was entirely built of red stone very much in the gothic
style. We also saw two market wagons quite new to us in their construction,
being small houses. We had not been long in the house when Wm. Norris sent

us word that if we wished to visit two places of worship an opportunity was now afforded, & on going down we were introduced to Judge Bristol who kindly procured the keys of an Episl. & a Presn. one which we visited. The former had a turret of sandstone the body of the building being of brick. It was built in gothic style, the ceiling being beautifully arched from the top of each pillar which was composed of 4 smaller shafts. The pulpit was painted white & the sounding board ornamented with a great deal of carved & stucco work giving it to our quaker eyes a very insignificant, trifling appearance, somewhat resembling the paper hangings we see hung up to catch flies. The windows were conically arched & the glass cut into diamonds instead of squares. In this there was a neat organ, but none in the Pres. both were heated by stoves & the paint consequently much smoked. I enquired of Judge B. whether he knew S. McCall from Caro[lina]. he did & offered to walk with me to see her but it was too late as I expected to be in the Stage in an hour. These places of worship together with ~~another~~ Congregational one were situated just opposite to the Tontine on the Green & these with the new State House (an adjacent edifice apparently of white stone with lofty columns at each end supported on a flight of steps) & the College buildings on the other side presented an uncommonly fine assemblage of public buildings. After dinner we set off for Hartford in a crowded coach. It rained almost incessantly so that we were obliged to be satisfied with such views of the beautiful scenery while we were passing up the Connecticut Valley as we could obtain by lifting the side curtains which it was well we had the control of for we were the only ones who seemed to care about looking out. The road sometimes run along the bank of the river, sometime further off, but was almost constantly between two chains of hills, at one time clothed to the top with verdin at another broken by little farms or handsome country seats diversified with fine trees fruitful fields & green pastures where sheep & cattle were quietly feeding. In our way we passed thro' Northford 10 miles from N.H. changed horses at Durham 8 miles further & passed thro' the beautiful village of Middletown 6 miles beyond— in looking back upon this after having left it some miles behind—it was truly picturesque, the houses being scattered like sheep upon the distant hills. There we alighted for a few minutes, left 3 of our passengers & took in a new one. Nothing worth noticing occurred until we reached Weathersfield when the clouds gradually broke away & a most beautiful rainbow appeared in the sky—it completely spanned the eastern hemisphere being very much elevated on account of the Sun being very low. After riding 4 miles we entered Hartford followed by repeated discharges of cannon whh. were fired on account of Monroes decease whh. took place on the 4th. Our horses literally ran into the town but as the way was clear no accident occurred & they were easily reined in when we reached the City Hotel which is a very fine establishment. After supper being weary we retired to bed.

July 7   After breakfast we rode to Thos. Perkins & left our address for Catharine Beecher who was in School, returned & begun our journals—she called about 2 O'Clock & arrangements were made for our being accommodated at T P's the next morning. Spent the afternoon in writing—after tea went to take a walk saw some very handsome large buildings, with beautiful gardens attached to them. The State house also, whh. is a handsome edifice in the middle of a square with a row of pillars on two sides & a statue on the top holding the scales of justice equally poised. In our way home called at J T Walls & left our certificate—he called a short time after & at his request we went home with him & spent the evening quietly & pleasantly.

July 8   After breakfast rode to T Perkin's where we were very kindly received. At 9 O'Clock went with C Beecher to her Seminary where we remained until 1. Here we met with a trial for the School was opened with reading the Scriptures & prayer at whh. we kept our seats. At dinner the family stood round the table while the blessing was asked but we sat & no doubt appeared like fools in their eyes. Went again to the School at 2 & continued until 4—then returned & as we were fatigued & the weather continued rainy did not go out ~~at all~~. The tea was handed round & immediately after, the doors were closed & T P read a chapter in the Bible & offered up a prayer at which we again remained seated. 12 scholars board here, they are very genteel in their manners & appear to be under excellent management, the house is as quiet as tho' there were neither young children nor boarders in it. T P & his wife are quite the gentleman & lady in their deportment. Spent the evening pleasantly in company with C B. & M[ary] P[erkins] they are very sociable & put many queries to us relative to our Society—but they have not yet found out why we sit at prayers & grace & I fear they will be tried when they discover that we are in so doing, bearing a testimony against forms of worship—opportunity I have no doubt will offer for us to explain our views on this subject & I trust we may be strengthened & favored to do it with meekness & wisdom.

July 9   There being no School on 7th days we have spent our time in writing. C B invited us into her study & we spent some time agreeably there—it is a neat parlour with a small Library—commands a beautiful view from the West & South windows & communicates by folding doors with her chamber & dressing room which are literally a double closet & can hold nothing but a bedstead, bureau & washstand—at night the doors are thrown open, in the day they are closed. She has very sociable manners & has been in our room several times today & converses freely & agreeably. Mentioned to us that 4 of her Scholars had gone to Alabama to open an infant School & a seminary there in Huntsville. She tho't I might prepare myself to become a teacher in 6 months remarked that her scholars were taught to feel that they had no right to spend their time in idleness, fashion & folly, but they as individuals were bound to be useful in Society after they had finished their education, & that as teachers single women could be more useful in this than in any other way, so ~~that~~ many of her pupils tho' quite independent had become teachers simply from the wish of being useful. Tho't it was great folly to think of teaching the Latin grammar in order to learn the English language, & believed this idea wod. be exploded as education advanced. She thinks that in 6 weeks a girl may learn enough Latin to understand the classification of language which is all that is necessary. After dinner took a walk with her to Lydia Sigourney's & while I remained in the grounds she went up to deliver my letter of introduction. When returning home the conversation turned on the moral & religious education of children. She could not believe that children well managed would ever turn out badly, in all the instances that had come under her observation in which the children of religious parents had done so, she had found there was some defect in the system pursued with them—either they were treated too strictly or too leniently or the parents differed in their views & the child was bro't up under a contending instead of a harmonising influence ~~of~~.

July 10   Went this morning to the little meeting 3 miles off but 2 men & one woman who were plain attended & a few young persons, it was poor indeed. The ride there & back was very beautiful and we enjoyed it much as this was the first clear day we had had since we arrived here. The weather is not like Summer but Fall. Passed Wadsworth's cottage, it is built in Italian gothic style & is truly picturesque being surrounded by trees. The pillars running up the gable ends are nothing but the trunks of trees with a limb extending from each & forming a natural arch in the middle—the well barn &c. are all in the same style. Spent the afternoon in reading. In the evening our friends came into our room & we passed our time very agreeably. Mary thinks I must be something of a Catholic because I live so simply. We have been quite amused to find how our letter was received here & what surprise our unique appearance occasioned. C[atharine Beecher] says she was quite astonished on opening it at the date & general style tho't it must be from two Jews until she came to that part in which we said we were members of the Society of Friends and Mary Perkins begged we would arouse her confusion in receiving us the day we called for she had been absent when our letter arrived, & had not heard of our intended visit, & never had seen a quaker before. She had never heard such an introduction in her life & was lost in utter astonishment at having Angelina Grimké & Sarah Whitall presented to her. But she behaved with great politeness tho' evidently embarrassed & indeed I have been quite surprised at the behavior of the people here & the boarding scholars particularly—none would know but that they were accustomed to our manner & appearance.

July 11   Accompanied Catharine Beecher to her School both morning & afternoon & as I have kept a particular account of it on a separate piece of paper shall pass it over here. Before tea Nancy Perkins called & after tea Charlotte Young one of the teachers who has treated us with great kindness. Spent the evening in my room writing.

July 12   Went to the School this morning—made our first attempt at drawing maps were much fatigued & returned before it closed. After dinner laid down a long time & at 4 set out in an open carriage to visit the State Prison at Weathersfield. The ride was pleasant affording a beautiful view of the surrounding country. Our two friends C B & M P accompanied us on horseback. On arriving at the prison we passed thro' an extensive meadow in front of the main building which is of brown stone. We were first shown into a very large & lofty area with 4 tiers of windows—in the middle were double stacks of cells 4 stories high 50 cells in a row, making in all 200—these apartments were very small & the beds were all strapped against the walls—when let down there seemed to be no more space left than would admit of a person standing beside them—this building had long piazzas extending the whole length in the 2d, 3d & 4 stories— the whole were whitewashed excepting the pillars supporting the staircases—all the doors were painted black—separate from these were the womens cells constructed on the same plan. We next saw the kitchen where the cooking was done by steam, their supper consisted of a broth made of pease indian meal & meat with bread—this broth was carried to their cells in wooden vessels where each prisoner was sent to eat it. We then entered the female working room where 18 were engaged in binding shoes—there sat in perfect silence & were overlooked by another female—if any of the prisoners spoke they were remanded to an empty cell & allowed nothing but bran bread & water. After this we were conducted into the different workshops thro' the yard on two sides of which they were arranged, one was a two story, the other a one story building—here some were working in iron, others in mahogany, others in leather, in some 20, in others 60 men were at work not a word was spoken & each shop was watched by one man, visitors were scarcely allowed to speak to each other in their apartments & never to a convict, if anyone wished to see one of them particularly, he was called out of the shop & their conversation took place in the presence of one of the officers. After passing thro' these we returned ~~thro' there &~~ being invited to remain to hear the religious instruction which was given them, we returned to the Guard room & stationed ourselves at a window ~~where we were~~ one which we had a full view of the range of shops at the extremities of which were 2 elevated towers before which were stationed two armed men as guards. Here we made many enquiries & found that in order to prevent conversation the same rule was adopted among the men as among the women & that in case of an insurrection the keeper of each shop was ordered to shoot the first man dead who attempted to move from his work. This excited very dreadful feelings in my mind & I could not compare the Penn. system with this & mentioned some of the particulars. Some observations were also made on the Auburn plan one individual remarked that this prison being visited by one of the keepers of the Auburn Prison, he remarked an individual who had formerly been under his care & enquired of the keeper whether he had not a great deal of trouble with him, upon being answered in the negative, he then queried of the man himself why he behaved so well here he replied, you treated me like a dog & so I acted like a dog, but here I am treated like a man so I act like a man. We were shown an old black man who was standing at the extremity of the second tier of cells waiting for his supper, he was imprisoned for life for poisoning or attempting to poison his master & had been incarcerated 23 years—was too old now to work being 108 or 10. This institution was founded 4 years since, contained 180 male convicts & 18 females & so profitable had their labors been that near $8000 had been paid over to the Treasurer above the expenses of the prison—every visitor was required to pay12 cnts. 6 O'Clock now arrived & we turned our eyes eagerly towards the shop doors when 5 files of men appeared (every individual in a file having his right hand in the shoulder of the one immediately before) & walked closely up to the middle of the yard where there was a board walk—here each file was examined by their keeper every man lifting his arms & quietly submitting to the search, before them stood their buckets all numbered, so that without counting the men it was easy to ascertain whether they were all present. Then at a signal were all uncovered, then covered & then each taking his own on his arm walked slowly into the spacious building before described, a vacant space being left in front of the cells—here they all stood in regular files & at a signal sat down on their buckets, for there were no other seats provided. The chaplain then begun to impart religious instruction by reading a few verses & then commenting upon them in a simple & correct manner I tho't then a few more & soon. No doubt vocal prayer was offered, but we left the prison before the Scriptural instruction was over. No female visitors are allowed to be in this apartment whilst service is performing, we were only spectators by looking thro' the grating of the door in the guard room—& this privilege I think must produce a hardening influence on the prisoners & ought not to be allowed instead of which we were rather pressed to stay. I can hardly describe my feelings on seeing the files of men marching from their workshops—it was a melancholy sight indeed to see some of my human beings brought into bondage by crime—some incarcerated for life—they looked so degraded & many of them so hardened, here the man of gray hair & the boy of 16, the white & the black, the native & the stranger met together— they were all dressed alike in dark colored clothing—here they all have an opportunity of seeing each other & knowing who has been a violater of the laws of the land—& tho' I think this system is far superior to that of the old prison at New Gate yet it seems to me greatly inferior to that adopted at the Penn. Penitentiary. Since writing this have been told that the money received from visitors goes to the Institution & that after the service of prayer is over in the evening— the prisoners march up the stairs & along the galleries & each stands before the door of his cell when at a signal given they instantly disappeared & a dozen keys are heard turning at the same time—the cells are 7 ft. long 7 high & 4 wide when these secured a guard is placed in this building who wears mockasons & as his footsteps are never heard no prisoner knows but that he may be close by his door—no attempt had been ever made at an insurrection & a measure of success has crowned the efforts of the Warden Pillsbury for reformation. Conversation is not entirely prevented for we saw 2 men speak to each other several times while they were standing in the yard. The salary of the Chaplain is $___. They receive religious instruction twice every day & hear preaching on First day. On returning home passed thro' the meadow and sometimes were in wilderness with a creek on each side sometimes in the midst of corn & potato fields or rich meadows with a beautiful prospect beyond of high hills fruitful fields & pretty houses. From one part of this road had a very good view of the wharves on the Connecticut & the bridge over it 360 yards long but this was old & dark in its appearance to add to the beauty of the prospect. The steeples & turrets & public buildings were very handsome, rising above the fine trees & inferior houses.

When riding into the city our friends pointed out the oak under which the Hartford Convention was held—it was a fine tree on the declivity of a hill on the top of whh. stood the house of then Secretary Wylley this had once been hollow & admitted of 3 persons sitting round a table within it but is now filled up. On our return found two friends of the name of Parsons. J[ohn] W[hitall]'s daughter also had called[.]

A substantial portion of the diary (approximately twelve lines) are intentionally blotted out. It apparently describes the beginning of a conversation between Mary Perkins, Angelina, and Catharine Beecher. The diary continues with the same entry describing the rest of the conversation.

The conversation then became more serious & after M had retired, I read the beautiful & touching piece of poetry written by E K after the decease of the young man she had been engaged to, dear Catharine soon became convulsed with agitation & it was not difficult to perceive some tender string had been touched & when the piece was finished & after a little silence she remarked that her case had been very similar & enquired whether we remembered the loss of the Albion 8 years ago and then mentioned that she was engaged to Professor Fisher who was lost to her. She went on to say how this affliction had been blessed to her & how completely the whole course of her life had been changed by it, that she had been uncommonly wild & tho'tless living without a tho't of religion, but since that time had been an altered character. Remarked that such an idea had never crossed her mind that he would never return & that when she received the letter from her father containing the sad intelligence, she could compare the state of her mind to nothing but a large manufacturing establishment in which the whole machinery was suddenly stopped, such was the perfect vacuum, the entire cessation of interest in everything she experienced. About 11 she left us saying that she had never expected to say a word to us on the subject but it seemed to relieve her to do so. Received a letter from Sister today.

July 13   Went to the school & try to draw maps. While there two of C's friends called on us & one of them invited us to tea tomorrow evening & we expect to go. Received a letter from Drayton. Went to the Deaf & Dumb Asylum, it is now superintended by the former Principal of the one in Phila. The exercises here were very tedious to me, for there was nothing of that variety in the exhibition which I had seen in Phil. & I was very glad when it was over & we were shown into the girls parlor—here we saw the one who is deaf, dumb & blind

also—she found out by feeling us that we were Friends—she threaded her nee-
dle for us and her work was very neat, she was sewing up a seam—we were told
that her sense of smell was so natural that she could select her own clothing from
that of the other girls when they came in from the wash she knew all the scholars individually & was generally content. While with the Exhibition room Dr.
Comstock came in & was very polite having been introduced to us at the School
he tho't we were Sisters & was quite astonished when told I was Thos. Grimkés
sister, why sd. he I did not know that Mr. Grimké was [from] a quaker family. I
said he was not, but only had 2 or 3 Sisters who were Quakers. Went into the
boys room, from the 4 windows of which we had very extensive & beautiful
prospects, none of the hills however were more than 600 feet high—the view of
Hartford with its 3 Presn. Steeples, very tall, one in the middle of town & the
other two at equal distances on either side with the other turrets &c. scattered
among the trees & houses made a fine appearance. Next we went into the boys
workshops where they were making mahogany tables, desks, boxes, &c. & leather
shoes, in the ware room there was quite a handsome display of furniture. 123
pupils are now in the Institution at an expense of $115 each—the boys work
5 hours & receive instruction 5 hours every day—the girls keep their own room
& do all their own work, but are not employed for the benefit of the Asylum.
Paid the Morgans a visit as we were going down to J T Wells where we took tea
& returned home before dark.

*Again a portion of the diary has been marked through. Interestingly, it is again a
description of a conversation involving Mary Perkins. It is not discernible whether the
entry was defaced shortly after it was written or later. It would be interesting to know
whether Angelina intended for the lines to be made unreadable. After five lines the
entry continues.*

I have been told that the blind girl at the Asylum might be restored to sight by an
operation, but there is no possible way of making her understand this & of
course she would make violent resistance to so painful an operation. She became
blind at 4 years old from an attack of scarletina.

July 14   Went as usual to the School this morning and took tea at a friends
called Watkinson, found several persons had been invited to meet us. We enjoyed
a walk in their large garden & a pretty view of the town & river & country from
the top of the house. Sat by a very intelligent man with whom I had much interesting conversation on the subject of Prisons & other public Institutions. Was

very glad I had been to the Penn. Penitentiary & I could say I had seen one of the convicts myself hope I was able to remove some prejudice which existed on account of its being supposed to be a system of total unalleviated solitude. Returned home before dark. Catharine & Mary spent the evening in our room, had some very interesting conversation on religious subjects—parted about 11. Have found that we could not come to Hartford under more favorable circumstances. The character of Quakers stands very high & the object of our visit being that of Education has tended to interest persons in us as it is one of such uncommon interest here. I hope we may ever remember with gratitude the attention we have received here. Were invited out this evening for 7th day but declined.

July 15   Went as usual to the School but finding nothing particular to attend to soon returned & spent the morning in writing. Received a letter from Sister Anna. In the Afternoon C accompanied us to the Insane Retreat. It is a white stone building 150 feet long by 50 wide & can accommodate 50 patients. It is on a farm of 17 acres & we saw the second class of patients working in a corn field & the worst class walking over the grounds under the care of a keeper— another class was shown us all females some were doing nothing others were employed in quilting. We did not see the convalescents because the presence of strangers produced an unhappy effect upon them. Dr. Todd is the Principal of the Institution. He has been very successful (in restoring his patients) (under the divine blessing) to reason. His treatment is moral as well as physical & medical— the patient is never confined unless it is necessary in order to prevent his hurting himself or others—the straight jacket is never used, but one which confines the hands only not the arms also. We then rode round to the summit of Rocky Hill from which we enjoyed a pretty prospect—the descent was so precipitous that we tho't it safest to get out of the car coach & walk down. Reached Lydia Sigourney's at 5—this is a very beautiful situation on Little River close to the Mill dam, the winding walks & shady trees, the flowing river & the water fall all combine to render this place interesting & lovely. We went to Washington College accompanied by Lydia S. C B. C[harlotte] Y[oung] and some others. I never was in such an institution before, but cannot say much for the whiteness of the walls or the cleanness of the floors. The Library contains I was told about 6000 volumes but appeared more extensive from the fact of a private individual having deposited his books here during his visit in Europe. After ascending 5 flights of steps we reached the top of the building which commands a beautiful & unobstructed view of the surrounding landscape, the Connecticut here & there making its appearance thro' the trees. Took tea at L[ydia] S[igourney] & here met with a young Greek who is educating at this College & is supported by Sigourney. C Young begged me to speak with him for we were great curiosities in his eyes, he never before having seen a Quaker—he soon gave me an opportunity of doing so by taking his seat by me, & I had known Stephinini & corresponded with Jonas King, it was quite interesting to me to meet with him—he is very intelligent, spoke much of Greece & said he expected to return when he completed his education. Returned before dark & met with H[arriet] Beecher at home who had arrived in the afternoon. She is very sociable & tho' I am glad she has come before we leave Hartford, still I cannot help regretting we have lost the pleasure of seeing her in the School. But I ought to have said how lovely a woman Lydia Sigourney appears to be—a perfect lady in her manners, agreeable in conversation & prepossessing in her exterior appearing to combine wealth & beauty— refinement, talent & religion in one beautiful assemblage. Spent an hour in Catharine's parlour but being much fatigued we retired at 9.

July 16   This day anticipated with so much pleasure by the youthful company whose party we proposed joining in an excursion to "the Tower" about 9 miles distant, at length arrived & the Sun shone brightly on the prospect of our innocent enjoyments. About 50 of Catharines scholars were to go & about 8 O'Clock the barouches began to assemble at the Seminary & each being numbered & every girl knowing the number to which she belonged, the arrangements were soon made & the lively procession moved off accompanied by Catharine the head of the party on her fine white horse Rolla—she wore a green riding dress the contrast was handsome—she is an expert rider & altogether the Cavalcade made in imposing appearance. John Whitall & S[arah]—H Beecher & myself begged leave to go before in our hack in order to avoid the dust & after a pleasant ride the day being uncommonly cool for the 7th month we arrived at the Talcott Mountains. This most elegant spot has been fitted up by Daniel Wadsworth a person who has a handsome establishment in the town of Hartford & also a pretty farm about 2 miles from the city, for the purpose it would seem of not of selfishly enjoying it himself only, but of generously affording strangers & visitors an opportunity of beholding Nature in one of her most engaging & lovely forms. Upon alighting from our carriage we were led thro a shady walk some distance when a beautiful lake expanded itself before us, it is about a quarter of a mile long & as wide—35 feet deep & is situated on the top of a very high hill enclosed on all sides by verdant trees, sometimes the rocks would rose in gentle slopes from its banks & sometimes they were more bold & perpendicular, but a broad pathway extended almost all round it—which we pursued but for a while when the little white boat house caught the eye on the opposite shore & the Tower lifted its head above the trees some way behind it—this looks like an antique stone edifice & appears to be built of the same rocks which lie scattered in wild confusion, but picturesque beauty all over the mountains & is fine object for the poets pen or painters pencil. As we wound our way still further round this rippling sheet of water we first saw the bath house a neat little white build-ing with its tapering spires—then the dwelling house built in Gothic stile its base being hidden by the tops of the trees which grew on more level ground. When we reached the northeastern part the path led into the woods & on coming to a rock we gained a more elevated station & looked down upon the lovely scene below us. We soon left this spot & descended again to the brink of the lake & perceived that all the shallow part of it was covered with green leaves & white blossoms. At length we reached the Boat House where we took some crackers and raisins. Our situation was soon arrested by the sound of voices in the woods & finding ourselves in a few moments surrounded by the lively group who had just arrived began to wind our way up the Mountain leaving them to talk over their little adventures & give way without restraint to the feelings of pleasure which beamed in every countenance. We had not pursued our toilsome path long when turning a little to the right we found ourselves on a steep precipice which commanded a fine view of the lake on one side & Farmington Valley on the other with its winding streams & little villages. We turned again into the woods & soon reached another rock—but going on we at last arrived at the tower the great object of interest as we all promised ourselves a charming prospect from the top of it. We now perceived that this seemingly brown stone antiquity was a wooden edifice but all acknowledged it to be a good imitation of what it was designed to represent. ~~With~~ Altho' weary with ascending the Mountain some of us immedi-ately begun to ascend the stairs which after winding round & round at length brought us to the top ~~of this~~ when looking round I found myself encompassed on all sides with a complete amphitheatre of hills & mountains whose fertile bos-oms were covered with fields of yellow grain, or verdant grass, with villages, cot-tages, orchards, or forest trees, all scattered in beautiful variety below & around us, with here & there a steeple lifting its aspiring head above the grave yard & the cluster of houses lying at its ~~foot~~ base, & there too, the Connecticut or the Farm-ington winding its way through the valley. On our side Mount Holyoke stood out in bold relief on the northern sky—tho' 40 miles distant and West Rock on the southern 30 miles off. Hartford, Litchfield, Farmington, Northington & Avon could all be seen beside many other groups of houses & the Lake too, that most lovely feature perhaps in this assemblage of beautiful scenery spread its rippling bosom to the gentle zephyrs & the bright rays of the Luminary of day—there too was the dwelling house embosomed in trees & there a bold projecting rock. After feasting our eyes for some time we begun to read some of the multitude of names carved in every direction about us even on the floor for there seemed to be room no where else but we found none that we knew & concluding we should not like ours trampled under foot returned from our exalted station willing to leave no trace behind us of having once occupied so elevated a place in the world. Pursuing the same shady path thro' th' woods we slowly turned our footsteps towards the house where seating ourselves flat on the stones we were soon encircled by the juvenile party who came up in little bands of 6 & 8—some eagerly engaged in carrying the provision baskets to the Saloon where we were to partake of the repast we all felt ready for—others set down & joined in social converse & one produced a little musical box which played sweetly for us. Harriet Beecher now came up & began to describe our dining parlour. It was long with green tapestry & carpeted with mosaic work & on the west side was hung a beautiful picture painted to the life representing the sloping hills & verdant trees the fields, villages & orchards which we had just been admiring so much from the top of the Tower. About 12 we were all called to dinner. The parlour quite equal'd the description & we seated ourselves on the graceful reclining setters & partook heartily of the sweet, or wholesome food before us just which best suited our taste. The Farmer had kindly provided us with ice—the driver brought us water from the well & our kind friend Catharine Beecher presided over the Table & I sent round the Lemonade and dishes, so that we had a plentiful meal I believe & again separated, but not before a messenger was sent to our old friend John Whitall requesting his company at our plentiful board, for he had not rendezvoused with the rest of our party, he however declined, having already eaten of crackers & raisins. Some of us went one way & some another, I accompanied H B & two others to the South Rock. This is a hill nearly opposite the Tower, its summit was clothed with trees, about half way from the large blocks of stone seemed to have been hurled upon it—or rather I should say the hill itself seemed to have been torn to pieces by some dreadful convulsion of nature by which these solid rocks were separated & hurled one upon another in wild cohesion while around the lower part of the hill were scattered thousands of small stones, apparently the fragments of the larger blocks which were piled above them. Here the trees were interspersed most beautifully affording us a refreshing shade after our toilsome journey & I soon found a seat where I could recline against the yielding branch of a young maple & enjoy the view before me—here by the lake before me—one side the neat white dwelling house with the bath house before it & the sloping hills & fruitful valley behind—in front of the Tower lifted its proud head above the trees—on the jutting rocks before it, were to be seen groups of girls in pink & white dresses & the boat house before them & on the other side of the lake were skirted with verdant trees & a pathway running on its brink. Here I sat a long time & changing my position sat in a still more awkward retreat & H & myself had a long talk about Friends being now left by our other companions. She took several sketches of the scene & about 3 we set off to meet our Company who we found sitting on the grass waiting our arrival. After partaking of some ice lemonade we got in to our hack & again headed the Cavalcade—the girls being busily employed in decorating the barricks with branches of trees. The ride in was warm & dusty & being much fatigued we gladly reposed ourselves on the bed until tea wh we had about 6.

July 17   Went to meeting this morning tho' it sprinkled rain & were repaid for doing so, not only by the convenience of having done right but J[ohn] W[hitall] appeared acceptably in testimony—two old men sat under the gallery both of whom were so much afflicted with rheumatism as to be obliged to walk on crutches, it was an affecting sight. JJW kindly invited us home with him but dear I was not well enough to admit of our venturing out except to meeting in such very cloudy weather so we declined—rode round to see the house once occupied by Richard Jourdin—it is a wooden building 4 rooms on a floor now but we were told that the roof had been altered so as to make 4 chambers, it was a lintel roof formerly. Simeon Arnold now resides in it. Tho't ourselves much favored in getting home without a heavy shower from the lowering clouds. We read & wrote in the afternoon when tea was over. I went to see JJW for it had cleared off & I had said if it did I would call. I also paid Parson a little visit, this was contrary to my usual practice but I tho't circumstances might excuse it. In the evening packed up.

July 18   We received a joint letter from S B T: it was very kind in her to write, to me particularly. Went to see a wool & card manufactory where the machines were moved by the power of Cur dogs. We were very much surprised & gratified by the inspection of it. First we entered a small apartment in which were 5 large dogs treading on an inclined plane of jointed wood which was continually turning as they incessantly walked up hill as it were, 4 of them needed nothing to keep them in their place, but seemed to work voluntarily, one had a leather collar round his neck, but they needed no one to watch them & worked in this way for near 2 hours at a time when they were relieved by another set—every dog knew his name & his place; upon inquiring whether they did not sometimes come off this plane, we were shewn a trap door just behind one of the places where they stood the unruly dog was put & if he came off he must fall into it this hurt him a little & frightened him so much that he very soon learned to keep in his right place. I was glad to find they were all fat & seemed to be kindly treated; at first they were fed entirely on meat, but this made them so ferocious that they were continually fighting—now they are fed on indian meal principally & a little meat. In the next apartment to our wonder we saw 18 machines all set in motion by Canine power & on examining them found the machinery very complicated but beautifully exact & regular—on one side stood a wheel round which was the wire this was cut & bent & hammered into the leather before, & the holes all punched & the teeth bent on the other side with astonishing quickness & exactness & think that all this was done by one machine & the whole 18 were set in motion by 5 dogs was very surprising & novel to us. We were told that a Bostonian by the name of Wittemore had invented it 30 years since but had kept it a secret. The purchasers of the patent were ruined by it from not knowing how to manage the machine—it sold for $70,000—and it was only in the last 6 or 8 years that it had been worked—each one cost $500. Next we went to see some ear trumpets but not thinking they would fit a friends plain cap did not buy them. Then we went to the Seminary to see C. Young & after a kind farewell from the teachers set off with C. B. to pay our visit & were very tired & warm when we got home. Finished packing & about 2 O'Clock C & myself set off to walk down to the boat expecting to go to Springfield this afternoon, but after waiting there 2 hours had to return, on account of part of the machinery being broken was rode up in the Stage & passed the handsome brick building newly erected—the basement story is appropriated to the Market the others to a City Hall Court room &c. the front is supported by lofty columns and the whole done in imitation of white marble. On reaching home found that S[arah Whitall]'s father had been to let her know the Steam boat could not go after she had been kept in suspence on hour, so we hardly knew whether she or we had fared the best but disappointments are good for us & I tho't it so much better to be thus detained than to have had the pipe break in the river that I was quite satisfied to return & feel it a favor to be again seated in my comfortable chamber writing my journal.

July 19 Spent the whole morning at home writing my account of the School off fair. About 2 the stage drove up to carry us to the Steam boat—on our way down called to take in some other passengers when a man stept up & told they need not get in as the machinery had again given way—all felt surprised & disappointed; hoping however to be able to get conveyance by land if we could not water, we drove to the Hotel & found our friend waiting for us & other travellers—the news was soon announced & we alighted to wait until arrangements could be made for our accommodation with a Stage. In about a quarter of an hour we were called out of the room & those who got in at the hotel of course chose the seats they liked best—however when we called for our other passengers we soon heard the declaration of "I can't ride with my back to the horses or I shall be so sick"—so Sarah & myself both gave up our places, she had the full benefit of the warm sun which shone immediately on the side of the coach & I was nicely packed in between her cloth riding dress & her fathers cloth coat—however we only laughed at our warm births & every thing went on pleasantly. We passed thro' Windsor & Suffield & had a very pretty view of Enfield on the opposite side of the river. Changed Stages half way & crossed three rivers—the Windsor, the Westfield & the Connecticut. S & myself changed places where we changed stages for I tho't she must be very tired of holding up her parasole, this being the best way we could think of for enjoying the air while at the same time she was shielded from the sun—the thermometer was 88 in the stage—9 persons inside & 2 passengers outside. About 7 O'Clock we reached the bridge over the Connecticut. We were told it was more than a quarter of a mile long & it really seemed so there is nothing elegant or neat in its appearance, being covered ~~in~~ with wood which looked as if it had never been painted, nor did I think we were very secure in passing over it, for the boards rattled & creaked beneath our well loaded coach. Sometimes we were almost in the dark from the shutters having blown too, & the only object of interest I could find in this gloomy structure was a transient view of the setting Sun who was enthroned apparently on the tops of the trees & threw a broad column of glowing fire into the depths of the river before us. After our warm & dusty ride we were very glad of some water & altho' refreshed by it found it rather trying to wait for our supper until half past 8—after partaking of it two of us retired to our room, but were so tempted by the pleasant piazza which ran across the second story of the house that we went out to enjoy the moonlight. I was soon left to enjoy my walk alone, but hearing Catharines voice also in the chamber I went in not wishing to keep the light burning on my account. I was the last to be ready for bed & was just going to step in, when a servant came to inform C that some of her friends were below—we immediately proposed her seeing them & laid very still in our beds while they had a social talk together.

July 20　Rose this morning much refreshed by a comfortable nights rest, but tho't instead of going to walk round the town of Springfield. I would stay at home & write my journal as I should have a good deal of fatigue in riding to Northampton & going to Mount Holyoke. Springfield is 26 miles from Hartford. There is a hill in this town at the foot of which rises a good many springs of water & one of these runs for some distance thro' ~~the~~ a Street under ground being arched over. Here is the U S Armory a flourishing Seminary under the care of Julia Hawkins once a teacher of C Bs she opened this School with the assistance of two of Chas.' scholars.

July 20　Had the promise of an extra stage at 9 O'Clock but had to wait until past 10. We had an extremely dusty ride of 20 miles to Northampton & arrived about 2, having passed thro' West Springfield & South Hadley Falls. We had promised ourselves the pleasure of ascending Mount Holyoke in the afternoon, but were prevented by rain—this mountain & Mount Tom had been at interval very interesting objects to us as we rode some times on the banks of the Connecticut & sometimes a little higher up. We are now staying at a Hotel which commands a fine prospect of these hills. After tea we were walking in the upper piazza enjoying the scene but I soon returned to my pen again being anxious to get my copying finished. Sent a note to T & A Napier informing them I was here. About sunset S came to tell us there was a rainbow, upon which I again went into the piazza. The scene was truly charming. Before us stood Mount Holyoke clothed with verdant foliage seemingly to the Summit & behind it darted up a broad pencil of white rays reflected from the setting Sun in the west—this looked very bright & beautiful—but did not suppress the appearance of Mount Tom upon which was resting the side of the rainbow while variety of coloring contrasted finely with the pure white light of the horizontal rays. Above were floating fleeces of white & yellow clouds on the asure sky & all seemed to promise a fair day of our anticipated visit to the mount. We were enjoying the beauties of Nature when I saw my Friends coming up to the house & ran down to greet them—they regretted they were boarders but hoped Sister & myself would come next summer & pay them a visit when they would be in their own house—they proposed going up to the Mountain with us in the morning & after a pleasant visit took their leave. I retired to my room & spent a comfortable evening in writing to S.B.T.

July 21　The sun shines beautifully clear & promises a fine view from Holyoke. After breakfast my friends T & A Napier called in a barouche to take us up the Mountain. I went with them leaving the rest of the party to follow after.

Crossed the river in a team boat where it is a quarter of a mile broad: & soon after we began to ascend the mountain, 4 of us alighted & walked up the rest of the way. We however rested where the carriages stopped & the rest of the party came up before we began the footpath. Never had I clambered up such a hill before, however it was not as fatiguing as I ~~had~~ expected & we all arrived safely at the top one after another—our friend John Whitall bore the walk up wonderfully & said he was not tired, which I believe none of the rest of us could. When seated in the house which has been erected for the accommodation of the visitors, we began to look around & were disappointed at finding the atmosphere so misty that our view was very circumscribed & not near as extensive as it had been at the Tower—but this did not prevent my enjoying what could be seen of this panorama of beauty. The winding of the Connecticut is very beautiful & serpentine, intersecting a large tract of rich meadow land where grass grew spontaneously & the farmer had but little trouble even with corn & eye of potatoes —these fields were spread like a finely shoded carpet at our feet with here & there a pretty village rejoicing in the abundance which surrounded it—from this level ground the high hills gradually sloped up to the distant sky forming an amphitheatre for some distance around us. Changing our position we saw Mount Tom before us which lifted his head too high for us to see anything beyond him— at his base glided the peaceful stream which runs between this mountain & Holyoke here it turns & returns in such a way as to form a pretty peninsula shaped like a fan this is meadow land adorned (as the rest of this low land) with single trees scattered here & there in picturesque taste & beauty. In the distance the valley seemed to extend for many miles & terminated in hills envelopped in mist. After partaking of some lemonade & cake & having our names registered on the books we began to think of commencing the descent which some tho't would be more trying & dangerous than the ascent, but I did not think so or find it so, for ropes on poles were fashioned from tree to tree in all the most difficult places & I could have got down in a very short time had I not stopped to wait for my two friends who being much older than myself were not quite as active. A little past 11 we reached our carriages & resuming our seats our party took the bridge road & we had a most delightful ride (cheered by pleasant conversation) of an hour & a half. We passed the neat little village of Hadley & rode at the foot of Round hill in Northampton & then turned & rode on the declivity. The two elm trees planted by President Edwards before his house were shown us here he had lived for many years & here his son President Edwards & Dr. Timothy Dwight were born & here too the devoted Brainard closed his life. His house was taken down & a large yellow brick building now stands on the spot. The elegant mansion of ____ Bower from NC was shown us—it is a wooden building with wings supported in front with round pillars & behind with square ones. There are other handsome private houses in this town & the public one at which we staid is also a very fine one indeed. We took dinner at 1 & after resting until 3 set off to Worthington 20 miles off. The road passed thro' a most beautiful & romantic country for a considerable distance at intervals it lay on the side of the mountain with a deep valley on one side with Westfield River running at the bottom of it over an extremely rocky bed & on the other by a sloping bank, on rocky precipice of about 200 feet covered with forest trees—we all enjoyed this ride very much for the interest was kept alive constantly either by the wildness of the scenery above & below us, on the extensive prospects of fruitful fields & distant hills clothed in living green which at times completely encircled us. This afternoon too we had a fine ~~prospect~~ opportunity of seeing the Sun drawing up water into the Clouds over a broad belt of copper colored sky which skirted the horizon bounded by deep blue mountains. About dark we reached our destination—& one of the party had so much rheumatism in her head & neck that she at least was glad of it. This was not a regular stopping place & therefore we were not entertained in the style we had been accustomed to on the road & were somewhat amused at the simplicity with which our chamber was furnished, it having nothing but what was absolutely necessary to comfort & that of the plainest kind. However we had a good supper & enjoyed an unmolested nights rest notwithstanding our many fears to the contrary.

July 22   After breakfast set off on our journey & continued to ascend the Housack[1] Mountains for 7 miles until we reached Peru which is situated on the highest ridge—the scenery continued rich in beautiful variety & I enjoyed it until about 10 O'Clock when I began to feel so exceedingly weary & sleepy that I had but little or no comfort for several hours. We stopped at the valley of Pitfield about 11 here some of our party wishing to visit the Shaker villages it was agreed to go round 3 miles further & pass thro' Hansuck & Lebanon. When we arrived at the latter I felt so fatigued that I did not want to take the trouble to get out of the Stages but rather than be left there alone I did so & went thro' the different departments of the establishment. Much neatness prevails thro' out & I felt repaid for the trouble of going over them & purchased some articles. We had not much time however to stay, & set off again. On entering the State of New York a beautiful view of Mountain scenery presented itself & Lebanon looked particularly pleasant to the weary travellers. Here we dined & resumed our journey about ¹/₂ past 2. We continued to pass thro' a very interesting tract of Country, but were now descending the Mountains. This afternoon saw the Catskill for the first time—they looked grand indeed being a great deal higher than any I had seen before. We made 10 miles in one hour. About 5 miles from Albany ~~the~~ some part of the iron work about the stage gave way—there was no danger attending it however, & on reaching a tavern it was propped on a rail & we proceeded onward—passed the barracks erected for the soldiers during the last war on approaching the Hudson the appearance of the city of Albany was very beautiful the houses are built on the slope of a high hill and have a fine commanding appearance—the sails on the river & the blush colored sky reflected the water with the broad pillar of light thrown across it by the Sun all added to the beauty & interest of the scene. We drove up to Congress Hall & our accommodations are to be sure a contrast to them we had the night we stopped at Washington, tho' I presume we shall pay pretty dearly for our handsome fare.

July 23   It rains today & we feel thankful we have not to travel in such unpleasant weather. Spent the morning in writing letters & talking by way of recreation—had it cleared should have gone to see the Cohoos falls about 2 miles above Troy, but it rains incessantly this afternoon & yet we are continually tantalized with the appearance of its clearing off for we have a great Sun colored dome just before our window & the enlightening effect it produces all around it is really singular. This is the gilded dome of the new City Hall which will be a handsome building apparently—our windows command a view of two public squares & I cannot help thinking from what I have seen of such specimens abroad that the Philadelphians are the only people that know how to make public squares in true taste & beauty beyond lies the Hudson with its hilly banks on the other side. I am sometimes surprised at the ease I feel in large Hotels. I feel as comfortable in them as if I was quite accustomed to travel & mingle in the fashionable crowd & care nothing about being a spectacle at table as I know we must both be. Today sat by a young man who was pleased to ask me to take wine with him of course I declined saying I was obliged to him but never drank it. After dinner our friend John Whitall came to our chamber door & with a countenance full of astonishment said he had come to inform us of a most singular request which had been made him by one of the young men. We asked him to walk in & eagerly enquired who it was. I guessed he wanted an introduction to us. I tho't he wanted to apologize for asking me to take wine, but no it was not one or the other, and our friend kept saying you never can guess for I never heard of such a thing, at last said Catharine he wants one of their caps: & what for he hastily enquired? why to get a pattern to be sure. Well you are a witch a witch I do declare, you must be a witch—how come you to think of such a thing. Why we exclaimed it is so in truth, yes he said he came to me & hoped to be excused for the liberty he was about to take & begged me to ask one of the ladies for one of their caps to send to the milliner to have one made by. We all set off in a full laugh & could scarcely believe our ears—but what was to be done. Why said I there is no doubt the man means to make fun of us and I should like him to know I think so. I was just telling the girls he asked me to take wine with him & believed then he was making fun of me. Sally said Oh no she did not believe he did & it was better just to tell him we did not feel liberty to do so without knowing what was to be done with it. We had many jokes & conjectures about the strange request during the afternoon & I wondered what I should do if I met him at tea tables. The bell rung at 6 & down we went. I was greatly relieved to find he was not there—but what was my surprise & sorrow in a few minutes to see him come in & seat himself in the same seat at the head of the table next to me. It was utterly impossible to contain myself—indeed C & S both joined me in a fit of laughter which lasted full five minutes. I dared not look up at all but shook all over, one man who sat opposite to us was as much amused as we were but the one who caused the commotion was as grave as a judge & offered me some cake with as good a grace as if he did not know at what we were laughing at. After tea enquired what he said to our message. J W told us that he said he had long been wanting a pattern of a quaker cap for a friend & had never before had an opportunity of getting one. But this we believe all a story of his own making, trumped up to conceal his sauciness for we do not believe his sober face to be a true index of his mind. Spent the evening in our room writing. Laforge.

July 24   As there was no Friends Meeting here spent the day in our chamber & tried to keep meeting there—read & wrote a little. After tea as S felt the want of exercise went out to walk with her father but as I did not remained in my room reading. The moon shone beautifully in the evening so we concluded to have no light & spent our time looking out on the lovely prospect before us & in friendly conversation.

July 25   This morning rose early & S & myself took a walk together by which she was much fatigued & has been suffering with headache from the effects of it. C took a delightful ride on horse back with one of her friends. After breakfast we took a hack for the purpose of going to see Cohoo's falls. On the way passed the handsome residence of Van Ransallier surrounded with a forest of trees—soon reached the banks of the canal on the McAdamised road—sometime rode between it & the Hudson, sometime both were on our right hand. Had a view of Troy on the opposite side. Passed the Arsenal the buildings of which occupy an extensive area of ground. About 8 1/2 miles from Albany saw the locks on the canal—some double ones—got out & saw one of them filled & the boat raised & passes up on higher ground—a little further was the junction of the Erie & Champlain canals—within a short distance there were 9 locks. The Western & Erie Canal has 83 locks which raise & lower the water 688 feet in all—it was to Buffalo a distance of 362 miles. About a mile from the falls (I think) we have a very pretty view of the bridge which is thrown across the Mohawk, it rests on two ledges of rock & 4 piers the sides are of diamond lattice work—this river unites with the Hudson on the other side of the bridge, they are then separated by a rocky island & again unites their streams below it. Here too we saw the rapids & in a little time the foaming cataract met our eye just before, it & the trembling rapids beyond. On reaching them we all got out of the carriages & approached very near the bank which is very perpendicular & 140 feet above the river—here we took our stand at different distances until finding as we tho't the most favorable position for viewing the falls we stopped to gaze on the sublime spectacle. I seated myself on the roots of a tree just above the abyss below them & in admiration & wonder for the first time in my life listened to the roaring of a Cataract waters as they were poured over a precipice 62 feet in height & about of a mile wide—this ledge of rocks extends completely across the river, but about the middle of a projecting rock in some measure breaks the uniformity of the falling sheet & over its sloping sides it runs in little streams leaving it almost bare—on one side of this the water falls about half way apparently into an abyss & another rock rising before it, occasions it to form up like boiling water & throw itself up in order to leap the barrier which would otherwise have stopped its progress. The whole of the rest presented an uninterrupted sheet of foaming water from the top to the bottom where a snow white spray (resembling the mist we sometimes see rolling from the mountain side) was thrown up perhaps 10 or 15 feet immediately below me on the surface of the water was a rainbow & all around had Nature planted the trees of the forest in wild profession sometimes bending over the Cataract & sometimes standing erect above the wall of rock which lifted them far above the rolling river below them. After remaining here about 1/2 an hour & being regaled by some pears our kind friend John Whitall had provided for us, we stept into the carriage & begun our journey to Albany—this road combines a great deal that is interesting—first it is Mt. Adamised then the Canals with their single & double & weigh locks & the boats continually passing up & down, the Hudson too is a noble feature in the landscape with its fruitful fields & thriving villages or towns—its fine dwelling houses & extensive Arsenal —the last however utterly failed to call forth either my approbation and admiration as its design was so contrary to those sentiments of "peace & good will towards men," which I believe ought to fill every bosom. The high hills in the distance too added much to the interest of the ride. We got home about 1 O'Clock & set off at 4 in the Steam boat Constellation leaving C B in Albany who said she would join us in New York. Had a very pleasant passage down the river, being much interested in the pretty island, sloping banks & distant Mountains which alternately or altogether met our view. At 7 we arrived at Catskill village & agreeing to stay here all night & go up to the mountain in the morning—we took lodging & are now seated in a very pleasant parlor writing—S her last letter home (she hopes) & I my journal, but our chamber does not promise to be quite so agreeable.

July 26   When we rose this morning found it rained so steadily that S & myself concluded there could be no use in our going to the Mountain as we should not see any thing to repay us for the ride. I mentioned to J W at breakfast what we tho't & proposed going on to New York—but this he turned a deaf ear to. Seated ourselves to write letters when he came in & said Angelina must not go from Catskill without seeing the falls come let us be off to the mountains for the Landlord says it is going to clear. This looked very improbable but still as both of us believed he was himself desirous of going tho' he insisted it is all entirely for my sake, we consented & about 9 the Stage drove up. As soon as I was seated I tho't I heard a well known voice but not liking to turn round & look at a person immediately behind me I waited until she spake again when being fully convinced it was Hatty Elliott from Charleston & turned & recognized her—we were both pleased to meet an old acquaintance & introduced our companions to each other. She was travelling with Robert Habersham & his daughter from Savannah. We soon joined in agreeable conversation & found another gentleman from New Hampshire who was equally sociable tho' none of us had ever seen him before. Our old friend J W was remarkably lively & afforded great amusement by his dry speeches & went on our toilsome journey with no other alloy to our pleasure than the distressing panting of the horses for the last 4 or 5 miles—for it rained but little after we set out & the breaking away of the clouds added a fresh stimulus to our good spirits & afforded us an opportunity of seeing & admiring the wreathes of mist which ascended from & rolled away from the brow of the mountains, which rose before us & appeared higher & more beautiful the more we approached them. Sometimes we caught a glimps of the Hudson, sometimes of the mountain house—sometimes were enclosed on each side by thick woods. At 1 O'Clock we reached the House which is situated on the ledge of a high perpendicular rock & overlooks a great extent of ground— this part of the mountain is 3000 feet above the river which is seen 8 miles off in a direct line ending its course among the hills & vales from North to South for a distance of 80 or 100 miles. In looking down upon the space between us & the Hudson, we found that all inequality of surface was lost in the distance, Mountains were levelled to plain & the smaller streams & lakes which ran among the hills & fertilized the valleys dwindled into little insignificant watercourses & ponds sometimes a foot or a yard wide—the houses looked like sheep scattered in the green pastures below us & the forest trees like bushes in the garden of nature & art. On the other side of the North river rose the Taugkannuc[2] and Saddle Mountains in Massachusetts & lower down a range of hills in the western counties of Connecticut. The prospect before us extended 100 miles in length & 150 in breadth—on the North & South rose two peaks of the Catskill higher than the ground on which we stood & therefore intercepted the view in those directions—but we did not stay long to look upon this immense picture stretched from side to side & touched with exquisite skill by the fair hand of Nature, but retired to take some rest before we set out for the falls. Dined at 3 & then got into a 5 seated Vehicle & after making some fun of the intolerable jolting we had over the stoney & slushy road & admiring the beautiful balm of gilead, black spruce, hemlock pine and other trees which crowded thick upon each side of the road at times holding up a verdant screen between bright rays of the sun & ourselves, we at last reached the place from which we were to begin our walk—this path way lay over rough stoney ground & by a winding course led us to the brow of a precipice where was erected a wooden platform, or kind of piazza at the side of which was to be seen the Catskill Creek, first rushing over a mill dam ~~then~~ a little behind us—then hurrying over its rocky channel & leaping the precipice over which we stood & after falling in the basin below a distance of 175 feet still keeping onward in its wild career & tumbling headlong over another rock 80 feet high & running along its rocky bed until it was lost in the impenetrable forest 260 feet below us. Toward the South and west, the ascending peaks of the Catskill lifted their verdant summits to the sky, & there shone the sun as he travelled over the blue of the sky with fleecy clouds scattered here & there as the dust of his feet. Eager to enjoy a still better view of the falls we soon left our stand & pursuing a path thro' the woods arrived at the head of the rude stair case which

led to the foot of the first fall. I descended pretty rapidly leaving two of my companions behind & just as I reached the bottom the flood gates opened above & a
much larger column of water rushed over the projecting rock which I now found
to be hollowed out in a semicircle 70 feet deep leaving a large space behind the
falls round which ran a foot path which appeared so narrow & shallowing as to
be extremely dangerous. I now went forward with Hatty Elliott R Habersham &
his daughter & as we approached this path he asked what we tho't of trying it. I
said it looked too perilous for me to attempt, but I should like to see him try it—
he accordingly led the way & as we followed on, all difficulty & danger vanished
& we soon found ourselves under the dazzling sheet of foam with the sun shining just opposite, but we stopped not long; impelled by an increased desire to see
this beautiful object in every point of view H & myself passed our guide & gaining a point at which the rainbow appeared most bright & complete hanging its
aerial & variegated form high in the air & gracefully bending down to the dark
abyss below, we stood still to gaze on the phantom of beauty. But this did not satisfy us we wound our way still further round & stood on a point of rock where
there scarcely seemed to be any foothold at all, but I believe where the mind is
so completely carried out of itself as ours was & so absorbed in admiration that
there is comparatively no danger for we had not time in looking at the deep
gorge below us & the shelving rocks which were built up from the bottom to the
path way on the brink of which we were standing, to think of the useful consequences of our false step; but does not this strikingly portray the conduct of the
tho'tless multitude who pressing onward in the crooked paths of sin & error
think not of the precipice on which they are walking nor the frightful abyss into
which so many are daily falling but continue to gaze on a phantom as delusively
bright & as fading as the rainbow. But this was not the only lesson I learned in
looking at the rainbow painted on the falling stream. I remembered it was the
token of that Covenant which God made with Noah; that He had set the bow in
the cloud as a standing memorial of his promise that the world should no more
be destroyed by a flood & when I saw it now, I could not but think that Man might
be reminded of this faithful & merciful promise not only by the bow in the cloud
but the bow on every glistening cascade of water. After gratifying our curiosity
as far as possible by traversing this pathway to the extremity, we began to return,
still stopping in our way back to take another & another look—but ought to have
said that R H followed us in his turn & went as far round as we did— ~~Whilst~~ and
then leaving us before we reached the Cataract descended into the basin of the
stream & crossed it on the rocks & met us on the opposite bank. While standing

on the extreme point of which I spoke before, I could hardly believe that the Steps I saw before me leading to the top of the rock were the ones by which I had descended, for they looked like nothing but ladders thrown from the top to the bottom of the step precipice. When we got back I found S sitting on a rock waiting for us to go up with her but our curiosity was not yet satisfied & H & myself proposed setting out to explore the path leading to the foot of the first fall. R H led the way but soon lost the path we ought to have taken, retracing our steps thro' the woods on the brow of the hill we at length reached it & I began the descent which was steep & slippery. Robert Habersham came after me & by dint of holding on to the roots & branches of trees & jutting rocks we at length reached the bottom not of the first fall but to my surprise & joy of the second, quite down in the very bottom of the deep gorge surrounded on the side by almost perpendicular hills & in front by the rock which was hollowed out 70 feet & over which the Cascade fell. As soon as I reached the bottom I took my seat on the trunks of some trees which were thrown across the stream for I felt weak & exhausted by the great exertion I had made but R H left me & I walked to the opposite side, I felt glad I was left alone & could enjoy in perfect silence the sublimity of the scene; silence, save the rushing noise of the trembling, foaming cataract—which urged its impetuous current from precipice to precipice imme-diately before me. As I looked upward at the place where it made its first leap, nothing was to be seen above but the pure bright azure of the vault of heaven, & the white stream looked as it was poured out by some water spout which had just broken & was emptying it contents on the top of the rocks. It fell in one unbro-ken sheet of dazzling foam, but from the place where I sat I could not see the basin ~~into which~~ below it but still nearer to me—it threw itself over another rock & rolling its agitated waters beneath me, it traversed the deep glade behind, & turning towards the South was soon lost in the thick shades of the forest. Nothing looked bright & shining but the white waters of the Catskill for the Sun was now too low to light up the dark & gloomy valley & here I could have sat for a long, long time but I was afraid of keeping our company waiting & proposed to return. I rose & began the toilsome journey up the steep & rugged hill—it is narrow, thought I just like the way of life & too narrow to admit of help from my human arm, here is a trial of my individual strength, I must stand or fall alone. With great exertion & patient labor I at last reached the foot of the steps when panting for breath I sat myself down to rest a while & take a farewell look at the falls of Catskill—after recovering a little I followed R H up the steep steps & O that I could with equal faith & patience pursue the upward course to Heaven &

arrive there as safely as I did on the top of the hill! We saw some of our party coming towards us—one told us that Hatty Elliott had gone to the foot of the first fall & her cousin turned back to meet her. I was extremely weary & took a seat on an old tree until I recovered a little from the exertion & then S & myself & another of our party set off to go to the Carriage where we found our friend J W & 3 others waiting for us. R & H soon came up & we were jolted back to the Mountain house but the ride was very pleasant being in the cool of the evening & a rough one, it was comparative rest to my weary limbs. On alighting we all went up to the top of the house to see the Sun set but this happened to be in a dark embankment of clouds, so that it afforded nothing remarkable, but what particularly attracted our attention were the soft sweet notes of the songsters of the wood singing their last requiem to the departing day. After tea were engaged in pleasant conversation with our Southern acquaintances but I felt as if rest for my body & reflection for my mind would do best for me & therefore retired at 8 leaving S to see the Moon rise. This I could see from my bed as our room fronted the east—there was nothing particularly interesting to me in her emerging from behind the distant Mountains like a ball of copper & as she gained a higher elevation throwing her somber rays on the Hudson, & this sometimes when she was quite covered with a cloud from our eyes. My imagination had been so powerfully anointed by my visit to the falls that my sleep was broken & after 2 O'Clock I did not sleep at all but waited to see the Sun rise.

July 27   This was very grand. The sky had been tinged by his rays for (two hours) nearly & after gilding the clouds which lay along the Eastern horizon he appeared between two dark ones just like a bright star so small a part of her disk was at first visible, he gradually throw back as it were the deep veil which shrouded his cheerful face & glanced his keen & piercing rays over the hills & valleys & thwart the placid stream of the Hudson & begun to gladden creation by his enlivening presence the little birds did not forget to welcome him back but chanted their simple notes of pleasure even before he actually appeared. We went down sometime before breakfast & enjoyed the view again from the piazza of the rich variety which was spread before our eyes—at table was pleasantly recognized by Dr. Phillips from Charleston—at $1/4$ past 6 JW.S & myself got into a barouche & in two hours & a quarter found ourselves transported to the village for as we were going down hill of course we travelled very rapidly the ride was very delightful affording us a fine opportunity of again enjoying the Mountain scenery. After waiting sometime in the Hotel on the wharf we went down to the landing. We soon recognized Catharine Beecher, & S & E Mason from Phil.

their company was very agreeable to us & I believe they were equally glad to see us. I enjoyed the wild & rocky hills which at times ran along the Hudson & sometimes completely enclosed it very much indeed. S M was very kind in pointing out all that was most remarkable as we passed along—the handsome country seats—the monuments at West Point Sing sing State prison &c. so that the day was spent agreeably. He also called my attention to Butternut Hill between 15 & 1600 feet high—on the west bank of the river—about 3 weeks since a man fell from the top of this & caught about 30 feet from the base but losing his hold was precipitated down & instantly killed. About 7 we reached New York. I think no one who has not been in the crowd of a Steam boat on it's arrival in this city can have any idea of the great press & bustle of such a scene. We took lodging at the American Hotel & being very weary retired to our rooms after tea & slept soundly tho' we were in such a noisy place.

July 28   Rose much refreshed & begun my journal before breakfast. One of S's old travelling companions called in to see her but at 10 we got into a barouche & rode thro' the city to see it. Some of the buildings are very elegant—the iron railings here are particularly handsome & costly—much more so than in Phila. & to a great many of the streets are wide & straight for a considerable distance. St. James Park is a beautiful square. Crossed in the Steam boat & rode thro' Brooklyn & returned about one very tired & warm—rested awhile when I again begun my journal. This afternoon took leave of C B who had determined to go to Boston—after tea walked down to the Battery this is a delightful promenade —returned at 8 & spent the evening in our room.

9

Divine Dispensation

August 3, 1831–June 25, 1833

Since her departure from Charleston, Grimké had not had to face much emotional turmoil. She had found a degree of solace in her life among Friends and no longer worried about what others thought of her appearance or her ideas. But as she returned from her summer excursion to New England, she was faced with important questions. She wondered what place she really had in the Society of Friends. Later she would question her place in any religious society. She also wondered whether she should become a teacher and whether she would ever become "useful." Angelina was clearly happier than she had been in South Carolina, but there was a restiveness that was reflected in the diary entries, and this got stronger after she returned from her trip.

The question that generated the most emotion during this period concerned her troubled relationship with Edward Bettle. The son of a respected and powerful family in the Arch Street Meeting, Edward had occasionally visited Angelina at Catherine Morris's home. At first Angelina didn't know how to receive him and worried about propriety and what people would conclude about their relationship. She alternately discouraged and promoted Edward's visits. Eventually, Edward stopped coming, and that too disturbed Grimké.

Sadly, Edward Bettle took ill and died in late September 1832. Angelina was thrown into an emotional upheaval she had not experienced since she left Charleston. Her grief eventually led her to become bedridden, but soon she recovered and looked upon Edward's death as a release from a potential domestic duty that she was never certain she wanted to fulfill. She even was able to admit that she was happier after Edward's passing. Undoubtedly she saw that a union with Edward Bettle would have prevented the pursuit of her public life, which she now began to envision for herself with more clarity.

August 3, 1831   Think it will be right for me to begin my journal again perhaps have lost much by not having written in it for nearly a year—for unwatchfulness has been the result. Have recently returned from a little excursion of about a month with S[arah] W[hitall] to visit C[atharine] B[eecher]'s school in Hartford. Have had my mind under some exercise as to my going there to prepare myself to become a teacher. Another subject of equal importance & solemnity had previously engaged my serious consideration & does still occupy much of my thoughts—but these two concerns seem to be directly opposite to each other so that I feel like the [unreadable] which was tried when two ways met. I feel the necessity of being still, of waiting until by the events of providence or the eternal evidence of the spirit my faith is made plain before me—until I am untied as it were & brought into the right way. Yesterday I tho't of Rebecca who when she felt the struggles in her mind went to enquire of the Lord. I felt these two concerns struggling together in my mind & would fair have queried too, "why is it thus"—for it seems as if both could not be right & yet as they have necessarily come before my mind I tho't they were of higher origin than my own willing & working. O that I may be kept still it is very hard to my nature to wait patiently.

August 21   Attended a very solemn meeting at Arch Street this morning S[amuel] B[ettle] spoke much to those who were in a state of insensibility. He rose with these words "Why stand ye idle all the day long" said he had been dipped into feeling with those who felt they were in a spiritual sense doing nothing in the Church, standing idle as it were, they felt their own weakness & were ready to exclaim I cannot dig, then spirits were willing but they had no ability to labor he warned such not to come to their beloved before the time—it would be far better for them to hang their harps upon the willows than to attempt to sing one of the Lords songs in a strange land—better for them to be willing to feel their own nothingness & patiently wait for the bubbling up of the living fountain & the lifting up of the light of his holy countenance than to stir up their beloved before the time, by impatience they might create animal excitement but these troubled feelings would be very different from the calm & peaceful flow of feeling which alone issued from the right source. He enlarged most feelingly on the necessity of lying here at the foot of the cross & being willing to feel our own weakness & the little way we were making in the divine life, yea, even our backsliding. Afterwards knelt & prayed most fervently that the Lord would remember the best of Zion. We could satisfy her poor with bread & would mine up Devils from the [unreadable] & [unreadable] to become as Mothers in Israel. Judge not the first, and Counsellors as in the beginning that we might not be given to reproach but that the Church might arise & shake herself from the dust of the earth. I believe this communion was for me & hope I may profit by it. When I told dear J[ane] B[ettle] about my prospect of going to Hartford to prepare to become a Teacher, she could not see it at all, tho't there was great danger in my throwing myself so entirely among Presbyterians. I felt much discouraged went to Wilmington that same afternoon & O how often was I made to remember the perfect clearness, & fulness & sweetness with which my other prospect had been opened on my view. No room was left for the doubting at all, for, it is a right thing, was continually sounded in my ear—& yet I was tempted to believe all this light was delusion of Satan but no, it was not, it was that evidence afforded by the Heavenly Father which it was sinful in me to doubt— & even tho' He may be pleased to withdraw the precious boon he designed bestowing on me, one account of my not abiding in faith & patience, yet I think I may truly say I did want to do his will not my own & was turned away from this thing by my fds. proposing the others &—E[dward Bettle]'s not coming to see me after my return to the City. It seems that they were all tried at my going away instead of staying at home to receive his visits they cannot understand it & I believe he felt discouraged & tried, & I have no doubt had no idea at all of my affections being engaged, or he could not have absented himself as he has done.

August 22 I feel most miserable today fear they must think me a most fickle & unmeaning creature. But I am not fickle my feelings towards him have remained unchanged even when I tho't he treated me with neglect. I was only persuaded by the enemy to believe I was required to sacrifice him in order to become more useful as a Teacher but all unrequired offerings are unhallowed & unacceptable offerings & I am left to suffer the loss of a friend with all the remorse of having refused a gift from heaven without any palliative excepting a faint hope & a little faith that if his attachment to me was rightly begotten he may yet return after these clouds of doubt & suspicion pass away. Saw clearly tonight where I had erred & believed it right, as I tried my friends feelings so much to acknowledge my error & tell dear J B that I had abandoned all my prospects of going away this seemed humbling as it would be equivalent to saying—I am now ready to receive E[dward]'s visits but dear Sister encouraged me to do in simplicity what my hands found to do & I was greatly relieved after determining to do so. Wrote her a note before going to bed.

August 24   This not appearing suitable in the morning being written too much under natural excitement—I willingly destroyed it & way opening for S to go to J B on business, I begged her to say what was right which she did.

August 25   This morning attended a very solemn meeting at Pine Street. I Gibbons appeared in supplication & my heart was melted believing I was one who was prayed for. In this monthly meeting great solitude was expressed by E. Evans for the young—much encouragement handed forth to the tried & faithful—much tender admonition to those who had lost their way, but did earnestly desire to return, & in whose hearts living desires had arisen to see themselves, just as they were & to become as passive clay in the hands of the Potter & be preserved & directed in the right way—& much more that was balm to my poor troubled heart. Was much impressed with the necessity of being willing to suffer now that I had erred tho' it was thro' unwatchfulness—not willingly. I expect my confidence in E's affection to be clearly proved by his absenting himself nevertheless I do now fully believe that he will seek divine direction in his movements & that whether it will be a week or a month it will not be in his own will. Have been enabled to pray that he may be directed by heavenly wisdom & not come before the right time. What a heavy trial it would be if he were taken with a fit of illness —how hard such a dispensation would be to bear just at this time—but I desire to commit ourselves into the hands of God as unto a faithful Creator & that his will may be done thoroughly done in us & thro' us is the trembling aspiration of my soul. Not because I am afraid to trust our heavenly Father but because nature shrinks from the furnace of affection.

August 26   Was favored with another solemn meeting this morning at Arch Street. E C preached a most beautiful, wakening, solemn sermon to young men—she remarked that some were there who had allowed some things to take such hold upon their afflictions of latter time as to produce lukewarmness & that if these did not let go of such things & give themselves wholly to God they could not be prepared to run of the Lords errands & do his work. I queried whether I must be given up by E & felt willing he should let go his prospects & try them on new ground if they should return.

August 28   Sat another very solemn meeting this morning. J Hubbard appeared largely in testimony & did seem to see our naked spirits before him— dear sister too threw in her two mites into the treasury—of latter times her tongue seems to have been loosed & if I mistake not a door of entrance is now opened in the hearts of the people to hear her, for a long time it seemed to me they were almost entirely closed to her communications, & it was a great trial to

me to see her rise, but now I can rejoice because I believe the cause of righteousness will be advanced by her faithful labors. This morning was enabled to
feel grateful that I was once more permitted to enjoy meeting.

August 29   Feel miserable this morning. What fetters of brass are to the
limbs of the body, so are strong feelings of interest to the faculties of the mind.
Can it be right for a christian to have their heart so engrossed by the subject of
marriage as to be able to think of nothing else? How far ought the feelings of
hope & fear as the views of the object of her affection to have place in her mind?
Ought she not to stand passive in quiet faith saying, not my will but thine be
done O Lord—or ought she not to bend to this oppressive exercise & go down
into the deep to be baptised into suffering in order to find out the thing that is
required.

September 16   Hope & fear anxiety & doubt are my daily, hearty portion.
At times am enabled to pray for perfect resignation to my Masters will, but others my strong natural feelings are tried beyond expression—how humbling to
any woman to feel that her affections are fixed on one who no longer pays her
any attention, tho' she may know as I do, that her own conduct has produced the
change in his. When under right feeling & reflect upon all that has passed, his
unequivocal attention my going away just after he began to visit me my saying I
was going back to Hartford & my going to his fathers house so freely & frequently, surely I cannot wonder he should think I did not care about him & therefore he should have withdrawn his visits. When I think on this thing I am forced
to say I have nothing to blame him for, but this is all the fruit of my own doing,
the work of my own hands & the least I can do is to submit patiently & cheerfully to the suffering I have brought upon myself. Then again I think these things
have been permitted in order that we may both try the foundation upon which
are moving—true affection like pure gold loses nothing of its real value or
weight by having tried in the fire & separated from the dross—so perhaps the
mysterious separation which has taken place between us for three months may
tend to purify the feelings of interest which have been awakened instead of
weakening & destroying them.

September 27   Have been thinking much this morning of a sermon
preached by J[ohn] L[etchworth] on first day morning. It was on the importance
of Saul who instead of waiting for Samuel as he had been commanded began to
offer sacrifices to the Lord. "Thou hast done foolishly"[1] was the language of the
prophet to him, as he assured him that Obedience was better than sacrifice & to
harken then the fit of ruin. How much have I been like Saul, if upon coming from

Hartford I had awaited in faith & patience for the regard of E's visits as I am sure I ought to have done I believe all would have been well but as he did not come immediately I gave up my mind to keeping school & tho't to suffer the unhallowed sacrifice of going back to Hartford & preparing myself to become a teacher. Often before J L rose did I immediately exclaim to myself in thinking of the course I had pursued. O fool that I was. The language of heart had been on 7th day night & has continued to be ever since. Lord let me suffer for I deserve to suffer. By yielding to the subtel reasonings of Satan I have been led captive at his will & did sin against the clearest light I know for myself from sorrowful experience that obedience is better than sacrifice, but O I think I can say I turned as soon as the conviction rushed on my mind that I had "done foolishly" & I desire to be thankful that I did turn before it was too late, & now I pray that I may be willing to drink the cup of suffering which I have mingled for myself, to drink it in silent sorrow & true repentance which is ever joined with the thankfulness for the chastisement. Sometimes I think E is only waiting for the right time to renew his visits & at such times I am permitted to feel the fullest confidence in his affections, believing that our separation has deepened & not destroyed the interest he felt in me, but when I look at myself & see my nakedness, my incapacity to fill the responsible stations of wife, mother, & mistress, I almost give up the idea of his return in despair, for surely he knows as well as I do how poor a creature I am & cannot still think of placing his own & his childs happiness in such unworthy hands. If I know my own unfitness, then is it not selfish for me to wish him to form such a connexion? if I really love him for himself ought I not rather to wish that at least to be willing that he never should return to me but this seems too much for my heart now. Then let me pray that the Lord would give me right feelings, for surely I do know not what to pray for as I ought—being ignorant of the end of their trials—scarcely knowing whether I ought to give up this thing entirely; or whether patient waiting only is required—but one thing I do know that at present I am to stand still & suffer.

October 5   When favored to view the circumstances within which I am placed with calmness I am led to conclude most certainly that if E's attachment is rightly grounded it will suffer no diminution at all from what has passed— & if it was not rightly begotten, it is far better it should have been thus closely proved before, than after an engagement or connexion was formal but I still do wish to be as in mind that my disobedience to the still small voice brought on the state of privation [unreadable] & to remember if it is turned into a blessing it is owing to that infinite mercy which is far from being deserved by me. Be still, be still is ever resounding in mine ears.

October 7   Went to meeting much tried at finding that my mind continued almost wholly engrossed with that subject which is at present the source of so much anxiety & trial, fear & hope it seemed impossible to shake it off altho' I was led to believe that those worldly cares were choking the good seed of the kingdom & hardening that exercise which appeared absolutely necessary to the growth of the divine life in my soul. Sat an hour somewhat humbled under the state of feeling & yet unable to raise the prayer for mercy on so miserable a sinner when S Bettle rose & remarked that the declarations of Scripture were true tho' we could not always realize them in our own experience. I have been thinking (continued he) of the words of our blessed Lord "Blessed are the poor in spirit for theirs is the Kingdom of heaven."[2] Now it is then tho't that for whom the blessing was pronounced are the very ones who feel unable to receive it, they are tho't so low as to be incapable of appropriating it to themselves; & feeling their own weakness & insufficiency of themselves even to feel their situation as they know they ought or maintain the requisite exercise they are almost ready to conclude that they are no longer under the divine care. My mind has been introduced into close sympathy in the meeting with some who are passing thro' the dispensation of barrenness and desertion. The apostle had the state to pass thro' & tells us he knew how to suffer want, that is he had learned to endure this state patiently to suffer with patient resignation, & I believe it is possible for the christian to learn in whatsoever state he is therewith to be content & to wait patiently upon the Lord. This & much more was said whh. suited to me & I was permitted once more to draw near to the communion table & partake of that bread which cometh down from above out of my fathers house—a sweet silence prevailed when E. Pittfield arose to comfort the feeble minded & support the weak, she pursued the subject S B had so feelingly enlarged upon & entered into sympathy with them who had been digging for water with the end of their staffs in the darkness, but found none, she encouraged them to dig on for they assuredly would come at last to the living fountain if they were willing to toil yet longer. All of us had our little cups to drink & sometimes we were ready to say "let this cup pass from me,"[3] but we should always add nevertheless ["]not my will but thine be done," ["]the cup which my father hath given me to drink shall I not drink it." For this encouragement of those who were under great discouragement she was willing to repeat a prayer of scripture which had occurred to her early in the meeting "Why sayest this O Lord & speakest O Faith, my way is hid from the Lord & my judgment is passed over from my God?[4] Hast thou not known, hast thou not heard, that the everlasting God, the Lord, the Creator of the ends of the earth fainteth not, neither is weary? there is no searching his understanding. He giveth power to the faint, & to them that have no might he comes with strength." She then went on to encourage such to wait upon the Lord, for assuredly they would yet have to sing a song of praise unto him, if they were faithful. S B had most beautifully commented upon the rewarding verse "Even the youth shall faint & be weary & the young men shall utterly fall, but they that wait upon the Lord shall receive their strength, shall mount up with wings as eagles, they shall run and not be weary, they shall walk & not be faint." Although borne down to the ground often times with a sense of their sinfulness & weakness, yet they that wait upon the Lord shall receive their strength & mount upward at seasons far above the quarreling, shaking cares of earth. These were the two gifted ministers closely united in travail of soul for the sinners in Zion, the poor in spirit, & a baptising time it was indeed to some present. S B appeared in solemn supplication at the end of the meeting & earnestly did he create for preservation during the few fleeting years that were to come that I involuntarily queried Will he be taken from us soon? & I was ready to say of him as John Feathersgill did of the aged & valuable minister who sat at the head of the gallery in the meeting attended as a young man, What shall we do when he is gone but I was checked by remembering that the Great Head of the Church was ever with us & that the memorial of that aged minister but proved a blessing to that meeting, 6 young ministers having been raised up after his decease. This consideration continues to rest with me.

October 9   Felt this morning that it was indeed a favor to have one day in every 7 set apart as a day of rest from worldly employments & desired I might be preserved from worldly tho'ts. It has been a day of much quiet, a solemnity has pervaded my mind & my heart has been tendered before the Lord under a sense of my sure unworthiness & his continued care & mercy. J L rose this morning in meeting with these words, "it is a great favor to have our love chaste" & tho' he applied it to our love to our holy Redeemer, yet it instantly struck my mind with so much force in reference to our love towards our fellow creatures that I have not been able to get rid of the impression, I have been permitted to pray that E & myself may examine our hearts & dig deep & beware that our love for each other is pure & chaste, that its foundation be laid on a rock (the Rock of Christ Jesus) not in the sandy foundation of mental or personal attraction or any rational advantages—that if brought together our domestic happiness may be able to stand against the floods of temptation & the storms of adversity which beat upon the heads of all in this vale of tears. Father into thy hands I commend our bodies, souls & spirits, do with us & by us & for us as seemeth good in thy sight, only guide us with thine eye here great & perfect resignation to thy will, whatever that will may be & prepare us to do all with thee hereafter.

October 13   Has graciously permitted this morning to drink again of the water of consolation through the instrumentality of Elizabeth Evans who came to our meeting this morning. Her ministry is indeed a stream of living water agreeably to the declaration our Lord "He that believeth in me out of his belly shall flow rivers of living water"[5] and may this win men "The mouth of the righteous is a well of life.["] She began by quoting the passage of Scripture "My soul is exceeding sorrowful even unto death, tarry ye here & watch with me."[6] In the most solemn & impressive manner did she hold up the example of our humble master as a man of sorrow acquainted with grief & queried how my sincere disciples would wish to be other than like her master. She poured the balm of consolation abundantly into the wounded heart testifying that tribulation was a token of divine power, & that anything which brought us near to the feet of Justice the place of prayer, was a mercy from God & should be cause of thankfulness, for we all know too well from our own experience that when prosperity attended us we are apt to sink down into a state of apathy & indifference so that even the best of us needed affliction & trial to temper our prosperity. When she saw those who had from time to time given proof of their allegiance to the King of Kings bowed under the weight of affliction, she rather required, believing they were visited & revisited in order to bring them to a sense of their own nothingness & to purify their hearts & cause them to see themselves just as they really are. With these she had been brought into near sympathy & trial to encourage them to hold on their way, who had drank more deeply of the cup of sorrow than any human being knows of, none but the heavenly Father knowing of the depth of their suffering. Much more did she say to the comfort of the tried & weary pilgrims in the faith flowing of gospel love, which seemed to come over my wounded heart like a healing ointment. O for true resignation, how my soul does crave for it at times—true resignation, not a state of indifference in which I may be contented with deprivation because I cannot help it & am unwilling to yield to the carroding feeling of anxiety & doubt, but a resignation which yields to suffering, willingly from a conviction that I do deserve it—thankfully because I believe I am chastened for my own good, & patiently because I am of all others the most unfit to judge of how long I ought to be left in the distressing state & silently because I ought not to seek alleviation in any way but by humiliation & prayer.

October 18   The language of my heart is that of Daniels "I have sinned, I have done wickedly but thou sheep what have they done?[7] Let thy hands I pray thee be against me," until the dispensation has done its work in my impatient heart.

October 19   Had been anticipating the satisfaction of going to 12th street M[onthly]. Mtg. for 3 weeks, but heard last night that E's brother was to pass meeting there today & therefore think I had better not go, as my motives wd. probably be misunderstood & I believe it best for me just now to be very guarded in my conduct & to avoid even the appearance of a desire to invite a return of attention which has been withdrawn as a punishment & fully believe from my Heavenly Father for my disobedience to the secret unfoldings of his will. I can see no other hand than His in my trials but they are very hard for me to bear— my temper has become impatient & positive under them & I have cause for daily, hourly repentance.

October 21   After the lapse of nearly 4 months E[dward Bettle] came to see me last night, find[ing] we were at Sister Anna's he came there & spent the evening. I hope & believe he has come in the right time. How humbling is this dispensation I am still passing thro'—my tho'ts all run in the channel of his name & no object can come before the view of my mind unassociated with him. He seems to be the clear & placid sky against which every object in the chequered landscape of life is drawn. O for preservation—how much I need it.

October 29   My mind feels truly solemn this morning. The vessel is below which is to bear my precious sister from me & I have prayed if consistent with our Masters will that we may be compelled to separate under a trying uncertainty as to my future prospects in life. But I can & do say Father unto thy hands I commit us & all our concerns "thy will be done."

December 12   Weeks & months have been passed in mental suffering. "Every heart knoweth its own bitterness" & whilst my countenance has been clothed in smiles my heart has often been filled with sorrow & sighing for daily, yea I most hourly do. I maintain a conflict for resignation to my present allotment. How strange is this even to myself when I look at the mercies & loving kindness which follow me every day—do I not deserve to be unhappy if I cannot be content with such things as I have, yes, I know I do, & it is a sense of my own base ingratitude to my Heavenly Father which distresses me for if I loved Him as I ought I would be willing that his will should be done, not mine, if I was as humble as I ought to be I should be grateful for the mercies received as to feel no inclination to reprove it that which is withheld.

December 24 Sat under two baptizing communications today from S[amuel] B[ettle] & T. K. The language of my heart is Lord. I thank thee, as I am so evil a sinner, that thou art pleased in thy infinite mercy to let me see it, & grant me grace to mourn over my ingratitude & idolatry, my hardness of heart & unprofitableness of life. I am deeply sensible that I am a poor sinner unworthy of the least of all thy mercies, much more of the greatest the mercy of God in Christ Jesus our Lord; He is an Almighty Redeemer, that my soul showeth right well & in the full & firm belief is all my hopes, for I know that no mortal, no angel can save me from my sins. I desire to be unfeignedly thankful my soul has been visited & revisited of bitter times. Oh how delightful once again to be permitted to drink of that stream clear as crystal which flows down from heaven to earth from Gods right hand, sometimes the waters of the pure river of life are quaffed by the thirsty soul as Gideons men drank from the river itself, at others thro' the living Ministers of the Gospel, who are like empty pipes conveying their soul refreshing streams thro' the Church & making glad the city of our God. Felelon says, "his condition is the best who is ready to suffer every affliction for the sake of God." Under my present trials I have sometimes tho't if this was religious exercise, if I was suffering for the Masters sake, I would cheerfully endure this affliction, but how deceitful are our hearts, how watchful our adversary to take advantage of these fleshy reasonings, for whatever be the trial we are called to bear, whether it be sickness, or the ill treatment of others or the effects of our own is as watchful & disobedience, all, all are born for the sake of Christ, when they are borne with the humility, faith & patience of Christ.

December 28 I never felt in better health & yet never did my life seem to hang on so slender a thread. I feel as if I was near the grave & I have often tho't S B's words in meeting last first day were applicable to me, "I believe he said that there are some here, around whose heads the curtains of evening are now closing." The subject of death has lived with me ever since, so much so that I have been paying some visits I tho't would burthen my mind should I be taken sick before they were paid. I think the feelings have been given to me to prepare me either for my own departure, or that of some dear fd. O that I or they whoever it may be, may be found watching when the cry of the bridegroom is heard. Lord I thank thee. I have lately been permitted to sit at the feet of Jesus & to wash them with my tears. I am a poor sinner & often feel as if I had nothing to plead, but the mercy, the unmerited mercy of a long forbearing God. The desire of my heart is that I may be directed in all things according to his will.

January 8, 1832   My mind has again been bro't under exercise on the subject of death & the language of my heart has not been Spare me O Lord, but prepare me O Lord for whatever thou art preparing for me. I am a miserable sinner & if I am saved, it will be this unutterable mercy.

February 28   Much of suffering & much of mercy might have been recorded in the weeks which have passed since I last wrote in this book. How well it is that we do not see the doubts & fears, the trials & temptations of that way which leads to the end of our wishes. Could I have seen the thorns & briars which I must pass thro before the object of attachment could be mine, the little interest I felt at first would have led me to say if I am to endure all this in order to possess him, I would rather not have him at all but the more I have suffered the more closely has my heart become bound to him, the longer we have been separated the greater seems to be the deprivation of his society, so that the love I bear him is not the result of excited feeling, but of the calm deliberate conviction that he is the friend designed by the Almighty Goodness to be earthly guide & counsellor, my companion in trvail & exercise, & partner in joy & sorrow. To receive such a boon surely great preparation & humiliation is necessary lest in holding the gift I forget the Giver.

March 5   For some weeks past have been looking forward to leaving the house of my Motherly Friend to make my home at Sister Anna's. Dear Sister S[arah] cannot see this step to be a right one & her last letter threw my mind into close & painful exercise on the subject for I hope I dread as much as she does taking a wrong step particularly one of so much importance. I answered her letter under much feeling & for several days, felt as tho' I had nothing to do but to stand still in passive silence. Yesterday the [unreadable] encouraging exhortation of Solomon rested much with me, "Ponder the paths of thy feet & all thy ways shall be indeed aright." The meetings were both solemn & refreshing to me, particularly that in the afternoon at whh. S B rose & offered much encouragement to the weary & heavy laden traveller who was ready to conclude he was not only lukewarm but had really backslidden from the truth. In the season of silence we have after tea, I was mercifully favored again to go down to the bottom of the well where spring the hidden waters of life & feel for myself that the days of my appointed time were nearly run out here & that tho' even given as a home it was about to be given away. J C spent the evening with us & truly the sublimity & sweetness of his spirit was to be felt. Altogether I have seldom passed so favored a day for which I desire to be truly thankful.

March 7   I think I see more & more clearly that this is no longer to be my home; The language of my heart yesterday was—"the Lord hath given & the Lord hath taken away, blessed be the name of the Lord."[8] When we are willing to "ponder the paths of our feet," we will always find that the right things lose nothing of their weight by being weighed over & over again in the balance of the Sanctuary. My mind feels oppressed with exercise, for the time seems to be drawing near when I shall not only meet my precious Sister once more, & leave this organized, quiet home, but when the subject which has so long engrossed my tho'ts & feelings will be more fully opened & it became my duty to determine whether I will become a wife, mother & mistress or not. O! for that pure wisdom which cometh down from above to help me in the awful decision, surely vain is the help of a man in such a case. To the Lord, the Lord alone do I desire to commit my ways in order that He may direct my path aright. Great are the conflicts I look forward to in entering into such a situation on account of E ill health & that of his dear little boy. Surely then things will continually remind me that the blessings are but borne & put me remembrance never for a single day to hold them as my own. That of myself I am entirely unfit to fill such station I am at times deeply sensible & that any sufficiency may be of God is at seasons the inspiration of my troubled soul. The prayer has arisen in my heart that as I leave each successive home which may be given me in this strange land I may be enabled to do so under feelings of gratitude & love to all under their roof—it was this I felt when I left this 18 months ago to go to T. Kite's—it was then I left his hospitable house & thus I hope to leave this in a few days. When I first heard unexpectedly that the vessel in whh. my beloved was, would be here in a few days, I felt exceedingly tried knowing that she could not have received my last letter on the subject of my leaving Catherines & fearing she would be unprepared for my continuing to think it was right to do so. I did not feel ready to see her, as it were & could not look forward to our meeting with that pleasure whh. it was so desirable I should; of myself I well knew I could not be prepared to meet her & I think sought to the Great Helper for right feelings & was favored on the 9th to meet her with real pleasure. We were soon left alone & she proposed reading a portion of Scripture which I did & we enjoyed a precious season of silence in which I felt thankful that we had one moment in the unity of the spirit & in the bond of peace; the desire expressed in my last letter to her seemed to be graciously granted, that we might meet in the love & fear of the Lord. As way opened in a few days I expressed to her my continued conviction that Sister

Anna's house was my proper home, she could not see it any more than before but said she had been made willing to submit to give me up this sounded strange to me for I so well knew the state of my mind that I did not believe she was losing anything at all—my feelings are so constantly absorbed in the prospect before me that I believe I can be nothing to any one, being almost wholly cut off from intercourse with the only one to whom I feel as if I could be anything. O! what a humbling dispensation to a christian, thus to have her mind so absorbed in an earthly object.

March 21   Dear Sister has given me up cheerfully tho' I believe she still stands in doubt as to the step I have taken she does not see it in the light I do. For some weeks I have fully believed that this was my right place not only because my board would be a help to Sister A but because I should be receiving visits whh. must either deprive dear Catherine of her parlor or make her often feel like an intruder in her own house—but this idea seems never to have struck her. The evening I expected to leave Catherines house to my great surprise dear Jane Bettle spent with us, it seemed to do my heart good to see her—in about half an hour [Edward Bettle] came in, my feelings on seeing him in our house after the lapse of near 9 months cannot be described tho' they may be understood by some who have passed thro' similar trials & anxieties. His conduct & that of his precious Mother seemed to confirm the belief I for some time had that he ment to renew our visits as soon as I should remove my home, & to my surprise Catherine made the same observation as soon as they left us, but Sister seemed never to have tho't of such a thing. I came home that night and have been favored to feel peace in the change, but last night we had some young company & I was betrayed into too much talking for which I have endured heaviness of heart, & I hope I always may.

March 27   This is indeed a sweet home to me because I am left so much alone. I came here not knowing the thing whh. would befal me here & desire to wait in passive silence the will of Him, who hath alone the right to form the clay into what vessel he sees meet. I have been thinking of the Y[earl]y M[eetin]g this morning. I want to feel more & more the impossibility of enjoying it without that preparation of the heart which is of the Lord. I want to keep out of the bustle & company consequent upon such an occasion & to feel that weak as tho' I was nothing to any one was anything to me. I want to go up to this solemn feast before the Lord with a lively remembrance of Him with whom alone I have to do & to sit in the great congregation an isolated being, ceasing from the arm of flesh & looking unto Jesus alone as the Author & Finisher of my faith. It is my grief & shame that so many of my tho'ts are spent on earthly objects & worldly concerns. O how my poor sinful soul cleaves to the dust & feeds on serpents food instead of on Angels. Truly I am in a strait betwixt two in outward circumstances & my Heavenly Father alone can preserve me from erring on the right hand on the left. I C spent last first day evening here, his spirit is inexpressibly precious it seems as if I could drink into it & feel the sweet influence of its purity & lowliness on my own mind. But under existing circumstances there is an alloy to his visit because of the peculiarly painful & delicate situation in whh. I am placed.

April 8   When I left the house of my precious friend to come here this language was strongly impressed on my mind "I go not knowing what shall befall me there" this has been speedily realized. I was looking towards an end to my trials and this selfish enjoyment of one to whom my heart still clings but Infinite Wisdom has ordered it otherwise & last week it opened on my mind to ask E Walton to come & spend Yearly Meeting Week with me this proposal she gratefully accepted when it was further opened to me that this was the home appointed for her permanently; & the concern resting weightily with me I proposed it to my Sisters & C W M who being willing I should move in it; I wrote to E who it seems had had the subject presented before her mind just at this time I had & as unexpectedly too. She had closed in with the offer, but desires it may rest with us only for the present. I think I can truly say & I do greatly prefer my Master's will to my own & can praise him for still holding back the promised boon from me & condescending to give me something to do for one of his dear sick children. I promise myself much satisfaction in being the companion & nurse of dear Elizabeth hoping I may indeed experience that it is better to be in the chamber of sickness than enjoying the selfish pleasures I had been anticipating. I have just finished reading "the Crook in the Lot."[9] I think I never read a book more in season to my poor soul. I can trace thro' its pages the line of my own mysterious experience, & tho' in looking at the state of my case I have suspected I was thrown into existing circumstances that I might feel for my beloved Sister & her friend, yet never before did I see it so clearly so satisfactorily. "A word in season, how good is it."[10] By reading this book I have been convinced of many things. 1st, that it was God who made the Crook in their lot, 2d, that I had nothing to do with trying to mend it for "who can make that straight which he hath made crooked," 3d, that my unhallowed attempts only plunged my Sister into still deeper suffering & made the crook even more crooked, 4th, that in my humiliation (my own prayers uttered in the agony of my soul when I saw her overwhelmed with grief & shame) have been answered, for "being in agony I prayed the more earnestly" that ~~the~~ if I had sinned I might see it, & that He would be pleased to punish me for it in the world, & not in the next. 5th, that my trials are designed not only to make me feel for them, but as a punishment to which I ought humbly to bend & for which I ought to be truly grateful—considering it is the work of God & not man—the chastening of a Father. This morning as I sat pondering on these things in meeting, I was struck with admiration at the exact suitableness of the punishment to the sin I had committed & the mercy with which the judgment had been tempered. For the first time I could say Lord I am now ready to undo the work I did as soon as thou art pleased to point out the sway & the time—if it be meet I should make restitution like Zacheus fourfold, O give me strength to do it, for truly I robbed thy dear children of far great riches than the perishing treasures of the world. I robbed them of peace & it was only of thy mercy that I did not rob them of that which Solomon says is rather to be chosen than great riches, "a good name." I adore thy Great Wisdom & Goodness and can kiss the rod & say ["]Lord for all I thank thee, most for the severe." These things filled my mind in the fore part of the meeting towards the middle I was startled by J L rising with these words Whether we eat, or whether we drink, whether we marry or given in marriage we ought to do all to the glory of God or words to that effect. I had never heard such an addition to the text before & it was delivered with so much solemnity that I tho't no one could have helped feeling it. My heart responded, let me not until I can do it to thy Glory—& often am I led in the secret of my heart to pray that the work of preparation may be fully done before we are permitted to come together, for that this is the Divine Will concerning us I continue to believe, tho' if I were to look at outward things I should say it cannot be, or why does [Edward Bettle] not renew his visits—outwardly there is no obstacles, but there is a barrier which Almighty power has erected & which he dare not overleap & I rejoice he does not attempt it, but is preserved from such an attempt.

May 19   For some time I enjoyed peace in believing the time had not yet come for E to renew his visits, I saw nothing of him scarcely & was freed from anxiety & trial but now that I often see him on account of his coming to take E[lizabeth] W[alton] to ride & he has paid us two visits I am again tossed & tried, my mind is wholly engrossed in thinking of him & for some days scarcely one good tho't has passed thro' my poor anxious mind.

May 30   I tho't I should just like to note the substance of part of a communication made in our meeting near two weeks ago by T K. After addressing a particular class he turned to some who had been passing thro' a deep & pressing

season of trial, desiring that such might be encouraged as the time of this probation was drawing to a close, and they would be favored to experience a change
of dispensation in whh. their hearts would rejoice & they would find that the
blessing they received would be sanctified to them by the Great Giver whose
every creature was good if received with thanksgiving. This was striking to me as
I had believed I did not suffer alone about—but that he was suffering with me &
had only been waiting for the right time & a little evidence that I was willing to
see him to come again. This week after J L also said a few words I think worth
recording tho' they were not spoken to either of us but as I tho't to J C who still
continues to visit me. He addressed one who was experiencing trial of mind
desiring they might be strengthened to bear the afflictions laid upon them & be
willing not only to see what the will of the Lord was concerning them but concerning others also. I feel tried at J's coming to see me as he does & have twice
lately left the room when he was here, for I do indeed shrink from the idea of
encouraging any man to pay me attention whom I cannot receive as I have reason to believe he wishes I should. O for preservation says my soul when favored
to breathe after any thing good—my mind is tossed & tried, subject to continual
disappointment & almost always struggling to appear not to feel what distresses
& perplexes me whenever I let go the shield of faith.

June 2   Last 5th day I was favored to sit a solemn instructive meeting.
S[amuel] B[ettle] spoke much to those in whom all sense of good seemed to be
extinguished & encouraged such to believe that the Almighty would yet clothe
those whom he had stripped. In the afternoon E W gave me a letter in which
much sympathy was expressed for the barren state of my soul. She quoted a text,
part of which had rested much on my mind "O that I were as in days past, as in
the days when God preserved me, when his candle shined upon my head, &
whom by his light I walked thro' darkness." This was indeed permanently the
case when I came out of the Presbyterian Ch. & that morning I had been reading over my correspondence with W McDowell & C M McIntire at that time, &
I could not but compare the personal state of my mind then to the insensibility
which clothes it now—my soul was then like a "well cultivated garden," but now
it is like "a garden that hath no water" & "an oak whose leaf fadeth." Then my eye
was single (I believe) & the glory of God was the great end of my actions, the
theme of my tho'ts, no earthly object then engrossed my tho'ts & affections, but
now how different. I was greatly troubled that day because E had not been to see
me for 10 days. I could not blame him for not coming, because I believed he tho't
he had once erred by coming too often, & that this time he was trying to avoid

that mistake, & yet the desire after his society is so strong that I cannot but feel troubled if I do not see him every three or four days. O these feelings of love, who can describe them—not even those who experience them—the thirsting of the soul after communion with the object of its sincere attachments, the sweets even of a look, the trembling anxiety, the timorous forebodings, the shrinking delicacy of feeling & yet the unbounded confidence of the heart O who knows them but those who who have felt them. He came that evening professedly to see his cousin & I am ashamed to say I felt as if I could not receive him kindly on such grounds, but these feelings were dispelled & we passed a comfortable evening there was more seriousness in his conversation & manner & I began to feel the influence of his spirit which I had much desired. He spent first day evening with us too the more I see of him, the more do I believe he is the man designed to be my counseller & friend.

June 18   When will I learn wisdom by the things which I suffer? This day [a] week [ago] E spent the evening here. I was engaged at C W M for he was sick & therefore left the house a few minutes after he came in & instead of coming home early I staid there until near 10 O'Clock & by the time I returned he was gone. I can hardly tell how my heart sunk when instead of finding himself here to welcome me, the parlor was dark and no one in it. At first I was exceedingly tried with him & tho't if he really had come to see me he certainly would have waited until I came home, or come to C W Ms for me, but when I remembered that I never had at any time (I believe) betrayed my feelings to him, & that he was (as far as I know) as ignorant now of the deep & lasting interest I have felt in him, as he was the very first time he came to see me; when I looked at these things I was constrained to take all the blame to myself & clear him entirely. And yet surely my heart was with him all the evening I would not voluntarily hurt his feelings at any time, but surely if I had wished to avoid his company over so much, I could not have acted differently from what I did & after staying near two hours, he went away no doubt concluding, at least that I did not care about seeing him. I felt my own disappointment very much, but I feel for him too now, because I have seen his Mother & brother since & am sure by their manner that they have been very much tried about it—he was unwell then & has since been too sick to leave the house. A new fear has come over my mind today. I am afraid that as they appear to know so little what my real feelings are & have been, that instead of imputing my sisters particular enquiries after his health to the tender concern I feel in him, they will think we are all making a cold hearted calculation as to his life & that I am just framing my conduct so as to keep his affection alive & yet prevent an open arousal of his feelings, lest I should be obliged to come to a determination before I find out whether his health will be restored or not. O how my soul shrinks from such selfish calculation on the holy & solemn subject of marriage. Such feelings could not find entrance in a heart so given up to love as mine. No! the language has been & still is, Lord give him unto me, even if I should have to be his nurse all his life, & at one time so improbable did I think his recovery that I scarcely even indulged the hope of ever being married to him even if I was engaged & yet my purpose & affections never wavered in the least. I cannot see how we ever are to understand each other fully for I am conscious of my own feeling that I am constantly on my guard to conceal them, whether this is right is a question I must soon seriously consider; but then again I feel so unfit for the station of his wife that I am constantly afraid of putting my hand to the work lest the work of preparation be not yet done & the Lord's time not yet come. O that I may see the path of duty!

June 19   How little do I deserve the goodness of the Lord. To my great surprize E & his dear Mother came to see us last evening, I was just going out when they came but I dared not do so afterward. T C came too tho' he had been only about a week before. I feel much tried at his visits on his own account, tho' I value his society very highly & esteem & respect him greatly—he does not appear to see the decided preference I feel. O that I may come out of this strait clear of all dissimulation & free from self reproach & condemnation from him. I hope I feel grateful for the returning health of my precious friend, he is very cheer ["]humbled at the contemplation of myself." It is said God hardened Pharaoh's heart, I think I know how. By permitting him to be tempted he fell into sin & sin hardens, not the gracious creator, my heart is hardened thro' the deceitfulness of sin, so that oftentimes I cannot repent, & so it was with Pharaoh. What judgments will be sent upon me I know not, but often do I think that let what amity befal me that might I should feel I deserved it & justify the Great Avenger of my sin.

June 24   Woke this morning exceedingly sad. It is but too plain that my heart is becoming more and more attached to E & find that my earthly happiness is altogether bound up in him, so that I am often greatly dejected simply because I cannot see him oftener. I am never permitted that unreserved spiritual intercourse which I so much desire. My heart was melted & softened by remembering that I was not so grieved at the absence of Jesus as at his, & yet I am fully persuaded that his constant presence would afford no pleasure to me without the approbation of our precious Savior to whom I could with tears appeal this morning in the language of Peter "Lord thou knowest all things thou knowest that I love thee."[11] The fear arose in my mind that I loved an earthly object more & the query was revived "Was crucified for you." But I do not— I feel entirely sure that Christ is the Alpha & Omega in my heart. Read Henry Martyn before breakfast & found my experience again, imbodied in words by him. In a dreadful storm at sea his Biographer says "He lay endeavoring to realize his speedy appearance before God in judgment—not indeed without sorrowful convictions of his sinfulness & appreciations for mercy in the name of Jesus, but, with a full confidence in the willingness of God to receive him." Such have in measure been my feelings since Cholera appeared here, but I have been ready to query Are these the feelings of the Christian? can this deep sense of sin consist with confidence & hope? Some say Paul was writing the experience of the unconverted sinner in the 7th chap of Romans—if so, there I am an unconverted sinner still, perhaps it will be right for me to cast away my hope & stand once again on the ground of condemnation instead of justification. Lord help a poor worm to see herself aright. Sometimes I think He who worketh all things after this counsel of His will, designs yet "to raise the beggar from the dung hill & set her among princes"[12] & that a time of treading down in the valley of humiliation must precede the elevation, a time of outward affliction & inward trial, a time of darkness & despair.

Afternoon   Attended meeting this morning for my mind had been sweetly solemnized for me to be willing to have it dispelled by idle conversation which I tho't I shd. be subjected to if I staid at home. It is my deliberate conviction that death can rob me of very little if his hand is laid on me, so poor & uncertain does all earthly happiness appear to me to be so glorious the rest of the righteous, but O! if I am to live & he lays his cold hand on the dearest object of my affections the world will be wilderness indeed, & I shall more than ever feel there is nothing worth living for but the glory of God.

July 15   E was here last evening. I cannot but admire & approve that candor which induces him to throw open his character to me by the free expression of his opinion on a variety of subjects—he seems to do it very designedly & thus to wish to show me what he really is. Feel very sensibly this morning the uncertainty of human happiness & its utter insufficiency to satisfy the cravings of an immortal soul. Nothing but Deity can fill "the aching void within" & I know that the most lovely & beloved earthly objects can afford happiness only in proportion as they are loved in & thro' the great Sourse of All Goods.

July 22   E W returned to us yesterday. I esteem it a favor that tho' her absence has been a great relief yet now I feel prepared to receive her; tho't as I lay by her side that as I had been unexpectedly released from the burden for 2 months I ought surely to be willing again to bear it & the desire arose that I might be enabled to let go my hold on my own concerns for a season & take hold of this work which I fully believe has been given me by my Heavenly Father to do. Has been very ill all day. One of her friends last night proposed her having a nurse, but dear Sister [Anna] & myself believe it is our business & desire if health & strength is granted to do to the last. This evening E mentioned her wish not to wear us out & yet a desire that we might be willing to nurse her to the end, and said she felt willing to tell us she had believed we would & that she had left us a full compensation for our services. I think I was never more surprised myself so, at the same time saying that it had all along been our wish to do so. Money can no more remunerate for the assiduities of affection & duty than it could purchase the gift of the Holy Ghost in the days of the Apostles. Nothing but the pure stream of gratitude & love can satisfy the demands of the heart.

July 23   Sincere desires have arisen that "as an hireling I might fulfil my day" for as such, I cannot help feeling myself to be now, & this is mortifying to the feeling of the natural man. This afternoon as I sat by her bed, the words of our blessed Lord arose before the view of my mind & again "inasmuch ye have done it unto me" & my heart was filled with a delightful peace mine eye with tears. I do indeed perform the most meanial offices for E & wait on her with the utmost cheerfulness, but this is all done from a sense of duty not from any feeling of love which would sweeten even a cup of cold water to the poor sufferer. I feel no sympathy for her, & therefore all my services seem dead because they lack the living principle of true love.

July 29   On 7th day evening E[dward] came to see me. We had a very satisfactory interview, the conversation being instructive & serious throughout. What then was my superior yesterday when E W solemnly reproved me for the volatility with which I had behaved that night she said she was much astonished to find I could leave her sick room & go down stairs & laugh & talk so loud—she said so possitively she had heard me that I tho't I must have forgotten & did not pretend to deny the charge. I felt tendered & told her how much I thanked her for her faithfulness & promised to think of it. Found from conversing with Sister A. that there had been a great noise in the Street which had disturbed dear E very much & which she could not be persuaded was in the street, but tho't it was in the parlor. I then remembered that when I went down I had opened one of the front windows & in this way the sound must have appeared to come from below instead of out of the street. Still however I was not satisfied, but endeavored to recall every topic of conversation & was upon reflection convinced that it must have been the noise in the street for I could not remember any thing which could have excited our [unreadable] at all. I felt in a hurry however to justify myself but desired to wait the right time, for "a word in season how good is it" to the order of our house, for the text rests with me by night & by day "Except the Lord build the house they labor but in vain that build it." ["]Behold I have graven thee upon the palms of my hands, thy walls are continually before me." Oh who can describe the sweetness of such promises when they are applied to the troubled heart in the power & demonstration of the Spirit. But O the hardness I have felt in Es mind today—it melted me to tears but my lips were sealed to her. I feel now as if I had cast my burdens on the Lord & that He was pleased to bear them, whilst I desire in childlike confidence to take the work he hands out to me from day to day & to do it for the love I bear him.

September 9   Amidst the perplexities & trials which have been incident to E W being with us I have had one strong consolation, the clear evidence that it is the right thing. My mind was brought under close exercise this morning in meeting about her, it seemed as if I could say in looking at our difficulties, "none of these things move me" and it presented very clear that I should have to write her a letter, describing some of the trials thro' which I have passed for her sake, & in christian love urging on her the necessity of taking up the loss & denying her appetite this is the only thing which has been denied her here, & instead of receiving it as a divine dispensation & binding her mind to her circumstances she is constantly struggling to bend her circumstances to her mind, but this she cannot do & therefore she is continually fretted & worried, because she thinks it so hard she cannot have just what she wants. This afternoon was strengthened by a communication from T H

Here there is a section of the diary that has been deliberately excised. The remainder of the page follows.

as if we were indeed walking in darkness about E W having no light as to how long our trials are to continue—no longer then is right I fully believe. O for patience to endure unto the ends. Much strength seem to be imparted for how true it is that ["]in the Lord Jehovah is everlasting strength."[13]

September 10   Had an open conversation with E W today—all was very satisfactory until I touched on eating—there was a strong spirit of opposition here a "pray thee have me excused["] in this "for it is a little one" but I believed it was required of me to use great plainness of speech & I shrunk not from sitting before her the bitter fruits which this indulgence had produced & then queried whether that thing could be right which had occasioned such discontent & disorder in our family. I urged her to look at these fruits & solemnly to consider whether it was not her religious duty to deny herself in what appeared to be the only thing which had been denied her here. She said it was the only thing, she knew, but seemed determined still to have her own way in this if she could by struggling for it.

September 13   Went out last evening tho' I was sure E[dward] would be here for now that everybody is talking about us I feel sometimes so tried at the embarrassing situation in which his not speaking to me places me, that I don't care whether I see him or not, came home late & found him.

September 17   Spent this evening at R E's. Have a heavy heart for too much talking great condemnation for not adhering strictly to the truth. I find it very hard to do this & daily err in this important particular.

At this point in the manuscript it appears that the upper portion of the page has been deliberately excised. The following is what remains.

& let me adore that Mercy which was [unreadable] such a time. A B sent him this message yesterday "I will keep him in perfect peace whose mind is still on me, because he trusteth in me"[14] & the same rested much with me for him.

September 23   Since I last wrote the floods of affliction have rolled over my guilty head, the judgment I feared has borne down upon me like the "blush of the terrible ones of the wilderness" & laid me prostrate in the dust. Death has snatched from me one whom I had fondly hoped would my friend & counsellor, my help mate in best things—but my Heavenly Father whom I love more than ever has in wisdom & mercy left me to look up to him alone as my head & husband. O I do humbly adore & kiss the hand that has smitten me to the ground—poor miserable sinner I deserve the stroke & far more, I know I do, therefore instead of wondering & murmuring I have been enabled to praise & bless his holy name—yes my prayer has been answered "in every thing I have been enabled thro' divine help to give thanks" my gourds are blasted—my pleasant picture stained, but let these earthly things be shaken, if so be it be found there are some heavenly things which cannot be shaken by the storm of affliction. Ah! my prostrate soul believes this & is comforted in the hope that the poor worm was permitted to glorify its Maker whilst in the furnace—the living desire of my heart has been that these things may deepen me in religious experience & strengthen my christian character. The 3rd. day after my friends burial I attended North Meeting, it was a time of refreshing to my soul—O A preached to me, I tho't— he said he had been bro't into sympathy with some who had a very narrow & difficult path to tread, but he would have them encouraged for tho' their road was beset with pits & nares he believed the Lord would be a Light to their feet & a Lamp to their paths & that they would be enabled to get along in safety & in peace. Last 3rd. day I attended again & W Evans said in the course of his communication that he wanted to encourage some, for that the Lord would give them a name far above any name that any earthly distinction could afford. O this name, on the white stone—how my soul did travail after it & desire it above everything else.

December 8   Thanksgiving & praise be rendered unto thee O Lord for all thy mercies which are more in number than the hair of my head. Since I last wrote it has pleased my Heavenly Father to lay me on a bed of sickness. I was most tenderly cared for by my dear Sisters & niece who did all they could to render me comfortable & the tears of gratitude often flowed & I could truly bless the Lord for all his mercies. I had every thing I could ask for & yet was unworthy of the least of the blessings that surrounded me & this sense of unworthiness sweetened the cup, when recovering from this attack of Dispeption[15] I went to spend some time at my beloved Catherines her society & that of dear Sister S[arah]—was a rich feast to my soul, so that I knew not how I should be willing to have them & contrary to all imputation I staid nearly two weeks. On my return home I felt the deprivation of their society more than I ever had before & the loss I had sustained in the death of [Edward] rushed forcibly over my mind so that in the anguish of my soul I exclaimed "Behold the goodness & the severity of God"—his goodness in that He wd. not permit me to destroy my own soul, his severity in tearing from me the object of my affections. My heart has yet at times to struggle hard after true resignation, for often does the tear start & the sigh arise in secret, for I feel my loss every day, tho' perhaps my dearest friends know it not. Last 5th day for the first time since my sickness I went to meeting. I was permitted to enter the banquetting house & my Masters banner over me was love. S B spoke on the subject of affliction & A Barker from the 131st Psalm. This was balm to my wounded heart. I was sweetly refreshed.

Between December 1832 and May 1833 Angelina wrote her tortured account of Edward Bettle's death and her struggle to come to terms with it.

May 13, 1833   The time will probably come when it may be of use to me to read the experience of these months of exercise in which my heart is often broken to pieces under a sense of that love which has followed me all my life long. The sorrows of my heart are like hidden waters in a deep well, unseen, unknown even to my dearest friends. God only knows the grief of my soul even now when I remember the wormwood & the gall. I have exercises & feelings to pass thro' on this subject which I dare not divulge to any human being secret baptisms which often beget the fervent prayer, that I may be purified in the furnace, and that this suffering dispensation may accomplish the thing whereunto it was ment, for I do believe if I am not measurably purified in these flames I must be destroyed by them. Save me O God for thy mercy's sake, & for the sake of Him who ever liveth to make intercession for poor sinners. Often do I realise that I am a poor miserable sinner. "God be merciful to me a sinner" for Months has been the prevailing language, sometimes the agonized prayer of my heart. And yet, for this secret of ["]the Lord is (only) with them that fear Him" there are seasons when I can exclaim with the Psalmist "The Lord is good to all them that call upon him"—yes & "greatly to be praised" & when the sweet feelings of gratitude flow in the strains of the poet.

> When all thy mercies O my God
>> My rising soul surveys,
> Transported with the view I'm lost
>> In wonder, love & praise.
> O how shall word with equal warmth
>> The gratitude declare,
> That glows within my ravished heart
>> But Thou canst read it there

Often during the last 7 months has my poor soul been visited by the day spring from on high. I have been permitted to sit at the feet of Jesus & to weep; & faintly to realize that my deep affliction has been a blessing to me, inasmuch as the tendency to lukewarmness has been checked, & the coal that seemed dead upon the alter of my heart has been blown by the storm of adversity into a flame for "He maketh the winds his messenger." But when I look at the loss I have sustained, with the outward eye all is darkness & despair & I am ready to exclaim, it never can be repaired, but I dare not utter this language save in the agonising conflict of a mind stung by the keen sense of present deprivation, & blasted hopes. It sometimes seems as if the lighting of Gods wrath had soothed & withered to the very roots the fair tree upon grew all the blossoms of hope, all the fruits of present joys but then again "I believe, O Lord help Thou mine unbelief" that thou art able to repair the branches made in my earthly happiness & to restore that which Thou hast taken away. But this, this is not the concern of my mind. "One thing have I desired of the Lord, that will I seek after; that I may dwell in the house of the Lord all the days of my life, to behold the beauty of the Lord & to enquire in his temple.["] This, this only is the fervent engagement of my broken spirit only let me come forth as gold from the furnace, only let the "broken vessel out of sight" be purified, & made meet for the blessed Masters use, no matter whether it be of stone, earth; or silver. Very, very often have I involuntarily exclaimed with Thos. More[:]

> O Thou who hearest the sinners prayer,
>> How dark this world would be,
> If when bereaved & wounded here,
>> We could not fly to thee.

I say involuntarily, because I do not like to make use of the secret expressions uttered by unholy & unfeeling lips, & yet this verse has followed me every where for weeks past & it is so appropriate to my feelings that I cant help repeating it again & again: for were it not for Divine Consolation I should even now faint under my affliction tho' I believe my dearest friends believe from my cheerfulness that I have quite got over the death of [Edward].

May 17   Altho' favored at times to wear the garment of praise, yet heaviness of heart is often the hidden manna given me to eat, & yet I cannot tell when it comes, sometimes I am ready to query with the Psalmist "Why art thou cast down O my soul & why art thou disquieted within me?["] for indeed after endeavoring to search my heart I often cannot tell Why this weight & burden is laid upon me, & at times I query, is this the baptism of the Holy Ghost & fire, if so, O that I may bear it patiently.

May 18   I have often remembered of late the language which was spoken in my ear, when I first arrived in Phila. With a heart touched with gratitude for my release from trials, I daily experienced at home I often exclaimed in the secret of my ~~heart~~ soul "What shall I render unto thee O Lord for all thy benefits" & the answer invariably was "The Lord will prepare himself a sacrifice." And he has, it was costly & precious indeed. Like the patriarch I have been required to offer the dearest object of my affections, but like him I did not find a ram to suffer in it's stead. No! it was actually taken & I daily feel the loss I have sustained. I cannot but regard it as a peculiar favor that I was permitted to commence the study of history immediately after my affliction. I believe it has been a great means of sustaining the poor mind, of diverting it from the sad contemplation of the bereavement it had sustained, & it is as much so now as it was then. As I begun to read with my neighbors I inse[n]sibly became very intimate with them & some of my fds. feel uneasy about this because the most serious & interesting had been disowned some years before, because she would not rise in meeting during the time of supplication. I never believed that either self will or obstinacy had been the cause of such a deviation from our established order, but a deep conviction of duty & tho' I felt no unity with the spirit which I believe had induced her to pursue such a course yet there was something so sweet, so meek & lowly about her that I could not help feeling demure to her & she was as unexpectedly & as strongly attracted to me & even more so, I think. My friends often asked me whether I had spoken to her on the subject—but I as often said that I regarded it as too solemn an one for me to touch without a special feeling that it was laid upon me from time to time my mind has been exercised about her & lately I have apprehended that when opportunity offered I should have open a conversation with her about it. This evening whilst sitting in silence at dear Catherines was brought reservedly to feel my loss very keenly & say as I often have it is only thro' faith I can say with the Psalmist "It is well"[16] to appeal with Peter Lord thou knowest all things, thou knowest that I love thee.

June 23   Returned last evening after passing 10 days with Catherine during the absence of my precious Sister. I am thankful I still know how to value such friends & do esteem it a peculiar privilege to be so welcome a guest under the roof of so valuable a woman. Whenever I have spent some time there & have again to return home I feel it a keen trial for I not only feel the loss of my friends society & that union of the spirit in the bond of peace which is as [unreadable] poured forth sweetening every little act of social kindness but I also feel renewed by the loss of him whose society for a few brief months rendered this home so pleasant to me & caused me to forget My mothers house (for C has been a mother to me in this strange land) in the enjoyment of his society, & yet such was the continual conflict of my spirit during that time, lest I should give to the creature the Creators due that I had no solid happiness, & I have often tho't on the whole I am happier since he was taken than I was before. No harassing doubts & fears pass upon my bosom peace now no earthly love interposes for a moment to usurp the throne of my heart but I feel & know Christ Jesus to be "my Lord & my God."[17] O I do reservedly feel that God "doth not willingly afflict or grieve the children of men,["] but that "in all our afflictions he is afflicted." He is a deeply sympathising friend being touched with a feeling of our infirmities. He only always sympathises with us, for his children are called to pass thro' baptisms which no human being knows of. The "heart knoweth its own bitterness"[18] & often times dares not disclose its sufferings even to Chn. friends. Today these words have revived several times "Thy Mothers children shall bow down before thee."[19] I don't understand then this afternoon as I sat in meeting bathed in tears I said with the Psalmist "my cup runneth over"[20] ["]my heart was filled with thanksgiving & the voice of melody."[21] I felt that the exercise occasioned by my afflictions had always produced the ~~spirit of~~ peaceable fruits of righteousness in my soul & thro' faith I believe they may be the means of preparing me for usefulness hereafter, but O how much depends upon my stillness now my patient abiding under the hand of the Potter whether on the wheel, suffering the drying shelf, or in the furnace heated of thine oftener than it is wont to be. Earthen vessels undergo the operation of the furnace last, gold & silver ones first. So we find now there are diversities of operations, but the same Lord. Some of his people He puts into the fire as soon as he lays his hand upon them it seems as tho' nothing could be done with them until they were purified, & the refining operation is repeated again & again until they reflect the images of their master from the unformed surface of the metal then they are taken out & the Great Workman fashions them according to the good pleasure of his will, some, apostles, some prophets, some evangelists some pastors & some teachers, for their own exaltation, or the applause of the world, but for the perfecting of the saints, for the work of the ministry, for the edifying of the body of Christ, just as the vessel of gold, & silver, & brass are all entirely subservient to the use of the Master & the accomodation of his household. These are trumpets sounding the alarm, censer sending up sweet insense to Heaven candlesticks bearing the light of truth snuffers, sometimes trimming the true lights & something extinguishing the false ones—cups filled with the new wine of the kingdom, laver containing the pure water of eternal life in which weary pilgrims wash their feet, fountains where the springing stream bubbles up to the lips of the thirsty traveller. But there are the vessels too in the house & not less useful I believe or less necessary because they are made of wood, stone, nevertheless they have never been in the fire—but the chisel & the hammer have done their work upon them & come of earth which have been put into the furnace last not first.

June 25   This morning I unreservedly feel that it is the blessing of the Lord which maketh rich & addeth no sorrow therewith not by the enjoyment of it, but by the absence of it. I feel unconscious of having bro't this miserable state of feeling upon myself by the commission of any particular sin, nevertheless I ought to pray "Set my secret sins before me in the light of thy countenance.["][22] Again I can truly say I am a poor miserable sinner. When shall <u>my</u> polluted soul ever be made white in the blood of the Lamb. O to <u>grace</u> how great a debtor I shall eternally be if ever I am saved. O Lord cleanse me from my sin for thy dear Sons sake.

10

Onto the Public Stage
December 1833–October 1835

Only fragments of Angelina's journal entries written after June 1833 are available. From eight loose pages the reader can detect Grimké's determination to achieve her place in the world and accept the "high and holy calling" that God had for her.

On these pages are her clearest statements on slavery yet, and she reveals that she had already decided to act publicly on behalf of the enslaved. She recounts her decision to send a letter supporting abolitionists to William Lloyd Garrison, a noted and widely despised abolitionist, who was then the editor of *The Liberator.* Her letter was subsequently published, and Angelina Grimké became an abolitionist as well. Unapologetic for her public acts and steadfast in her opposition to slavery, she seemingly without hesitation brushes aside concerns expressed by the leadership of the Arch Street Meeting and Samuel Bettle in particular.

Several interesting notes about these fragments should be mentioned. First, they reveal that once Angelina's letter was published, marking her first public act in support of emancipation, the diary abruptly ended. Second, the unusual spelling evident on these pages reflects her adherence to a spelling system that had been introduced by her brother Thomas Grimké, a self-styled educational reformer who was very close to Angelina. In one of the entries Angelina speaks of his unexpected death on a journey through Ohio.

∞

The beginning of this entry has not survived. Although its exact date is not known, based on the reference made in the entry following, it must have been sometime in December 1833.

Undated Fragment   deem us all my desire—only the means of spreading his gospel, & saving sinners is the first desire of my heart. Worldly honors or pleasures Ar. the small dust of the balance compared to these. At home I often had precious seasons of refreshment from the presence of the Lord, but in meetings I stand on the barrier mountains of Gilboa—why is there such a dearth in our land. Is the Gospel preached among us. Ar. we called to exercise repentance towards God & faith in the Lord Jesus Christ, or Ar. we called to the observance of our peculiar testimony as a society. Does not our ministry generally tend more to the casting off the branches than the laying of the ax to the very root of the corrupt tree. Truly my spirit thirsts after the naked Gospel Jesus Christ & him crucify'd. O that the Great Head of the Church would be pleased to raise up some among us to preach like Paul, who always sets his Master in front of himself & determined to know nothing amongst the people but Jesus Christ & him crucify'd.

May 12, 1834   Five months had elapsed since I wrote in this diary since which time I had become deeply interested in the subject of Abolition. I had long regarded this cause as utterly hopeless but since I had examined Anti Slavery principles I find them so full of the power of Truth that I am confident not many years will roll over before the horrible traffic in human beings will be destroyd in this land of gospel privileges. My soul has measurably stood in the stead of the poor slaves & my earnest prayers had been pourd out that the Lord would be pleasd to permit me to [be] instrumental of good to those degraded, oppressd & suffering fellow creatures. Truly I often feel as if I were ready to go to prison & to death in this cause of justice, mercy & lov, but perhaps I may be just like Peter who was frightened into triple denial of his Master. O! I think I do know my own weakness too well to suppose I can do anything of myself, but "thro' Christ strengthening me I can do all things" & I do fully believ that if I am calld to go back to Carolina, it will not be long before I shall suffer persecution of some kind or other.

June 15   My mind has been greatly exercised on the query, Is it right for me to unite with other denominations in the benevolent operations of the day? the great opposition felt by my wisest & best friends forced me into an examination of my experience on this subject—& I cannot help acknowledging that by mingling in such associations my attachment for & interest in the Society of Friends has been greatly weakened so that all exercise on their behalf has ceased. Now as such has been the result it affords an unanswerable argument to my mind that I had been essentially injured by such Societys, because when I look back to the exercise, convictions, & feelings with which I came among Friends I cannot doubt that this is the portion of the Lords vineyard into which I have been calld to labor, but if I love all interest and feel no exercise for Friends—how can I ever be prepared to labor among them. Another query arose If Friends take no part in the great moral reformation of the day, will it not be right to had them & go out with the duties which devolved upon me were prescribed by Him & tho' I had the sweet assurances of his help to assist me thro' difficulties I had never encountered before, & He did, I fully believe he did, for tho' my body was often weary, yet he spoke sweet peace to my mind. If it were not for some seasons of refreshment from the presence of the Lord, I know not what would become of my poor thirsty soul.

November 17   Last Month a deeply afflicting dispensation overtook us in the sudden death of our best beloved & most excellent brother.[1] Thro' mercy I was enabled to bow to the stroke & to kiss the hand which inflicted it, for tho' to all outward appearance he was taken under very aggravating circumstances, yet I experienced the secret "of the Lord to be wit them that fear him" & was shown that wisdom & goodness was markd on evry part of it & often did I forget my own loss of a Father Friend & Brother in the view I had of his glorious rest. Not a doubt rests on my mind as to his acceptance in the Beloved. My own loss too is nothing in comparison to that of my aged Mother, his wife & sons & some others. I weep more for them than for myself, yet I too had lost a great deal. The world too has lost an eminent Reformer in the Cause of Christian Education—an eloquent Advocate for peace & One who was remarkably ready for evry good work & works. I never saw a man who combined such brilliant talents, such diversity & profundity of knowledge with such deep humility of heart & such simplicity & gentle of manners. He was a great & good man, a pilar of the Church & State—& his memory is blessd leaving sweet savor on the mind.

December   Of late my mind at times has been coverd with much tenderness, contrition & humility. I feel a sweet freedom in approaching the footstool of mercy & pleading as a poor & needy sinners to had my sins blotted out & my heart purifyd. I find it a good thing to go into my closet & kneel down & pray vocaly. I believ I had had many a crumb by not using words in private devotion. My dear precious Sister [Sarah] told me so, & I was determined to try & the trial has been blessd in strengthening the things that remain that were ready to die & stiring up my luke warm feelings to true devotion & prayer. I can never be too thankful for such a Sister, she is the best friend I ever had & I never expect to have so valuable a one again, all things considered—she is a wise & good woman.

January 1835   My Heavenly Father has been pleasd from time to time to renew upon my heart the sweet evidence of his love & notice, Oh so precious to be able to say "My beloved is mine & I am his"—truly, great is the mystery of Godliness when we think of the greatness, majesty & power of Jehovah stooping to hold converse with such worms of the dust. My soul has often born to of late to desire to become a useful member in the Church Militant—to pray that the Lord would be pleasd to make me so, I know of myself I am utterly worthless, but his Spirit can qualify the meanest instrument & to had my heart again filld with love to God & love to the Souls his precious Son came down to.

The following two entries, written on a single page, have no identification as to month, and it is not certain whether there were intervening entries that are now missing. Given the contents of the entries and the one that follows, it is likely that they were written in August 1835. Certainly they were written after January 1835 and not long before those that follow.

26   Sat two lifeless meetings & O what cause for humiliation in some conversation after meeting with I. I. & M.A.S. my unsubdued will rose up in violent opposition because they could not think as I did about getting some of the prisoners in Arch St. to sign the Temperence pledge—a storm of passion arose & threw my mind into a sad state—the pilot seemd to had left the helm & all was in confusion—humiliation mercifully followd but not as deep as I had desired to be beaten with many stripes.

30   How humiliating to had so soon again to record my impatience & turbulence—had an argument on the subject of Slavery, tho' is so exciting a subject to me that I believ I ought to shun every thing like argument about it. I was realy rude to I. C. who defered a little only in passion with me. I never felt my tempter harder to control than now. I am most lamentably deficient in the crown of christian virtues—humility.

September   I believ it is right when we had passd thro' deep trials to record our feelings & exercises under them. It is now more than 4 weeks since I tho't it felt right to write W[illiam] L[loyd] G[arrison] a letter of sympathy & encouragement in regard to the efforts of Abolitionists & the violent opposition made to them. As far as I can possibly judge I believ that letter was pend under right feeling, in the spirit of prayer. I felt that it might involv me in some difficulty & therefore it was written in fear & after it was written I hardly knew whether to send it or not & therefore again implored divine direction at last I sent it to the Office & felt a degree of peace in doing so & as tho' I had nothing more to do with it than if I had never written it. I had some idea it would be published but did not feel liberty to say it must not be for I had no idea of my name being attached to it if it was. As 3 wks elapsed & I heard nothing of my letter I concluded it had been broken open in the Office & destroyd; this was just what I hoped would be done if it was wrong in me to had written it. I think I had no will at all about it, but committed it only to the divine disposal. To my great surprise last 4th day Fd.B[ettle]. came to tell me a letter of mine had been published in the Liberator. He was most exceedingly tried at my having written it & also at its publication. He wishd me to reexamin the letter & if I could to write to WLG disapproving the publication & altering some expressions in the letter. His visit was I fully believ prompted by the affection he bore me, but he appeared utterly incapable of understanding the depth of feeling with which it was written. The Editors remarks were deeply trying to him he seemd to think they were ravings of a fanatic & that the bare mention of my precious brother's name was a disgrace to his character when coupled with mine in such a cause & such a paper or rather in a cause advocated in such a way. I was so perplexd & astonished & tried that I hardly knew what to say & I said very little, declining however to write to WLG & expressing my belief that silent patient suffering would be far better for me than anything I could possibly do. That night I hardly slept at all & the next day I was sunk as low as I ever had been involvd in great darkness & desiring to feel utterly condemned if I had done wrong. I was truly miserable, believing my character was altogether gone among my dearest most valuable friends. My grief bound heart could not weep, but was sick of sorrow until evening, when I was enabled to throw myself as a helpless sinner at the foot of the Cross & plead for sight & for strength to undo, or to bear just what was required; I was indeed brought to the brink of despair as the vilest of sinners—a little light dawnd & I rememberd how often I had told the Lord if he would only prepare me to be & make me instrumental in the great work of Emancipation I would be willing to bear any suffering & the query arose, whether this was not the peculiar kind allotted to me. O! the extreme pain of extravagant prais to be held up as a saint in a public Newspaper before thousands of people when I felt I was the chief of sinners—blushing and confusion of face were mine & I tho't the walls of a prison would had been preferable to such an exposure. Then again to had my name, not so much my name, as the name of Grimké associated with that of the despised Garrison, seemd like bringing disgrace upon my family not myself alone. I felt as tho' the name had been tarnishd in the eye of thousands who had before lovd & revered it—but why enlarge—I cannot describe the anguish of my soul. Nevertheless I was helpd with a little strength and tho' I sufferd so deeply I could not blame the publication of my letter, nor would I have recalld it if I could. I believd

I had some right, that tho' condemned by human judges I was acquitted by him whom I believ qualifyd me to will it, and I felt willing to bear all, if it was only made instrumental of good. I felt great unworthiness of being used in such a work but remembered that God hath chosen the weak things of this world to confound the wise and so was comforted. Since this time my greatest trial is the continued opposition of my precious Sister S[arah] she thinks I had been given over to blindness of mind & that I do not know light from darkness & right from wrong her grief is that I cannot see it was wrong in one ever to had written the letter at all & seems to think I deserv all the suffering.

October   O the goodness & mercy of God. He has been graciously pleasd to deliver me from the trial & the apprehension of trial with regard to the writing of that letter. The storm seems to have gone over for the present Condemnation I do not feel & I think I had been enabled to cast the responsibility on Him by whose direction I think I wrote it. Latter times had been times of precious visitation to my poor soul, times of refreshing from the presence of the Lord— words of encouragement has been spoken by the Lord's servants at last I had receivd them as adapted to my state, but not without the earnest prayer that I might not be permitted to take what was not assigned for me. Times of opposition or times of proving and searching and digging, good and profitable times to the single eye & sincere heart. O I sometimes feel as if I am willing to do anything if the Lord will only purify and refine & make us useful in his Church militant & prepare me at last for him.

it surrounds Grimké's rhetoric, extends to the private as well as the public and includes the intuitive as well as the rational. Although the consideration of a private journey for personal discovery does not *necessarily* inform us about subsequent rhetoric, in Grimké's case it clearly does.

Private Struggles Won, Public Battles Engaged

Angelina's diary totals 337 handwritten pages. Almost 200 of those were written between 10 January 1828 and 10 October 1829, exactly twenty-one months. The remaining 137 pages were written over a period of six years. Clearly the regularity of entries dropped significantly. What was the reason for this diminished attention? It may be that keeping the journal became too tedious and time-consuming. It could be that once she arrived in Philadelphia she was too busy and simply did not have the time to devote to it. More likely, however, the urgency of self-expression and the need for renewal of spirit were no longer as strong as they had been in Charleston.

The fact that Grimké stopped writing as regularly as she had before, I think, reflected a change in her felt need to demonstrate self-sacrifice. Not only was the frequency of her journal keeping slowed, but the depth of her worry also diminished. No longer was she distraught over her situation, whether it was her opposition to slavery, her religious conviction, or her family conflict. Though she was still far from contented, by autumn 1829 she had already determined that she was a Quaker and was steadfast against the "depravity" of slavery. In addition she was convinced that she no longer belonged in her native state and had left Charleston. What then awaited her? What was she to do now that she had determined those things? No longer did she agonize over who she was, but what she was to become.

Always mindful of the obligations of her faith, Angelina sought to find sanction in the Word of God. The entries in her diary are replete with biblical references and examples from the faithful. Noticeably, these references diminished after she left Charleston. The reason, most likely, was not that she no longer required the guidance of the Word, but that the decisions she faced after moving were quite different than those she faced in South Carolina. In Charleston she sought personal renewal and her search was spiritual. By the time she arrived in Philadelphia she sought opportunities for service, and that search was more temporal than spiritual. Finally, she sought to define duty, and that search took her from the domestic sphere to the political.

She had tested her antislavery resolve in 1828 by confronting her brother successfully. But by summer 1831 she still had not decided what activity would occupy her life. She, no doubt, was still convinced that she was destined for a high and holy calling but still did not know what that was. When she started on her "excursion" to New York, Massachusetts, and Connecticut in summer 1831, she planned to visit prisons, manufacturing organizations, and schools, in particular the one in Hartford headed by Catharine Beecher. Even after that trip was over, Angelina still thought that her future might well involve "keeping school." But she never reflected much enthusiasm for it, and it was obvious that she had not yet made that choice.

Her tortured relationship with Edward Bettle, a man she considered marrying, confused her. It is obvious in the pages of her diary that she was never comfortable with accepting the role of wife and mother. She was clearly attracted to Bettle but was never able to make a commitment. She was never able to come to terms with what would be required of her if she married into the respected Bettle family. In a way, Edward's premature death released her from this trial. Even though emotionally she was injured by his death, she wrote soon after that she had been happier since Edward's passing. It is not insignificant that she recognized that she was now free to pursue *her* future, and not Edward's.

Surely the death of Bettle allowed Angelina finally to reach the destination her journey had been heading toward all along. It is likely that had she married Bettle or become a teacher, as she once contemplated, she would have been forced back yet again to a spiritual search to redefine her identity. Her closing of those prospects presaged an important aspect of her celebrated letters to Catharine Beecher, which appeared in print just months later.[3]

As early as 1828 Grimké had written in her diary of her antislavery feelings. She had even acted on them in small ways within the confines of her own home and among the disapproving but loving gaze of her family. Six years later she wrote that she had lately become interested in abolition. The difference is dramatic. Abolition required more than just action at home within the family; abolition was serious business that required a public act. It was more than making the plight of slaves more comfortable; it was revolutionary. Expressing her feelings no longer did anything to satisfy the cravings she felt in her heart. It is clear that by May 1834 Angelina was beginning to realize that it was time to do something, and do it publicly. She was now more interested in a remedy than she was in the problem.

The diary closed just as she stepped onto the public stage, perhaps prima facie evidence that what had begun seven years before as a private struggle of self-definition had become a search for useful methods of service. Within three years of the last diary entry Angelina Grimké became an important soldier in a very public battle. It could be argued that in those three short years she made more difference in the battle for abolition than any of her contemporaries.

A High and Holy Calling

July 1835 was a turning point for Angelina. She was led to write a letter to William Lloyd Garrison in defense of abolitionists. She urged forbearance in the fight to remove the sin of slavery once and for all. The moment for which she had struggled for seven years had finally come. Angelina had finally put her personal struggles behind her. She was ready to embrace the "high and holy calling" she believed that God had promised her. She knew what it was, finally, and no one would deter her from fulfilling it—not Friends, not public opinion, not self-doubt, not even her beloved Sarah. Once her letter was published, Angelina Emily Grimké was an abolitionist and a public figure. No longer did she "belong" to anyone. No longer did keeping a personal diary serve her.

Notes

Introduction

1. Katherine DuPre Lumpkin, *The Emancipation of Angelina Grimké* (Chapel Hill: University of North Carolina Press, 1974), 149–50.

2. Larry Ceplair, ed., *The Public Years of Sarah and Angelina Grimké: Selected Writings, 1835–1839* (New York: Columbia University Press, 1989), 319.

3. Ibid., 320.

4. Ibid.

5. Ellen Todras, *Angelina Grimké: Voice of Abolition* (New Haven, Conn.: Linnet Books, 1999), 8.

6. Catherine Birney, *The Grimké Sisters: Sarah and Angelina Grimké the First American Women Advocates of Abolition and Women's Rights* (reprint, Westport, Conn.: Greenwood Press, 1969), 5.

7. Ibid., 5.

8. See Lumpkin, *Emancipation,* 15.

9. Birney, *Grimké Sisters,* 15.

10. Robert Rosen, *A Short History of Charleston* (San Francisco: Lexicos, 1982), 75.

11. David Robertson, *Denmark Vesey: The Buried Story of America's Largest Slave Rebellion* (New York: Vintage Books, 2000), 35.

12. Stephen Howard Browne, *Angelina Grimké: Rhetoric, Identity, and the Radical Imagination* (East Lansing: Michigan State University Press, 1999), 1.

13. Kenneth Burke, *Attitudes Toward History* (Los Altos, Calif.: Hermes Publications, 1959), 203.

14. Richard Gregg, "The Ego-Function of the Rhetoric of Protest," *Philosophy and Rhetoric* 4 (spring 1971), 74.

15. Ibid.

16. Ibid., 74–75.

17. Ibid., 81.

18. See John Fletcher, *An Appeal to Matter of Fact and Common Sense or a Rational Demonstration of Man's Corrupt and Lost Estate* (New York: John Wilson and Daniel Hitt, 1810), 26–58.

19. Lumpkin, *Emancipation,* 59–60.

Purification and Perfection

1. According to Sarah's diary, Angelina destroyed several of Sir Walter Scott's novels. Obviously there had been a significant change of attitude about her reading

choices. Given the reference to this incident in Angelina's autobiographical sketch, Anna Braithwaite was probably responsible for this change of heart. Speaking of the Braithwaites' departure from Charleston, Angelina wrote: "O my heart clung to them, it was very hard to give them up, but their work here was done and they left us—about 10 days after I tore up my novels took the bows off my bonnet and the lace out of the cap and stuffed a boss with some lace veils, etc. I am sure I was strengthened by this." For further discussion of this incident, see Lumpkin, *Emancipation,* 31.

2. John 16:12.

3. This entry is X'd through in the manuscript but is clearly readable. The servant referred to was named Kitty. Gerda Lerner writes that the family would afterward refer to this incident when charging Angelina with being self-righteous. See Gerda Lerner, *The Grimké Sisters from South Carolina: Pioneers for Women's Rights and Abolition* (New York: Oxford University Press, 1998), 52.

4. Acts 9:5.

5. Luke 23:34.

6. Angelina had long had a difficult relationship with her mother. As the diary reveals, Angelina believed her mother to be distant and coldly indifferent. Her mother thought that Angelina was often too abrupt and unkind.

7. Henry was Angelina's brother.

8. Matt. 6:10, Matt. 26:42, and Luke 11:2.

9. In her autobiographical sketch Angelina describes the incident this way: "I believe it was the 12th month of this winter that I was strengthened to give up wearing a handsome cashmere mantle thinking it was too expensive ($20 was the price) and too gay (red) for a humble follower of the Master—this night I fully determined never to wear it again."

10. 1 Sam. 5:4.

11. Ps. 133:3.

12. Matt. 20:21–22.

13. Song of Sol. 6:10.

14. James 1:27.

15. Ps. 46:10.

16. Ps. 119:96.

17. Phil. 1:6.

18. Rev. 12:10.

19. 1 Pet. 1:8.

20. Eph. 6:12.

21. Ps. 46:10.

22. John 16:12.

23. Matt. 4:1.

24. 1 Pet. 4:2.

25. 1 Pet. 4:13.

26. Gen. 26:24.

27. Gal. 2:20.

28. Mark 15:34.

29. Ps. 22:16.

30. Eph. 4:13.

31. Gal. 6:14.

32. Ps. 31:11.

33. Ps. 31:12.

34. Ps. 26:4.

35. Ps. 31:12.

36. Ps. 46:10.

37. 2 Cor. 6:17.

38. Eph. 1:22.

39. 1 Pet. 2:2.

40. 1 John 2:27.

41. Mark 7:37.

42. William McDowell was the pastor of Third Presbyterian Church in Charleston, South Carolina.

43. Isa. 53:7.

44. Mark 3:22.

45. Josh. 4:5.

46. Acts 8:33.

47. Eliza was Angelina's sister.

48. 1 Pet. 3:21.

49. Ps. 123:2.

50. James 1:4.

51. Rev. 3:17.

52. Eph. 2:10.

53. Ps. 45:13.

54. Gen. 19:21.

55. Matt. 2:11.

56. Ps. 51:17.

57. Mark 4:34.

58. 1 John 2:27.

59. Heb. 9:14.

True Believer

1. I believe that it was during this seven-week hiatus that Grimké wrote an autobiographical sketch. She was about to leave Carolina, and this momentous event undoubtedly led her to review her religious and philosophical beliefs. The autobiographical

sketch allowed her to do that in detail. She was about to embark on a journey that would forever change her life.

2. Ps. 23:6.

3. Ps. 116:12.

4. Ps. 16:1.

5. 1 Tim. 6:17.

6. Matt. 26:45; Mark 14:41.

7. Isa. 66:12.

8. Ps. 116:8.

9. Matt. 24:20.

10. Gen. 31:3.

11. John 16:20.

12. Jer. 33:11.

13. Josh. 24:18.

14. 1 Pet. 2:5.

15. Ps. 31:20.

16. Exod. 14:14.

17. Ps. 40:3.

18. John 6:63.

19. John 7:46.

20. Ps. 103:1.

21. Ps. 139:14.

22. Phil. 2:16.

23. Ps. 127:1.

24. James 3:13.

25. John 14:16.

26. Angelina is referring to Catherine Morris. She had stayed with Israel and Catherine Morris during the previous summer in Philadelphia. She also refers to her sister Sarah.

27. 1 John 4:18.

28. Rev. 3:10.

29. 1 Cor. 10:13.

30. Rom. 5:3.

31. Matt. 5:3.

32. Matt. 5:6.

33. Ps. 50:21.

34. James 1:5.

35. Luke 9:35.

36. Isa. 40:10.

37. Ps. 46:18.

38. 1 Cor. 12:7.

39. Ps. 119:105.

40. Luke 9:35.

41. Ps. 46:10.

42. Phil. 2:15.

43. Josh. 9:21.

44. Josh. 7:1.

45. 1 Cor. 15:10.

46. Mark 8:24.

47. Isa. 42:19.

48. Prov. 4:23.

49. 1 Cor. 4:10.

50. Ps. 83:12.

51. Titus 2:14.

52. John 14:15.

53. Matt. 11:30.

54. Hicksite Quakers were more liberal than mainstream Friends. Interestingly, Angelina would eventually embrace their philosophy.

55. 1 John 3:16.

56. 2 Cor. 11:31

57. Mic. 6:8.

58. Luke 18:12.

59. John 16:12.

60. This event forced Angelina to confront slavery head-on. Not only was she forced to face the cruelties of slavery again, but she also had to confront her brother.

61. Angelina's efforts were successful. There is no evidence that brother Henry's heart was softened, but at least his mind had been changed and the slave was not punished. This success must have been an important encouragement to Angelina, and it steeled her for her "high calling."

62. John 14:27.

63. Gen. 31:3.

64. Selina was Henry's wife, Angelina's sister-in-law.

65. 1 Tim. 6:8.

66. The reference is to Angelina's brother Charles.

67. Isa. 51:1.

68. Josh. 24:18.

69. 1 Sam. 3:10.

70. 1 Cor. 13:8.

Trial and Triumph

1. Exod. 33:15.

2. Heb. 10:22.

3. Benjamin, a physician, was Angelina's brother.

4. Catherine Morris and her brother Israel Morris. Angelina had stayed with Catherine Morris when she had visited Philadelphia the previous summer.

5. Ps. 126:5.

6. The Rains were an elderly couple who lived near the Grimkés.

7. Ps. 119:49.

8. Ps. 119:51.

9. Ps. 116:17.

10. Matt. 6:10.

11. Jer. 45:5.

12. Exod. 14:14.

13. Acts 22:15.

14. Exod. 14:13.

15. Matt. 10:8.

16. Phil. 4:6.

17. Isa. 8:17.

18. Gen. 15:1.

19. Ezek. 11:16.

20. Jer. 45:5.

21. 1 Cor. 4:5.

22. Dan. 6:26.

23. Isa. 8:17.

24. Ps. 68:6.

25. 2 Sam. 22:34.

26. 1 Pet. 1:8.

27. Mark 9:7.

28. Matt. 17:9.

29. Mark 1:11.

30. Col. 3:3.

31. Hos. 2:15.

32. John 6:55.

33. Song of Sol. 5:1.

34. Isa. 1:10.

35. Exod. 33:14.

36. Ps. 106:24.

37. Rev. 3:10.

38. Luke 21:36.

39. 1 Tim. 6:17.

40. Ps. 84:10.

41. 1 Cor. 13:5.

42. Gen. 31:3.
43. John 16:20.

Strengthening of Will

1. Gal. 2:20.
2. Ezek. 11:16.
3. 1 John 2:16.
4. Ibid.
5. Phil. 2:3.
6. Ps. 119:76.
7. Ps. 37:9.
8. Ibid.
9. 1 Cor. 16:31.
10. Phil. 4:11.
11. 2 Chron. 20:21.
12. Ps. 145:18.
13. Deut. 31:23.
14. Ps. 138:8.
15. Gen. 20:17.
16. Matt. 26:38.
17. Matt. 20:3.
18. Luke 16:18.
19. Luke 11:2.
20. James 2:19.
21. James 2:20–22.
22. 1 Cor. 13:3.
23. 1 Cor. 13:4
24. Ibid.
25. Ibid.
26. 1 Cor. 15:10.
27. 1 Cor. 13:5.
28. Ibid.
29. Rom. 15:2.
30. 1 Cor. 4:10.
31. 1 Cor. 13:5.
32. 1 Cor. 13:6.
33. Ibid.
34. Ibid.
35. 1 Cor. 13:7.
36. 1 Cor. 13:8.

37. Rom. 12:16.

38. Rom. 13:10.

39. Eph. 4:15.

40. 1 Cor. 13:8.

41. 1 Cor. 13:13.

42. John 13:17.

43. Rev. 2:10.

44. Braithwaite was the Quaker who had visited the Grimké home in December 1827 and had such a profound impact on Angelina's religious convictions.

45. John 16:20.

46. Judg. 16:17.

47. Rom. 14:5.

48. Rom. 14:6.

49. Rom. 14:7.

50. Rev. 1:10.

51. Eph. 6:18.

52. Prov. 21:1.

53. 1 John 2:16.

54. Pss. 139:23–24.

Strengthening of Spirit

1. Gal. 6:10.

2. Acts 20:27.

3. Eph. 4:28.

4. John 8:15.

5. 1 Cor. 10:13.

6. Rev. 3:2.

7. Ps. 13:3.

8. Isa. 26:4.

9. Luke 13:8.

10. Col. 3:8.

11. Gen. 19:15.

12. 2 Tim. 4:2.

13. 2 Tim. 4:3.

14. Luke 10:7.

15. Ps. 17:5.

16. Matt. 8:20.

17. Rom. 15:27.

18. 1 Cor. 9:15.

19. 1 Cor. 9:18.

20. Matt. 10:8.

21. 1 Cor. 13:5.

22. Matt. 24:44.

23. Matt. 24:13.

24. Greenhill was the home of Israel Morris. Apparently, Angelina had visited there while in Philadelphia the previous summer.

25. John 1:13.

26. Matt. 10:16.

27. Prov. 15:17.

28. Jer. 47:6.

29. John 3:11.

30. 2 Cor. 6:18.

31. 1 Cor. 16:22.

32. Matt. 7:1.

33. Matt. 12:13.

34. 1 Cor. 2:15.

35. Gal. 5:22–23.

36. John 16:13.

37. 1 Cor. 2:16.

38. Isa. 5:20.

39. Titus 3:2.

40. Rom. 13:10.

41. Num. 10:32.

42. Isa. 53:3.

43. 1 Cor. 4:10.

44. 2 Tim. 2:24.

45. 1 Cor. 4:21.

46. Acts 7:51.

47. Isa. 65:5.

48. Matt. 24:44.

49. Ps. 37:7.

Out of Charleston

1. Deut. 12:8.

2. 1 Tim. 6:6.

3. 2 Cor. 11:3.

4. Rom. 12:8.

5. Grimké is perhaps referring to Edward Panton's *Speculum Juventutis,* which was published in 1671.

6. The margin note indicates a reference of 2nd volume, p. 292.

7. Rev. 7:9.

8. Exod. 12:5.

9. Exod. 33:4.

10. Exod. 33:5.

11. Exod. 33:6.

12. Gen. 24:53.

13. 2 Chron. 29:11.

14. 1 Pet. 5:5.

15. Col. 3:1.

16. Acts 10:25.

17. 1 Tim. 3:16.

18. Matt. 23:13–15.

19. Matt. 23:7.

20. Matt. 23:10.

21. Matt. 23:12.

22. Luke 9:48.

23. John 5:41.

24. Rev. 22:9.

25. Matt. 23:15.

26. Matt. 23:6.

27. Ruth 1:16.

28. Matt. 23:4–16.

29. John was Henry's slave who had previously run away. That incident led to a confrontation between Angelina and Henry that she recorded earlier in the diary.

30. Rom. 12:16.

31. Phil. 2:3.

32. Col. 4:1.

33. Gen. 9:25.

34. 2 Kings 17:15.

35. 1 Sam. 3:18.

36. Gal. 5:22–23.

37. Matt. 23:16.

38. 1 Cor. 15:10.

39. Eph. 4:20.

40. Pss. 121:1–2.

41. Gen. 18:14.

42. 1 Sam. 16:7.

43. 2 Cor. 6:17.

44. Isa. 40:12.

45. Rom. 3:13.

46. Num. 21:4.

47. Prov. 30:5.

48. Sally was one of the Grimké servants.

49. Job 14:14.

50. Matt. 6:10.

51. Rev. 3:8.

52. Exod. 13:3.

53. Ps. 16:1.

54. 1 Cor. 2:3.

55. In Charleston, King Street above Boundary was the commercial district and below Boundary consisted of slums. If they were discussing getting Charles a residence on King below Boundary, it would indicate certainly a surrender to baser elements than those to which the Grimkés were accustomed.

56. Luke 2:49.

57. John 15:19.

A New Life

1. Gen. 42:36.

2. John 14:3.

3. Isa. 33:20.

4. Isa. 36:16.

5. Matt. 6:22.

6. Ps. 37:7.

7. Angelina had stayed with Catherine Morris when she had visited Philadelphia in summer 1828. She moved in with Catherine again upon her arrival.

8. Rom. 5:7.

9. 2 Cor. 9:7.

10. Exod. 2:9.

11. Isa. 33:20.

12. Heb. 13:3.

13. 2 Sam. 1:21.

14. Isa. 59:3.

15. Gen. 8:22.

16. Job 13:15.

17. Isa. 50:10.

18. Ps. 22:6.

19. Matt. 6:10.

20. 1 Thess. 4:11.

Index of Subjects and Names

Index of Biblical Citations